井上雄彦

Takehiko Inoue

WE'VE MADE IT TO VOLUME 15 AND IT'S ALL
THANKS TO YOU, DEAR READERS. IT'S BEEN
THREE YEARS! (THOUGH ONLY THREE MONTHS
HAVE PASSED IN THE STORY—HEH!) ANYWAY,
I SOMETIMES GET LETTERS FROM PEOPLE
ACCUSING ME OF TAKING DRAMATIC LICENSE
TO MAKE THE GAMES MORE EXCITING. TO THAT
I SAY, NO WAY! A REAL GAME IS EVEN MORE
DRAMATIC. I HATE TO SAY IT, BUT IT'S
THE TRUTH.

Takehiko Inoue's *Slam Dunk* is one of the most
popular manga of all time, having sold over 100
million copies worldwide. He followed that series
up with two titles lauded by critics and fans
alike—*Vagabond*, a fictional account of the life
of Miyamoto Musashi, and *Real*, a manga about
wheelchair basketball.

SLAM DUNK
Vol. 15: HEAVEN & HELL

SHONEN JUMP Manga Edition

STORY AND ART BY TAKEHIKO INOUE

English Adaptation/Kelly Sue DeConnick
Translation/Joe Yamazaki
Touch-up Art & Lettering/James Gaubatz
Cover & Graphic Design/Sean Lee, Matt Hinrichs
Editor/Mike Montesa

© 1990 - 2011 Takehiko Inoue and I.T. Planning, Inc.
Originally published in Japan in 1993 by Shueisha
Inc., Tokyo. English translation rights arranged with
I.T. Planning, Inc. All rights reserved.

The SLAM DUNK U.S. trademark is used with
permission from NBA Properties, Inc.

Some scenes have been modified from the original
Japanese edition.

The stories, characters and incidents mentioned in
this publication are entirely fictional.

Printed in Canada

Published by VIZ Media, LLC
P.O. Box 77010
San Francisco, CA 94107

10 9 8 7 6 5 4 3 2 1
First printing, April 2011

Character Introduction

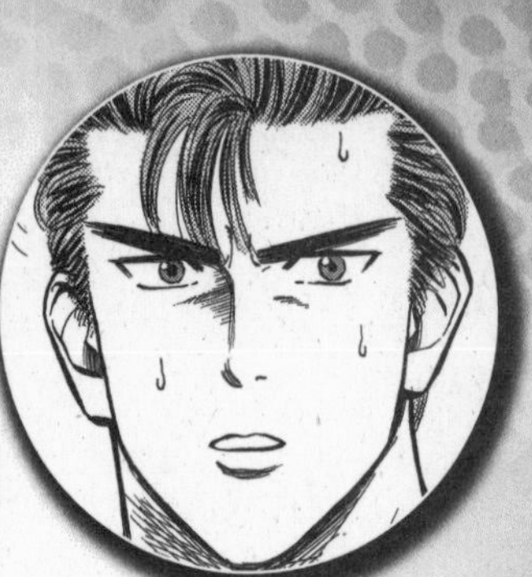

Hanamichi Sakuragi
A first-year at Shohoku High School, Sakuragi is in love with Haruko Akagi.

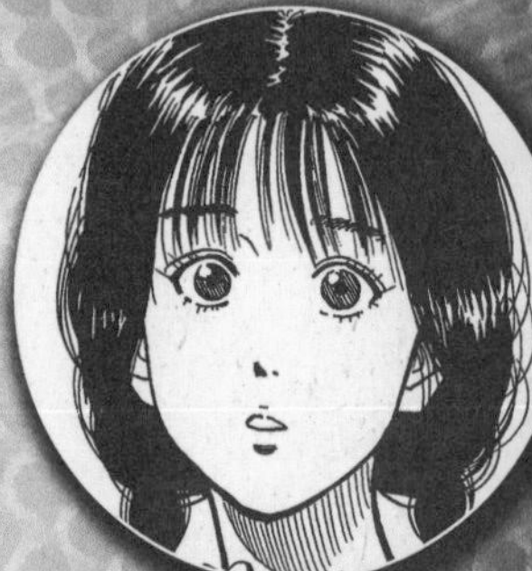

Haruko Akagi
Also a first-year at Shohoku, Takenori Akagi's little sister has a crush on Kaede Rukawa.

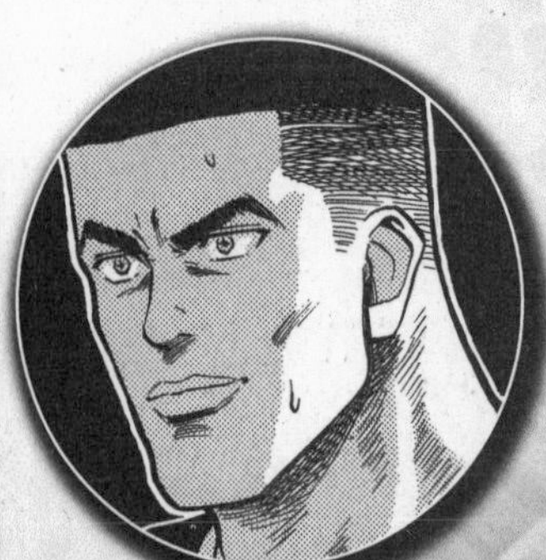

Takenori Akagi
A third-year and the basketball team's captain, Akagi has an intense passion for his sport.

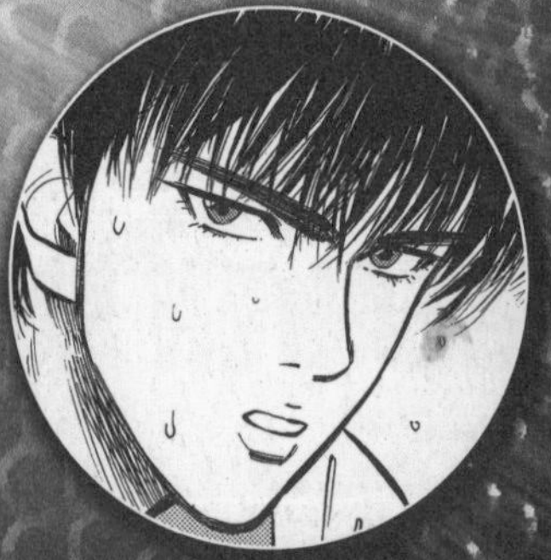

Kaede Rukawa
The object of Haruko's affection (and that of many of Shohoku's female students!), this first-year has been a star player since junior high.

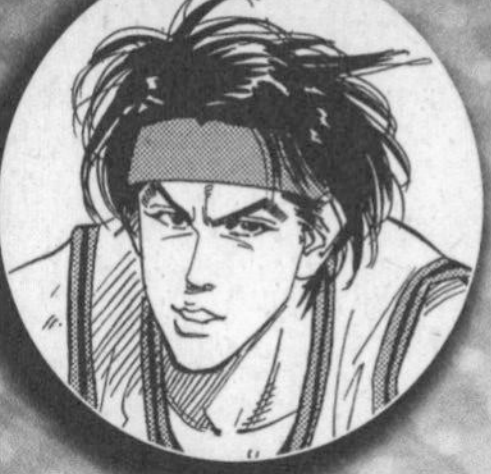

Kiyota

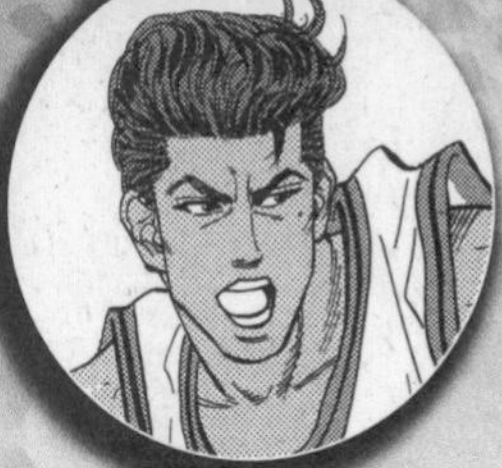

Maki

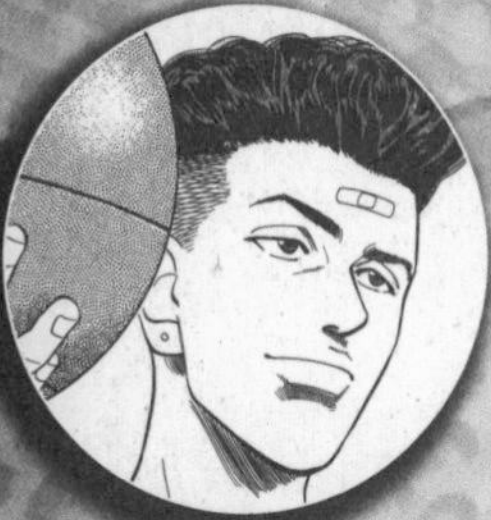

Ryota Miyagi
A problem child with a thing for Ayako.

Ayako
Basketball Team Manager

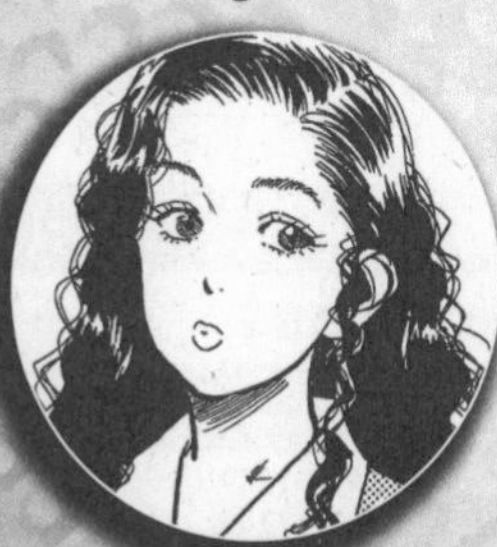

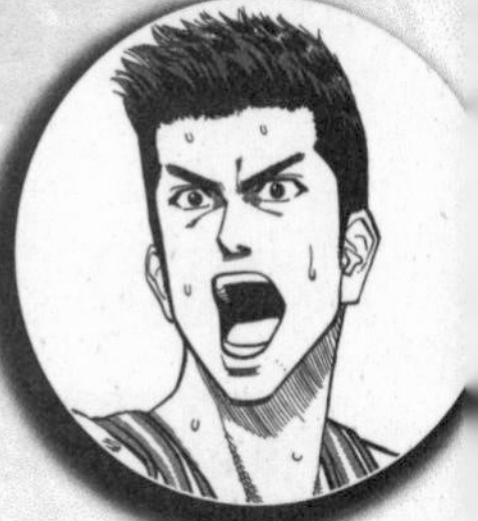

Hisashi Mitsui
An MVP during junior high.

Our Story Thus Far

Hanamichi Sakuragi is rejected by close to 50 girls during his three years in junior high. He joins the basketball team to get closer to his beloved Haruko Akagi, but the constant fundamental drills cause him endless frustration.

After a good showing in their first exhibition, the team sets its sights on Nationals and ex-problem-child Ryota Miyagi reclaims his position as Point Guard. Not long after Miyagi's return, Hisashi Mitsui—a junior-high-MVP-turned-gang-thug—finds he too misses the game and rejoins the team.

Shohoku advances through the prefectural tourney to face Kainan, but the players lose their captain to injury. They manage to tie the game in the first half anyway—thanks to Rukawa's brilliant performance—only to give up the lead in the second. Our boys try to catch up to "King" Kainan, but can they do so with only two minutes remaining?!

Vol. 15:
HEAVEN & HELL

Table of Contents

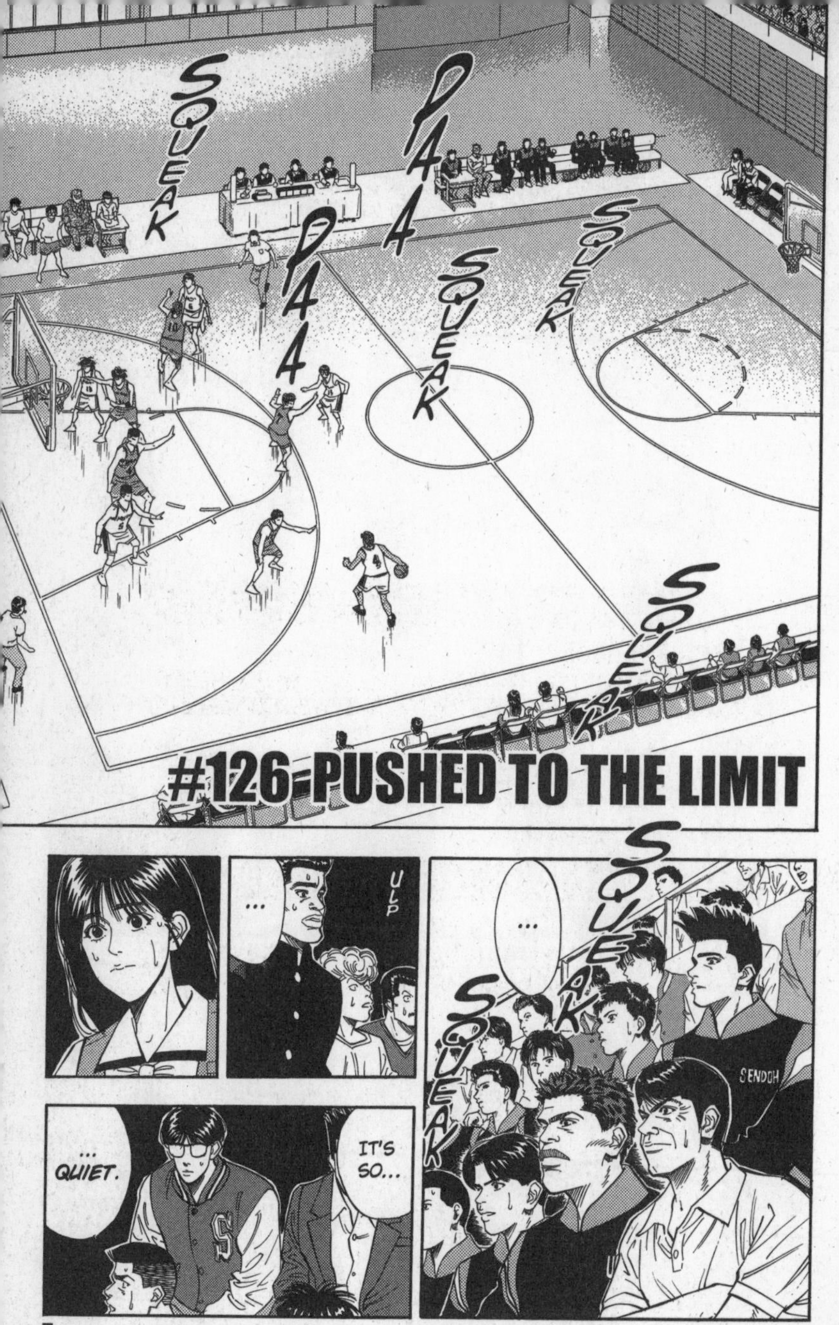
SQUEAK
DA4
DA4
SQUEAK
SQUEAK
SQUEAK
#126 PUSHED TO THE LIMIT
SQUEAK
SQUEAK
...
...
ULP
IT'S SO...
... QUIET.

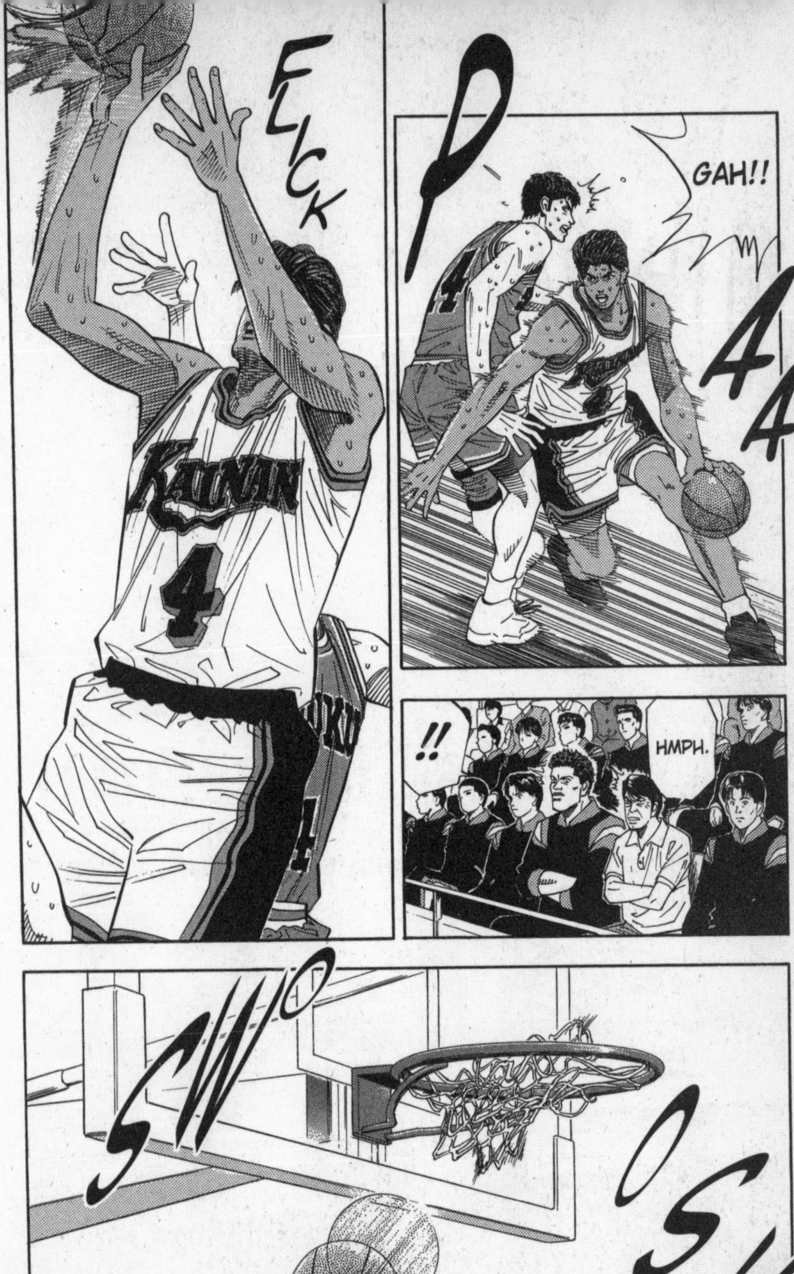
P
GAH!!
AA
!!
HMPH.
FLICK
SWOOSH

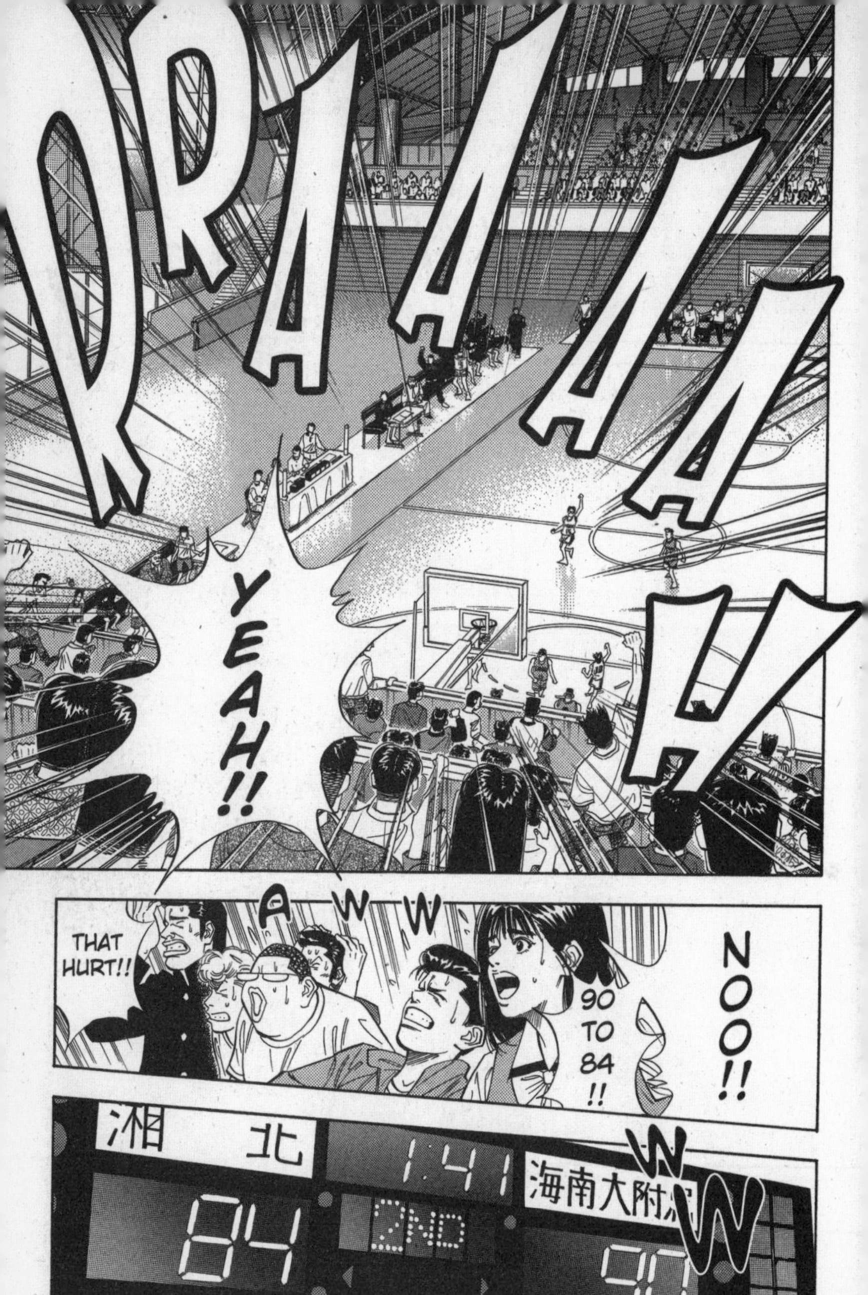
WAAAAAH
YEAH!!
AWW
NOOO!!
90 TO 84 !!
THAT HURT!!
湘北
1:41
海南大附属
84
2ND
90
WW

Scoreboard: Shohoku Kainan Dai Fuzoku

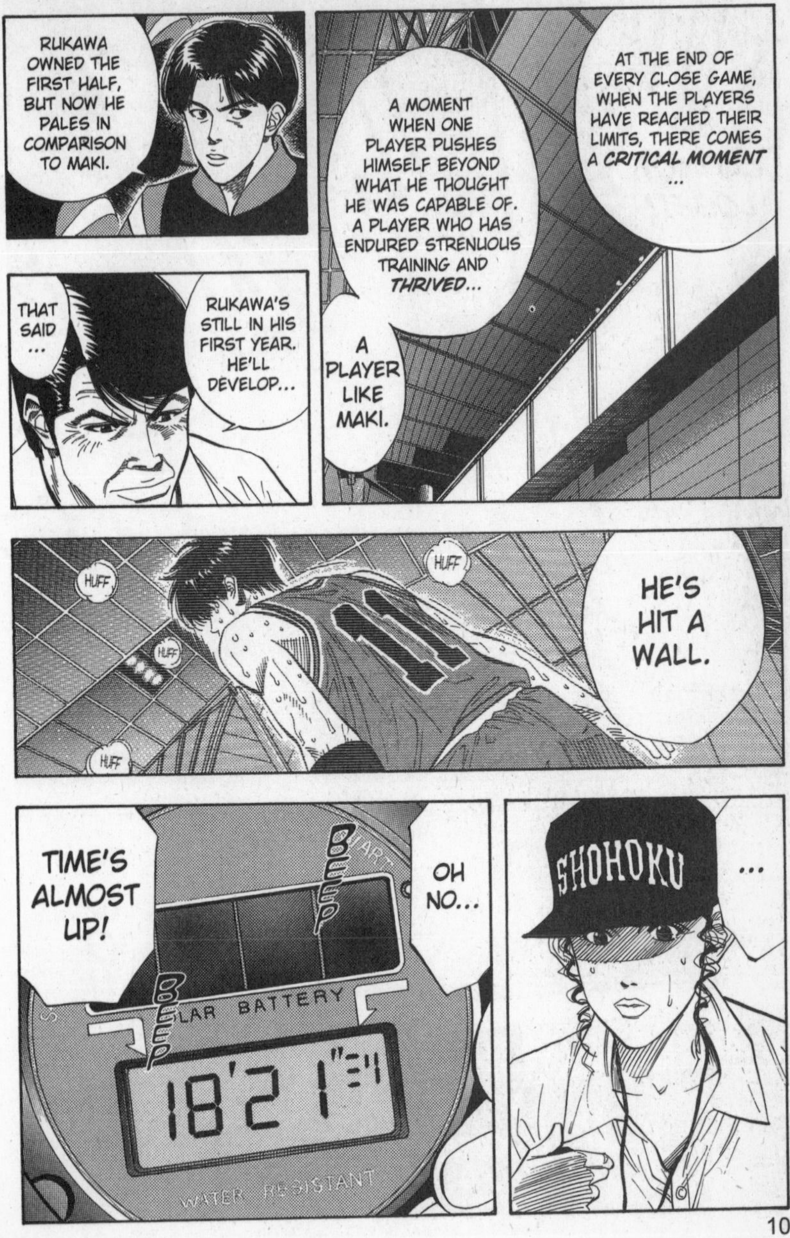
AT THE END OF EVERY CLOSE GAME, WHEN THE PLAYERS HAVE REACHED THEIR LIMITS, THERE COMES A *CRITICAL MOMENT* ...
A MOMENT WHEN ONE PLAYER PUSHES HIMSELF BEYOND WHAT HE THOUGHT HE WAS CAPABLE OF. A PLAYER WHO HAS ENDURED STRENUOUS TRAINING AND *THRIVED*...
A PLAYER LIKE MAKI.
RUKAWA OWNED THE FIRST HALF, BUT NOW HE PALES IN COMPARISON TO MAKI.
RUKAWA'S STILL IN HIS FIRST YEAR. HE'LL DEVELOP...
THAT SAID ...
HUFF
HUFF
HUFF
HUFF
HE'S HIT A WALL.
SHOHOKU
...
OH NO...
TIME'S ALMOST UP!
BEEP
BEEP
LAR BATTERY
WATER RESISTANT

READ THIS WAY

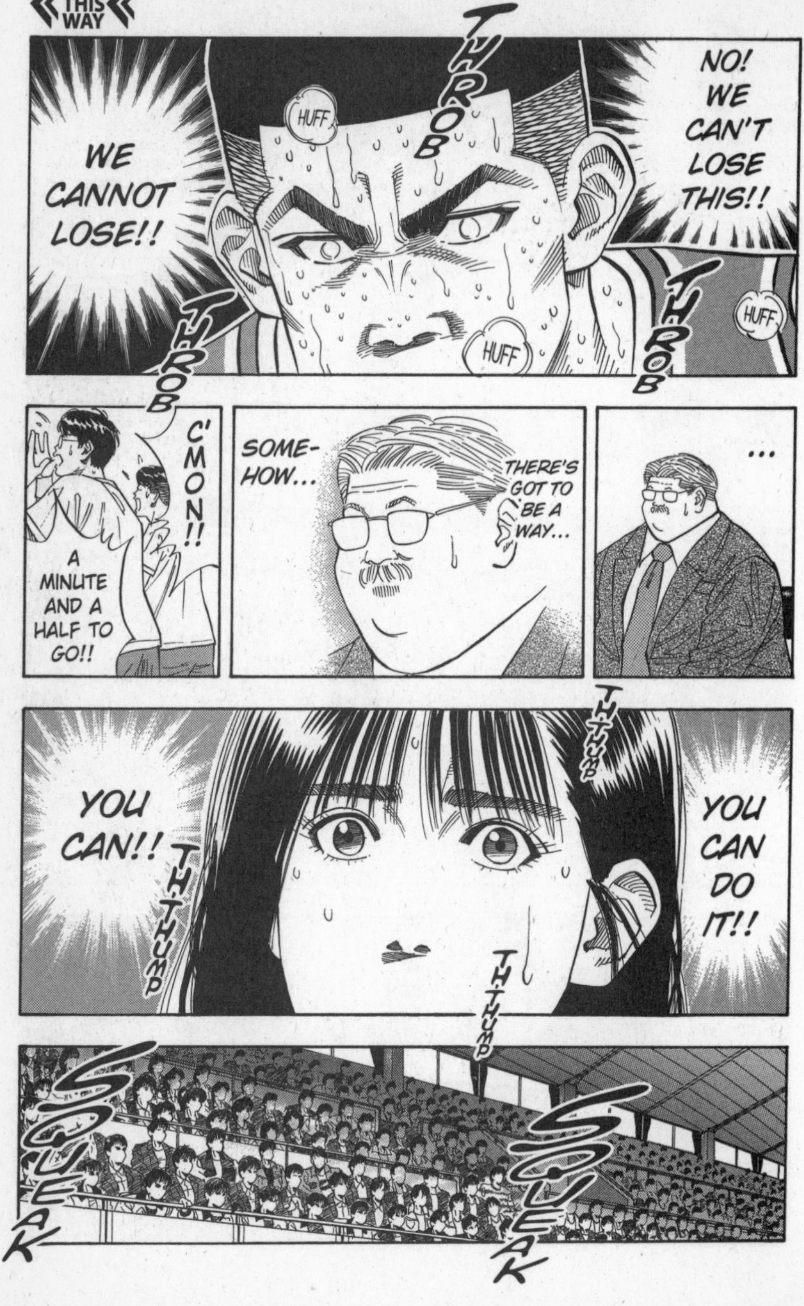
THROB
HUFF
NO! WE CAN'T LOSE THIS!!
WE CANNOT LOSE!!
HUFF
HUFF
THROB
THROB
...
SOME-HOW...
THERE'S GOT TO BE A WAY...
C'MON!!
A MINUTE AND A HALF TO GO!!
TH-THUMP
YOU CAN DO IT!!
YOU CAN!!
TH-THUMP
TH-THUMP
SQUEAK
SQUEAK

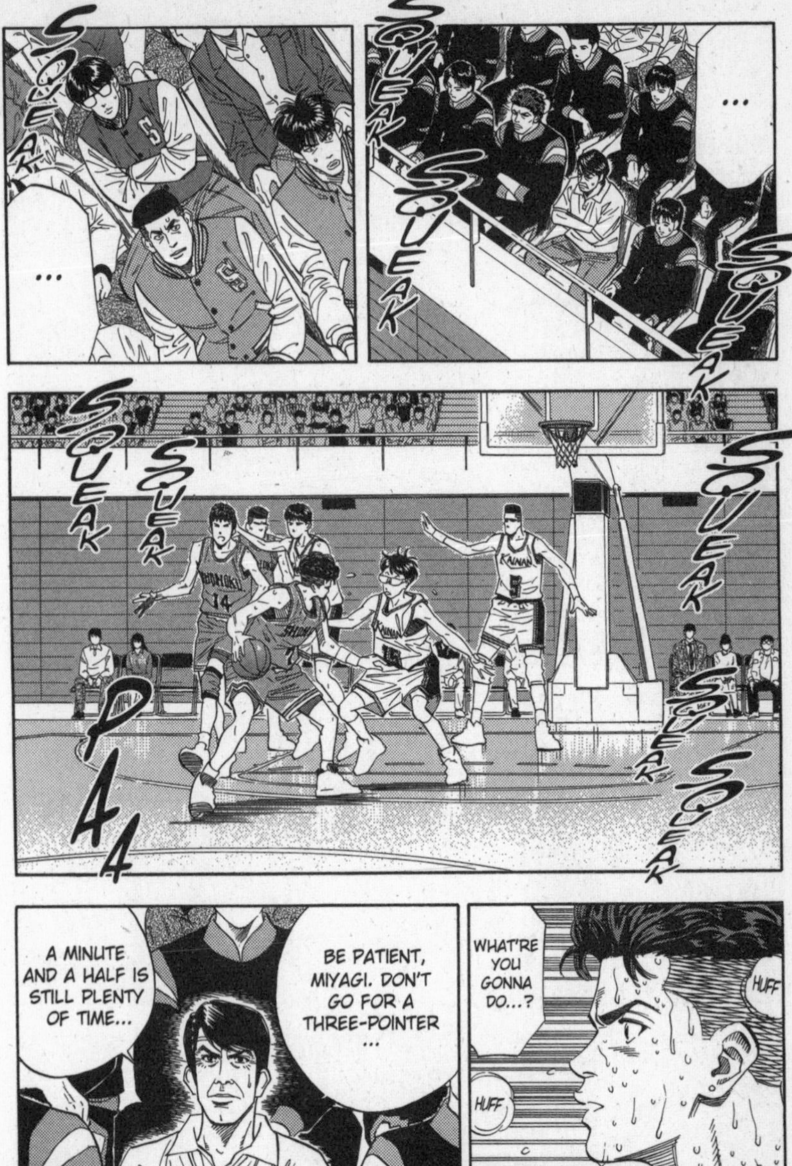
SQUEAK
SQUEAK
SQUEAK
...
...
SQUEAK
SQUEAK
SQUEAK
SQUEAK
SQUEAK
SQUEAK
WHAT'RE YOU GONNA DO...?
HUFF
HUFF
HUFF
BE PATIENT, MIYAGI. DON'T GO FOR A THREE-POINTER ...
A MINUTE AND A HALF IS STILL PLENTY OF TIME...

READ THIS WAY

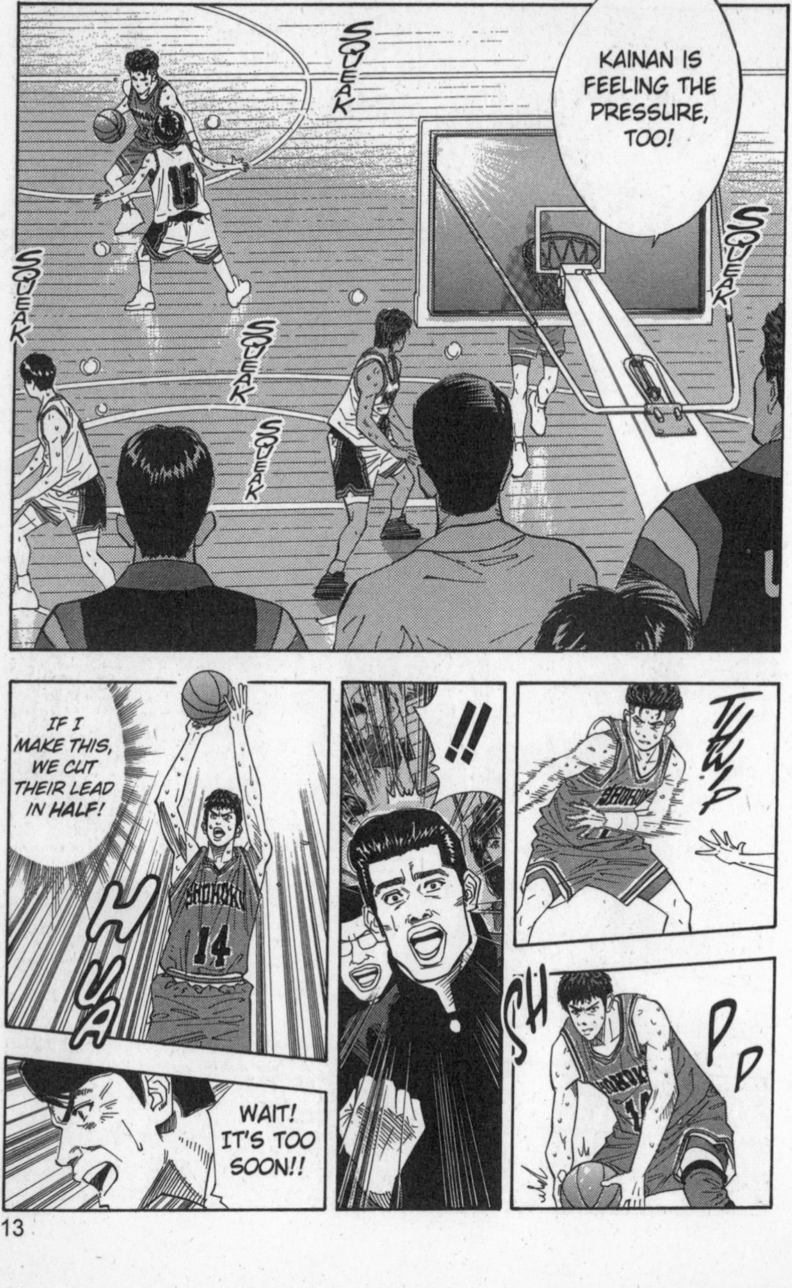
KAINAN IS FEELING THE PRESSURE, TOO!
SQUEAK
SQUEAK
SQUEAK
SQUEAK
SQUEAK
THWIP
!!
IF I MAKE THIS, WE CUT THEIR LEAD IN HALF!
WAIT! IT'S TOO SOON!!

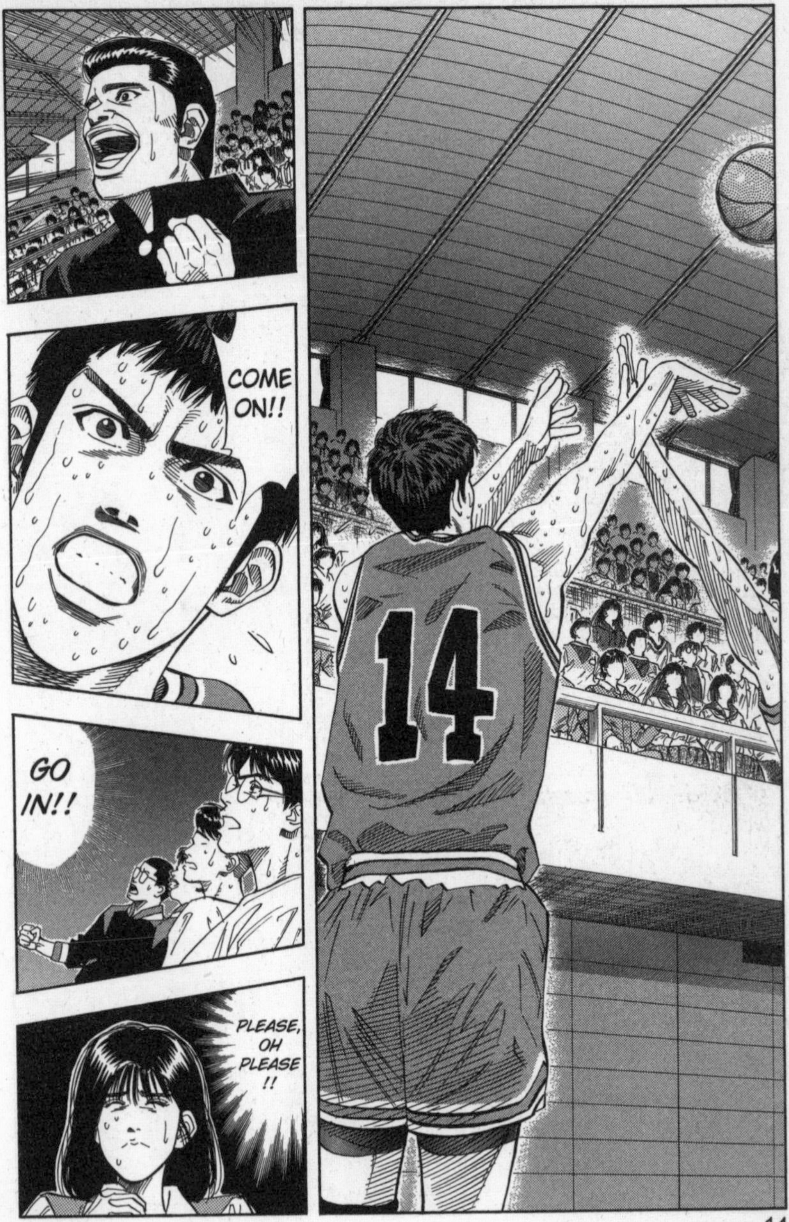
COME ON!!
GO IN!!
PLEASE, OH PLEASE !!

READ THIS WAY

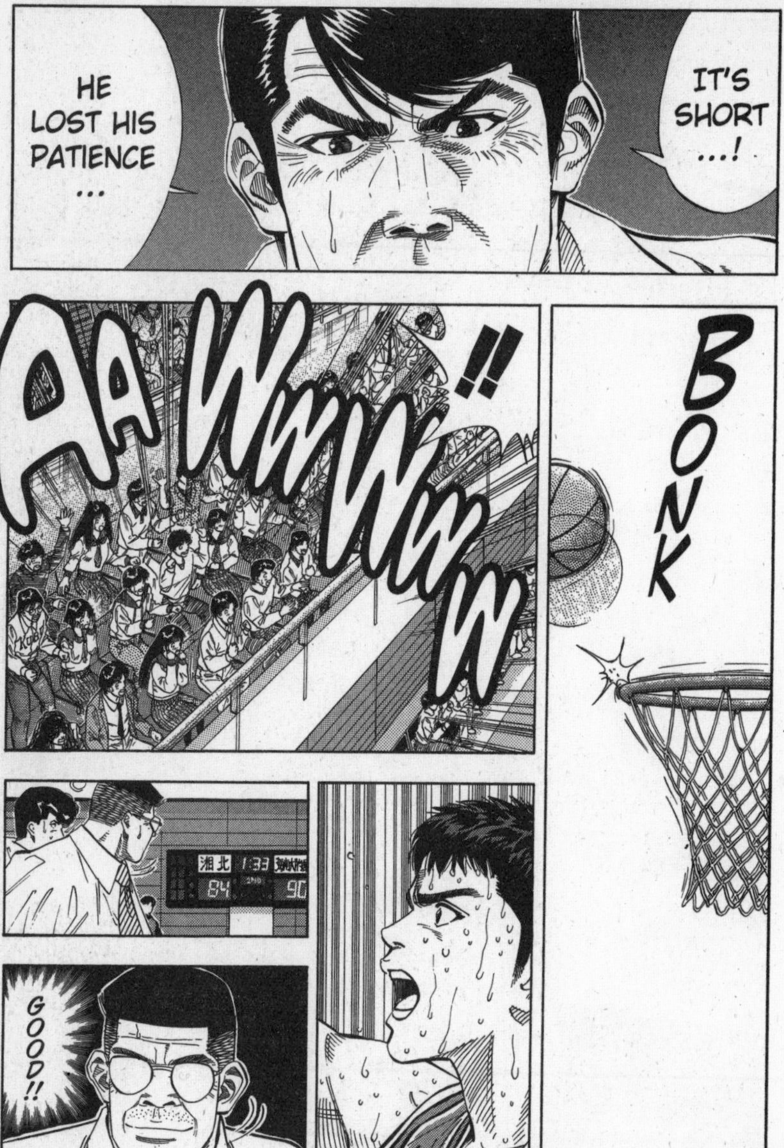
IT'S SHORT ...!
HE LOST HIS PATIENCE ...
BONK
AAWWWW!!
GOOD!!

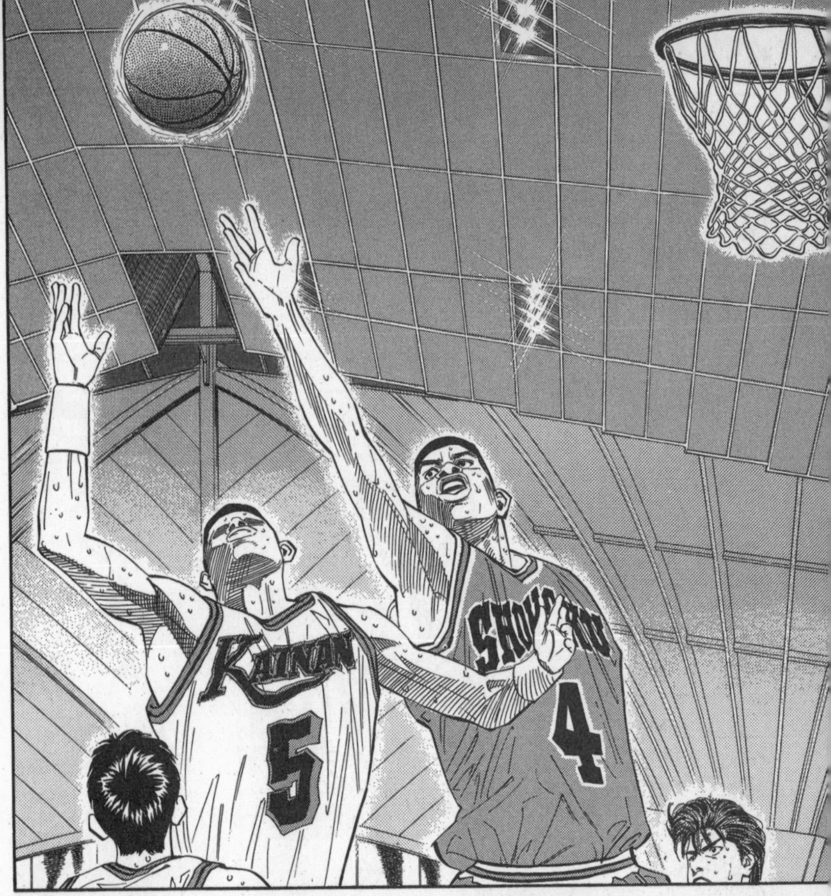
KAINAN
5
4
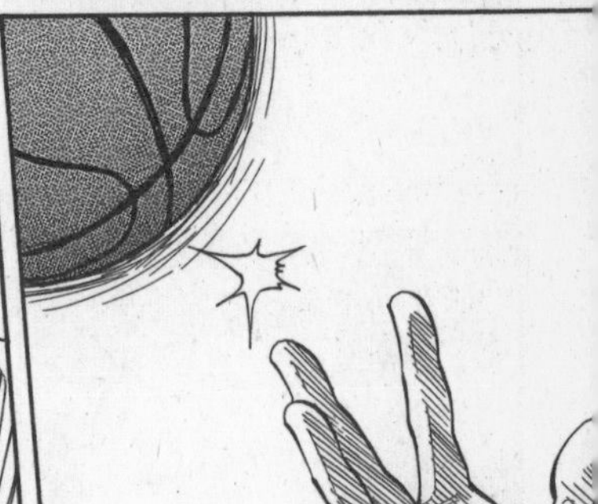
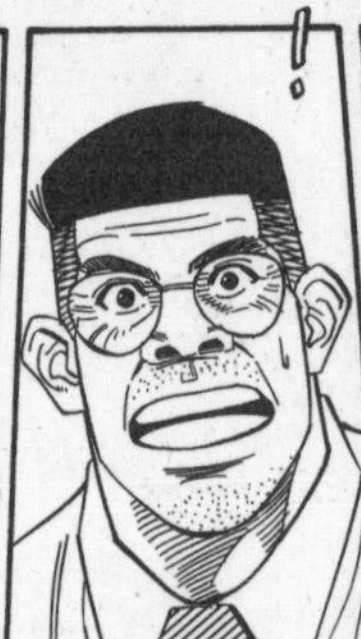
!
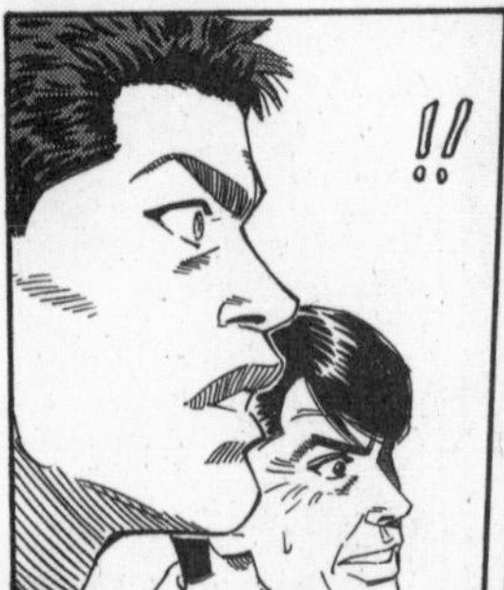
!!

READ THIS WAY

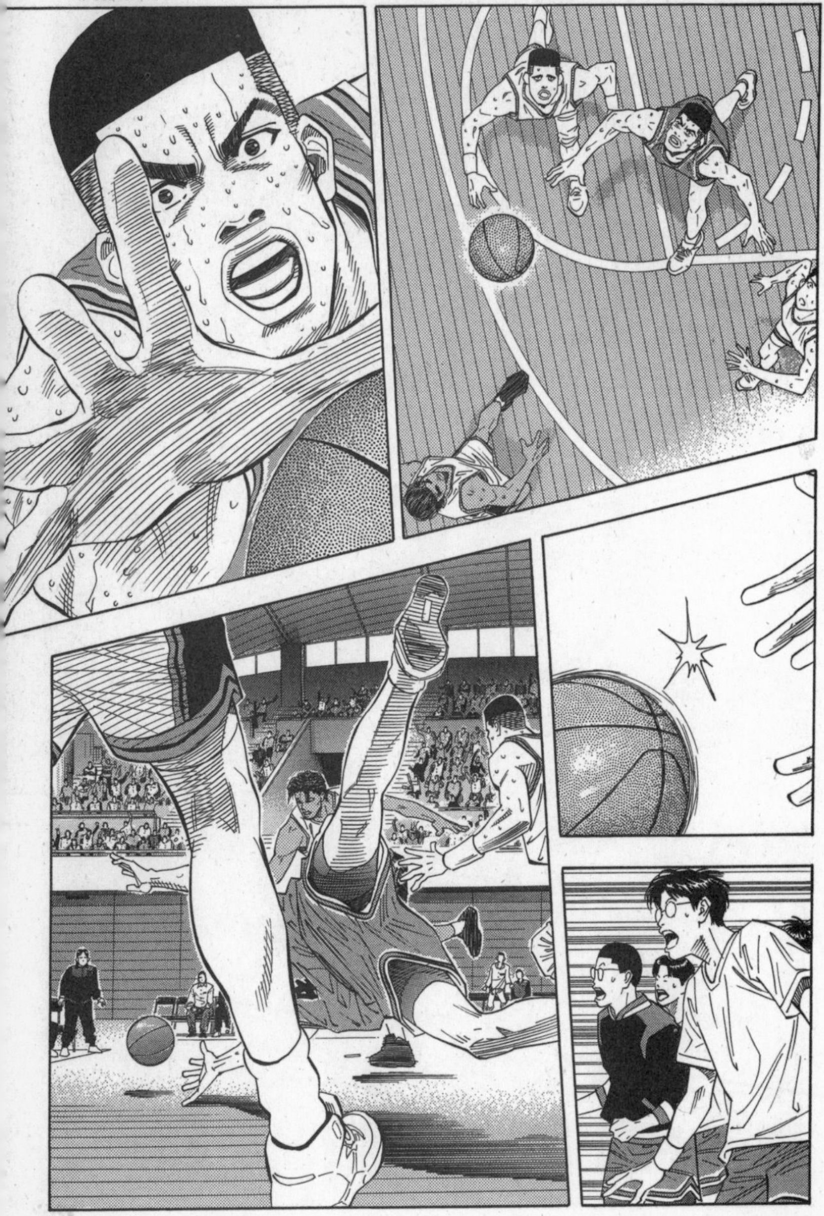

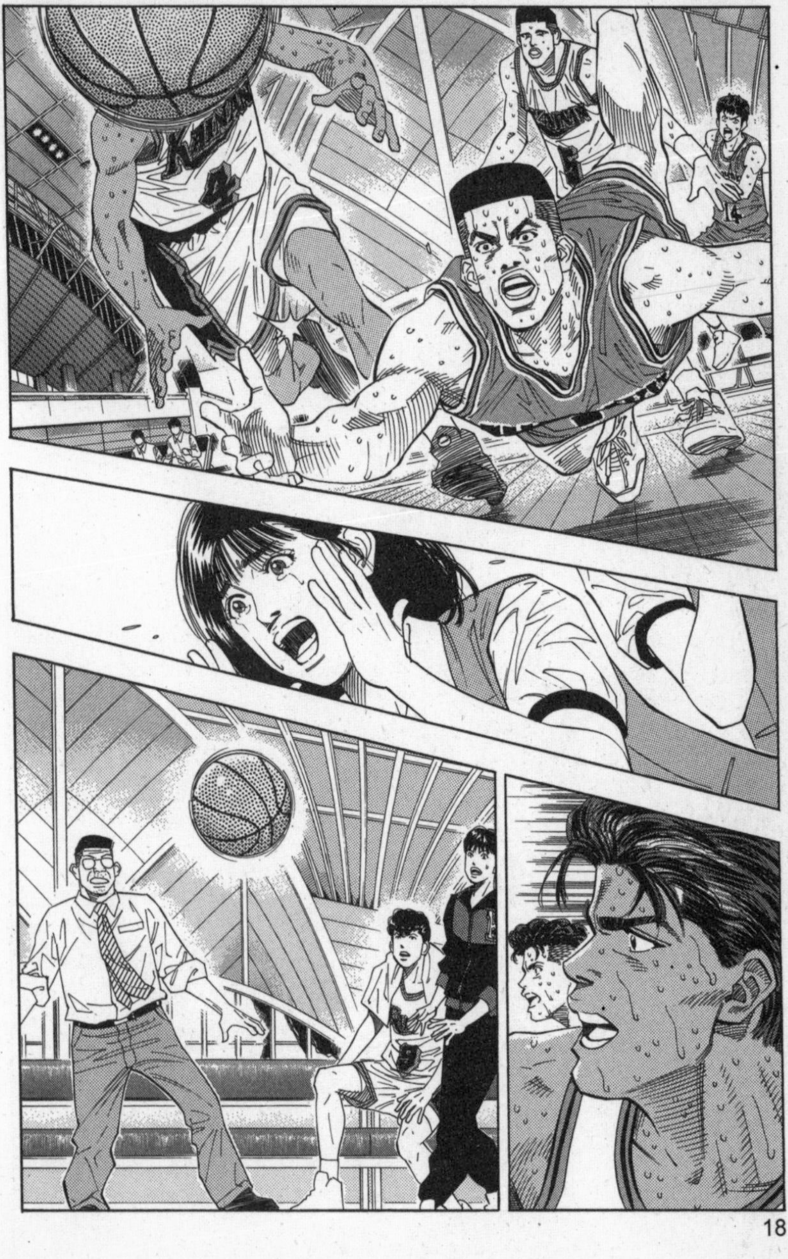

READ THIS WAY

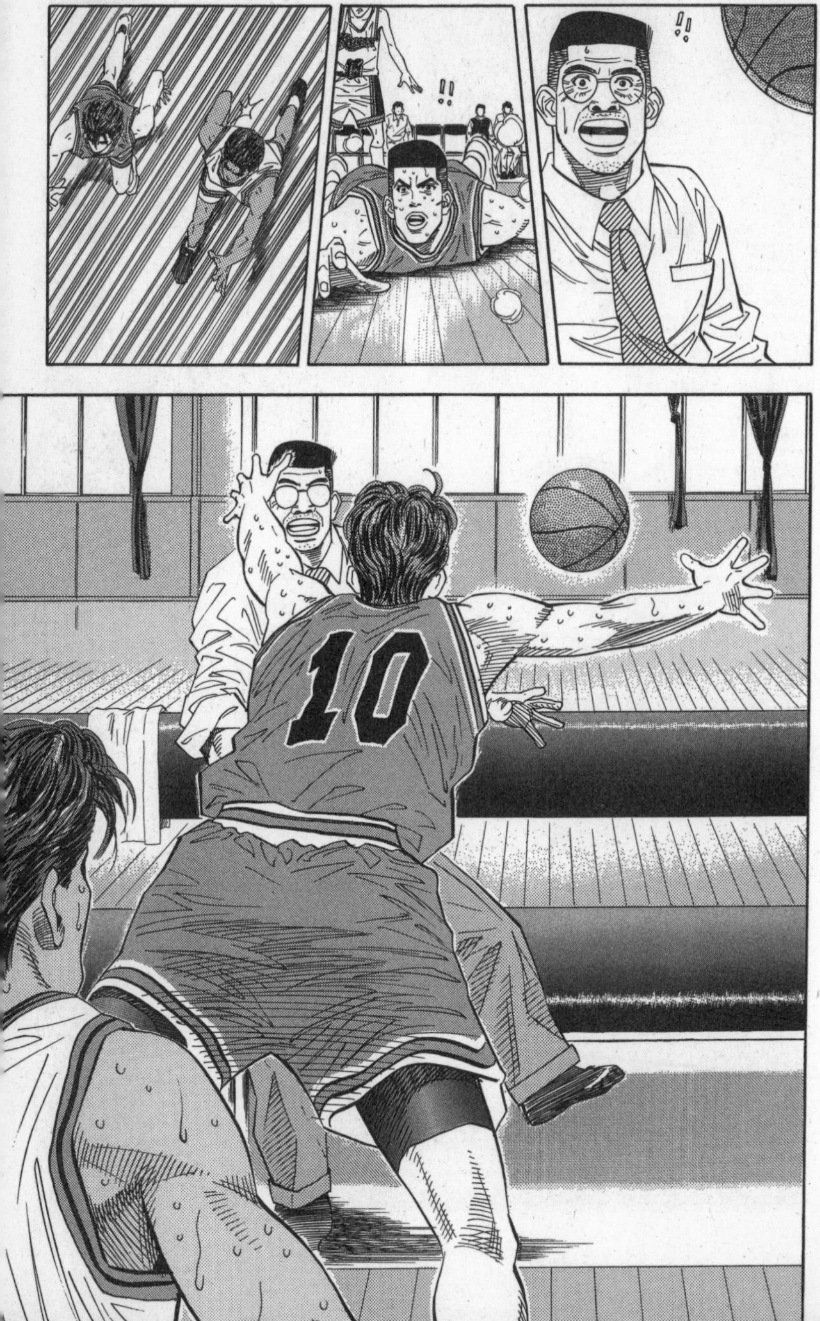
!!
!!
10

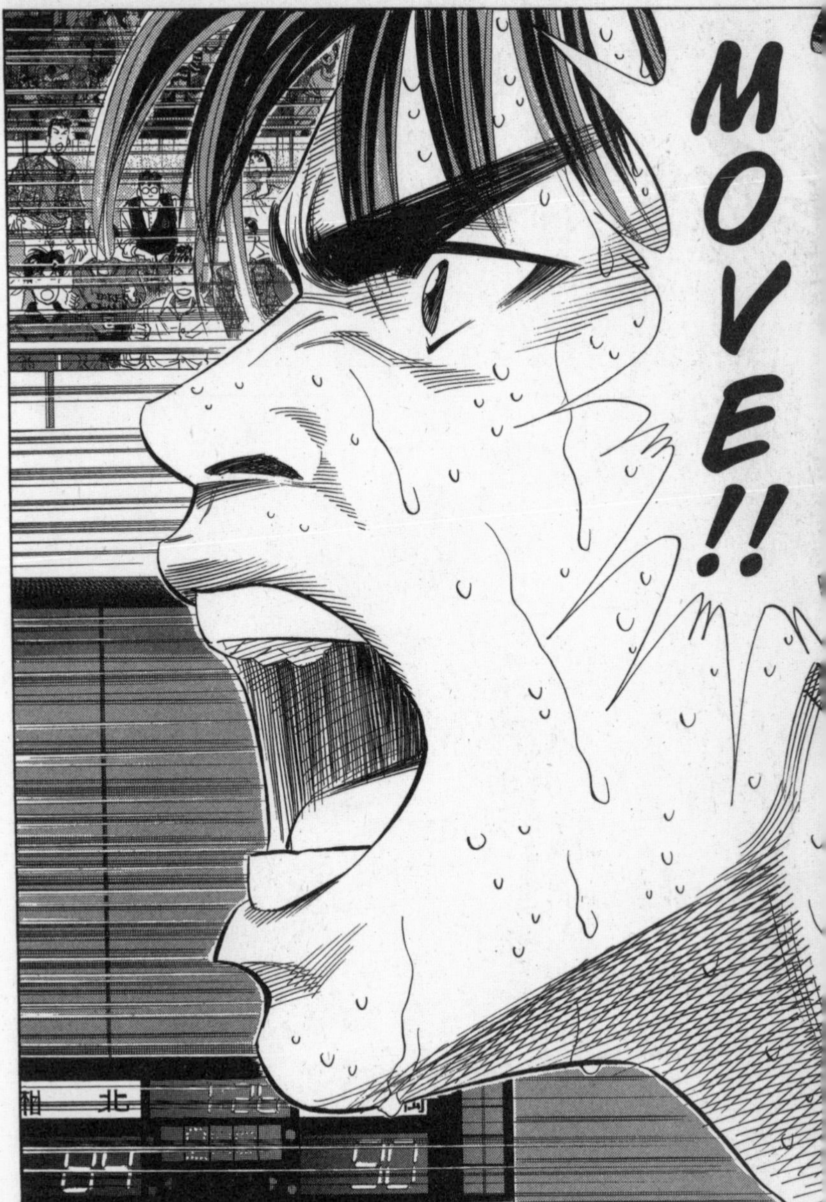
MOVE!!

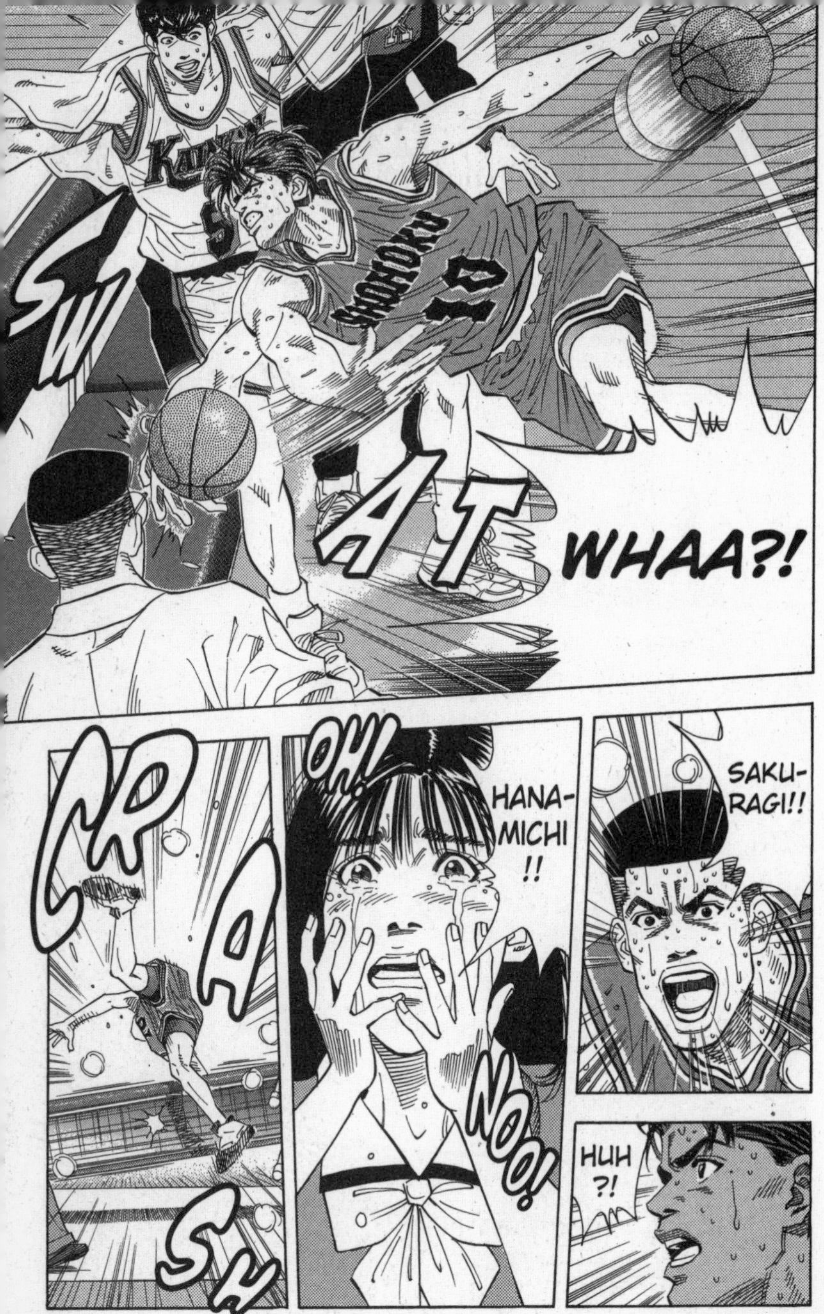
SW
AT
WHAA?!
SAKU-RAGI!!
HUH ?!
OH!
HANA-MICHI !!
NOOO!
CR
A
SH

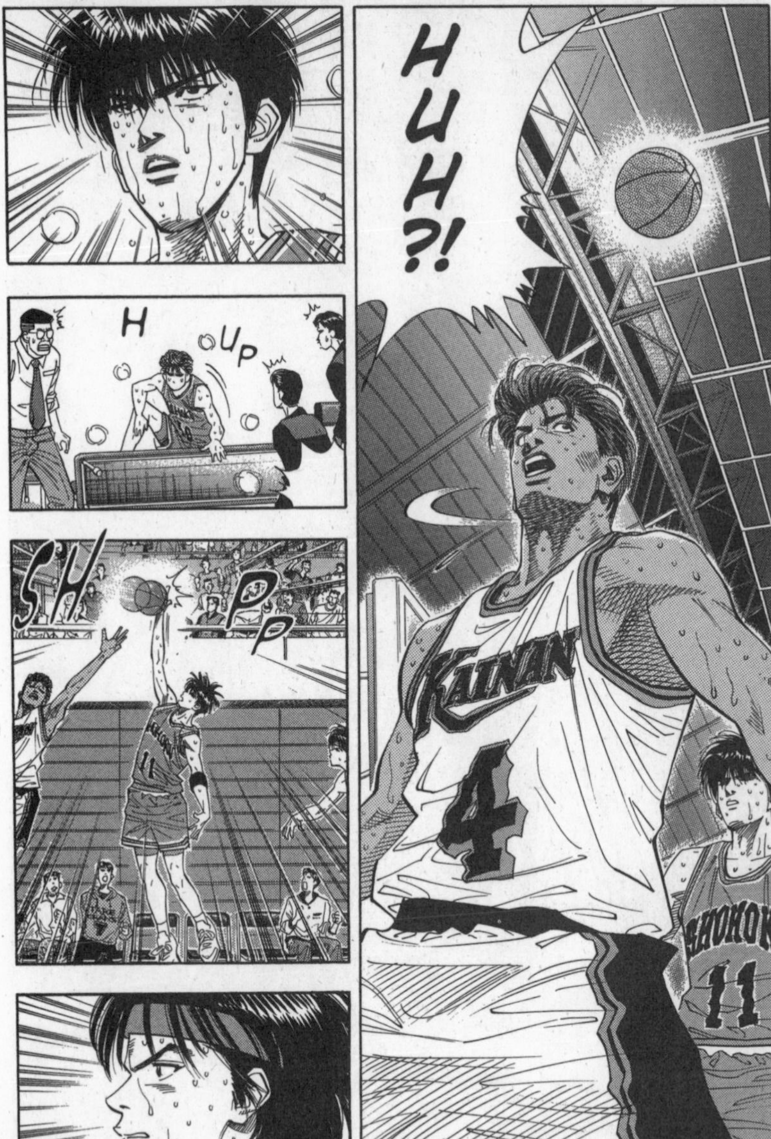
HUH?!
H
UP
SH
PP

READ THIS WAY

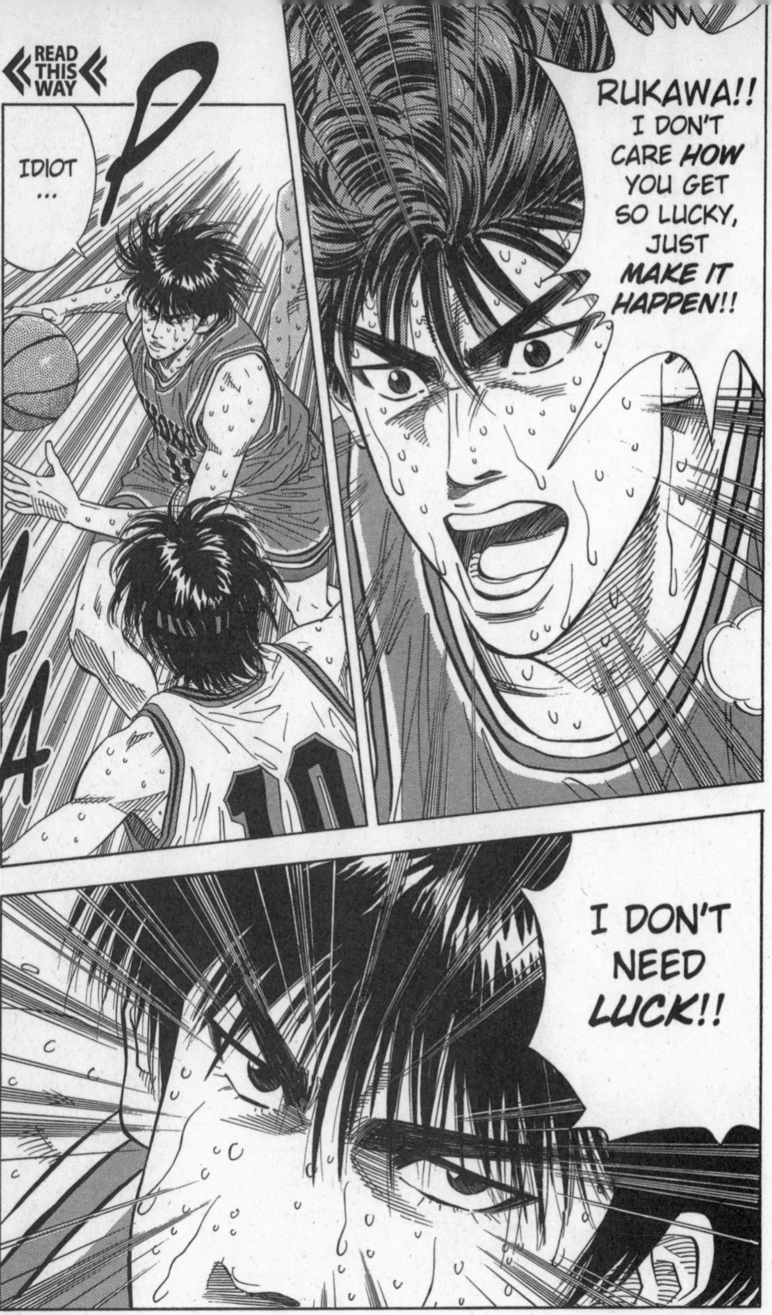
RUKAWA!! I DON'T CARE HOW YOU GET SO LUCKY, JUST MAKE IT HAPPEN!!
IDIOT ...
I DON'T NEED LUCK!!

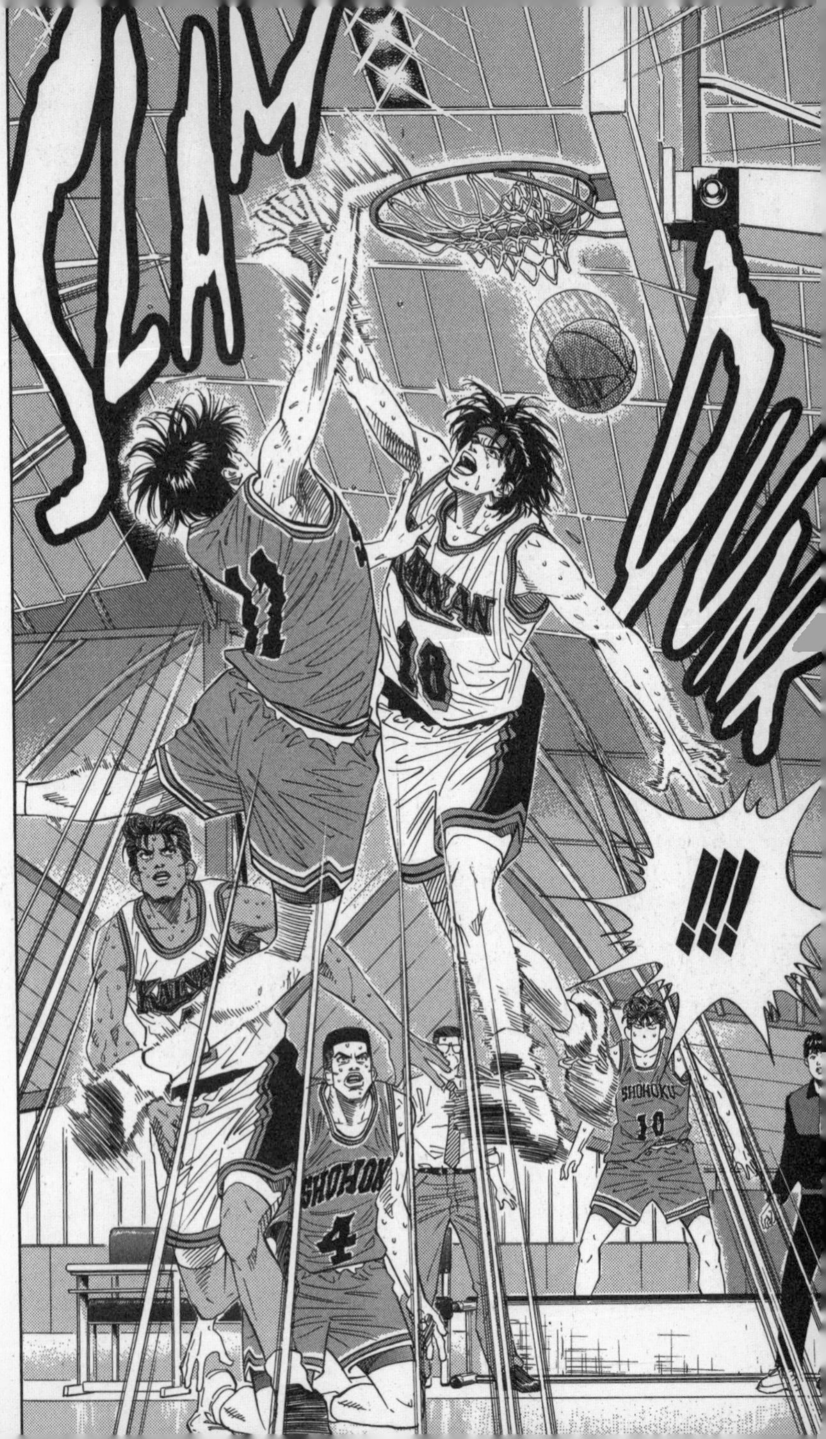
SLAM
DUNK
!!!

READ THIS WAY

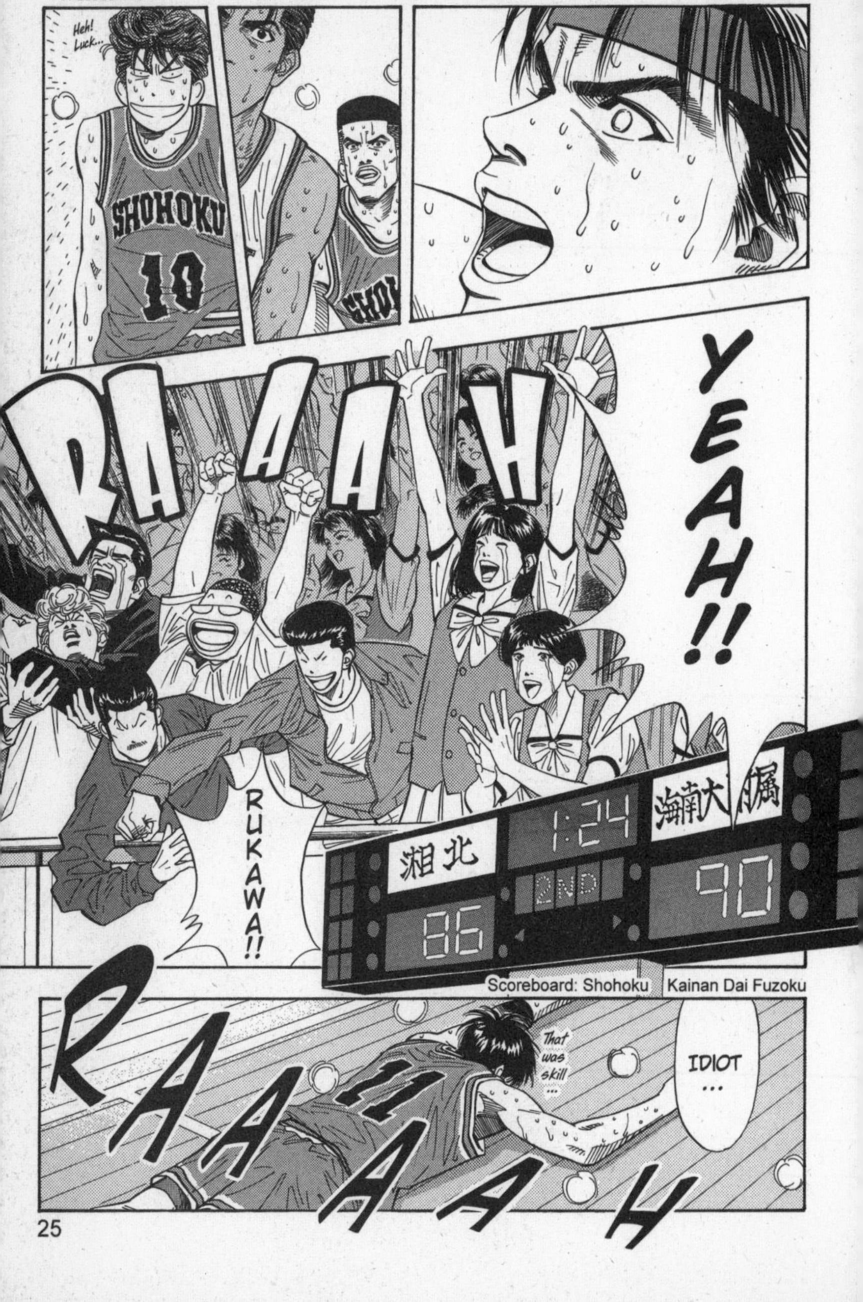

Heh! Luck...
YEAH!!
RAAAH
RUKAWA!!
湘北
1:24
海南大附属
2ND
86
90
Scoreboard: Shohoku
Kainan Dai Fuzoku
IDIOT ...
That was skill ...
RAAAAAH

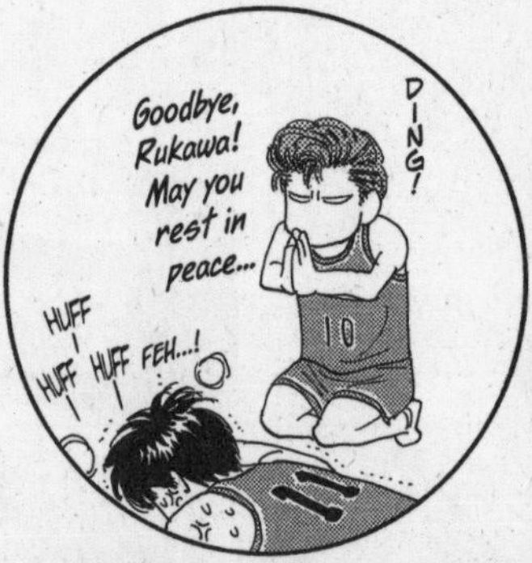
DING!
Goodbye, Rukawa! May you rest in peace...
FEH...!
HUFF HUFF HUFF

SLAM DUNK

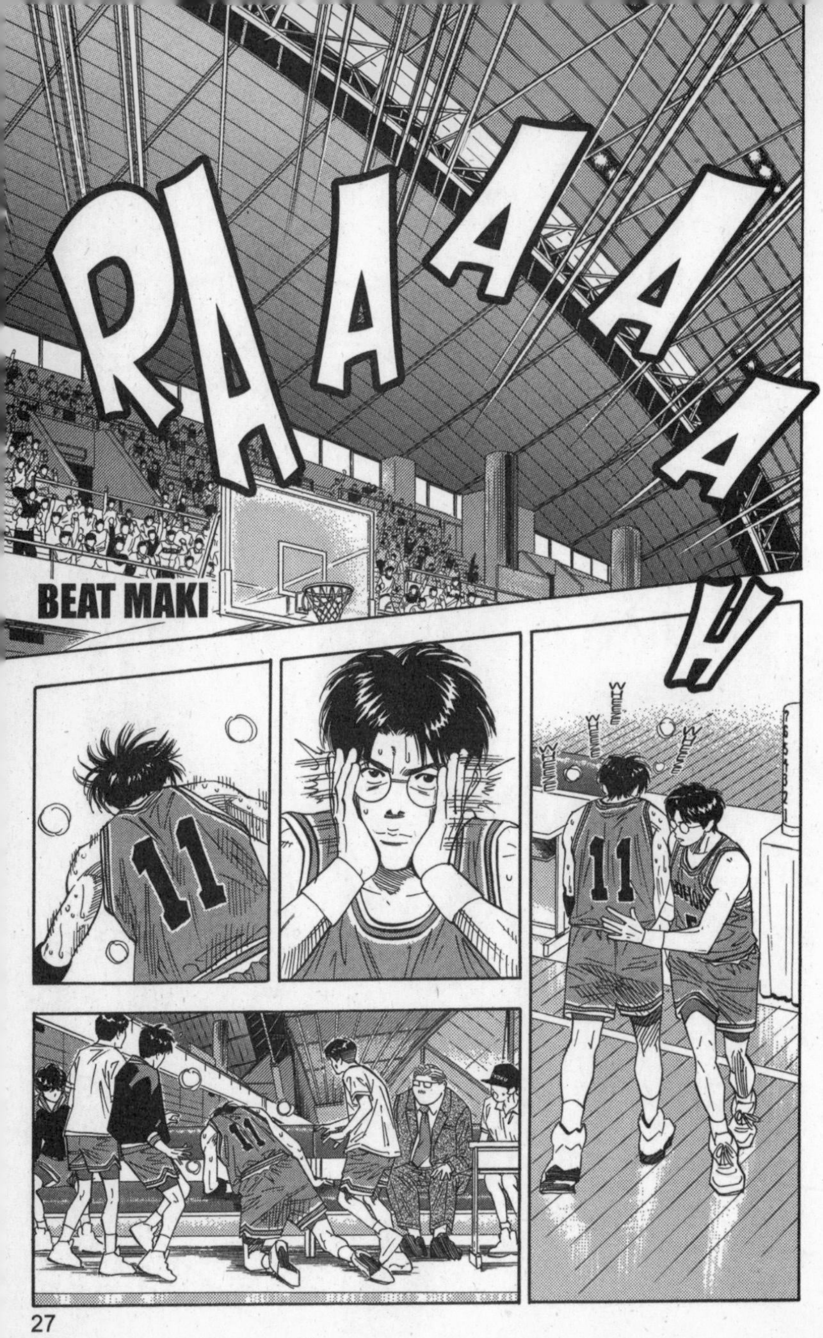
RAAAAA!!
BEAT MAKI

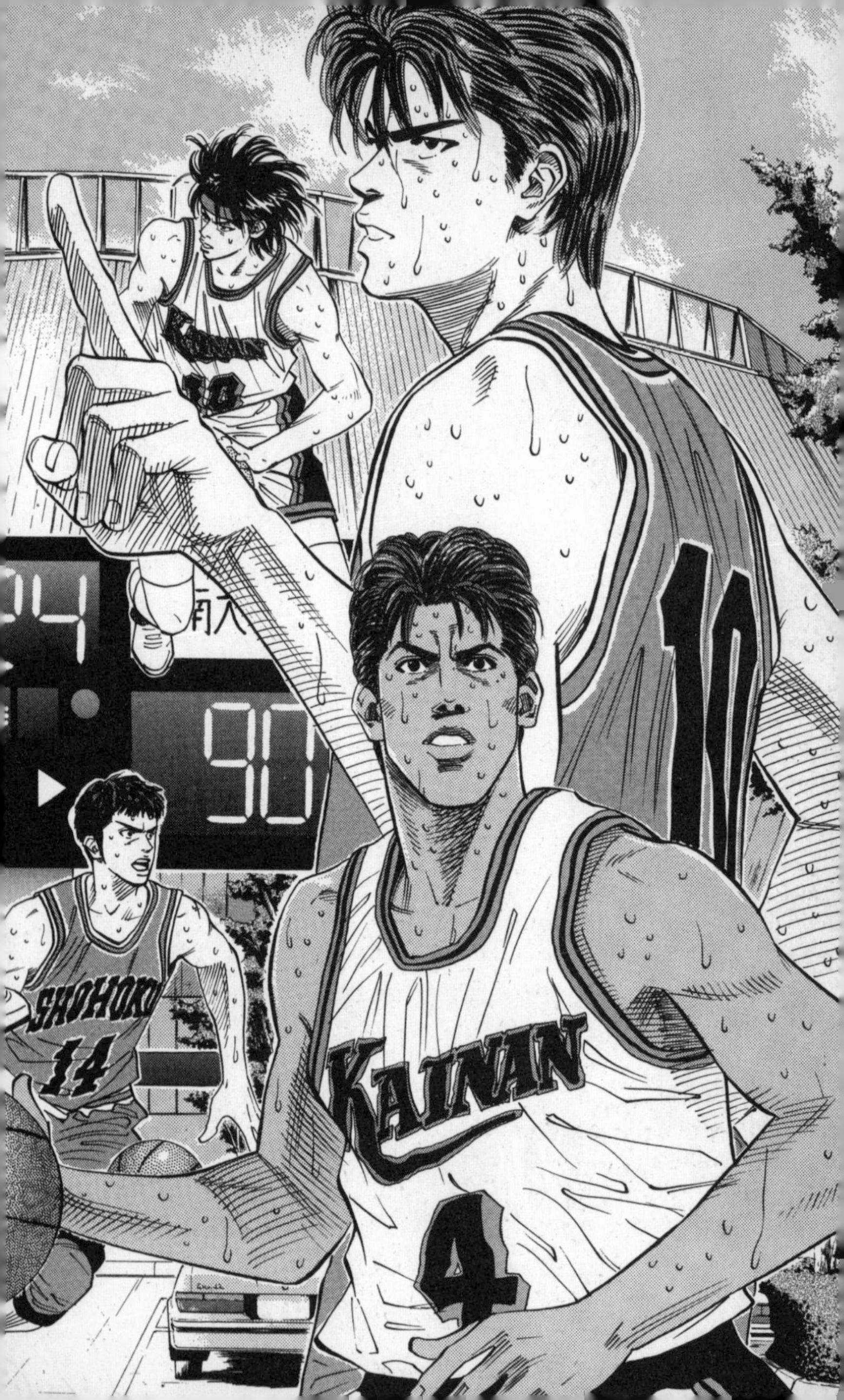
KAINAN
10
90
SHOHOKU
14
KAINAN
4

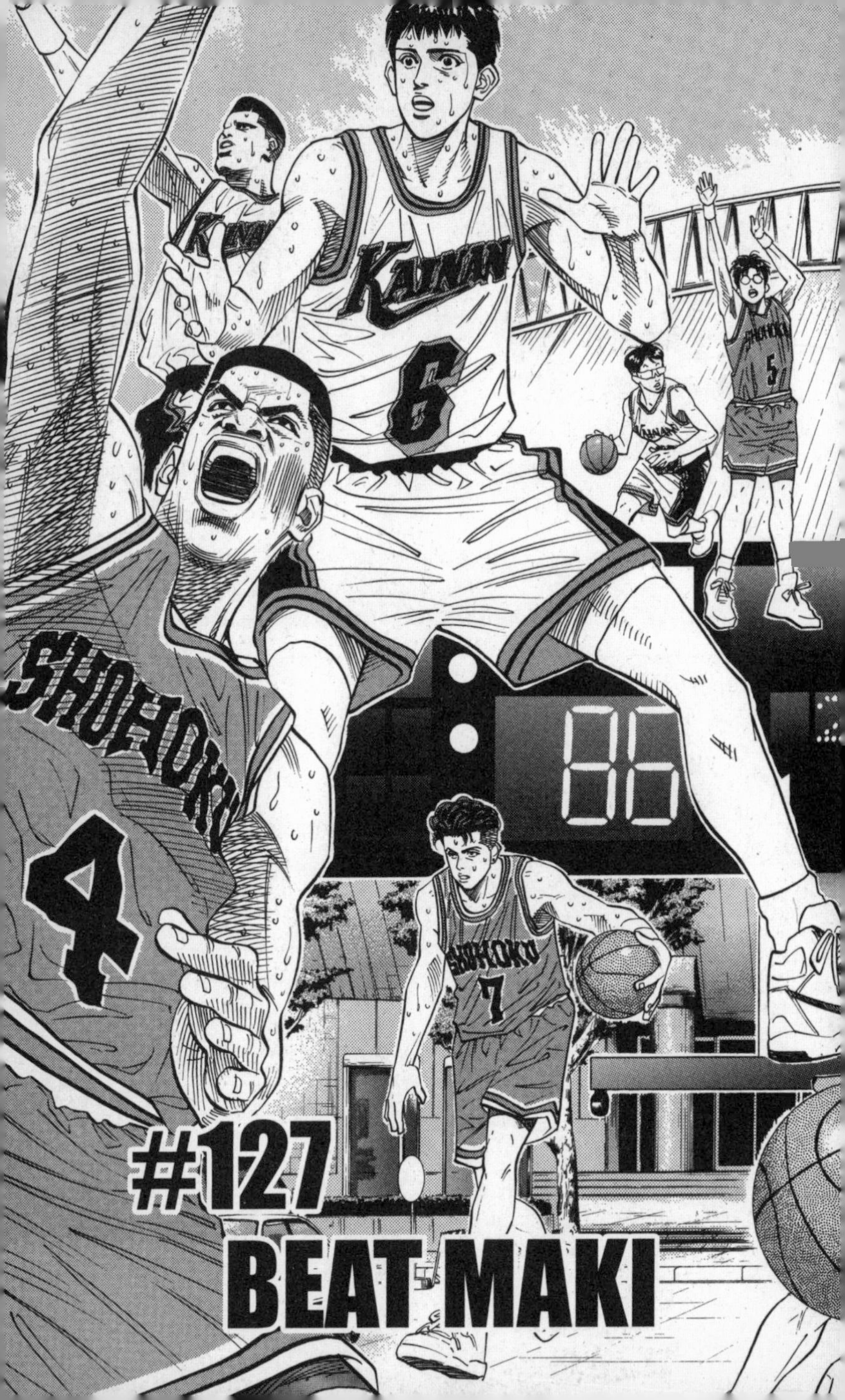
KAINAN
6
SHOHOKU
4
SHOHOKU
7
#127
BEAT MAKI

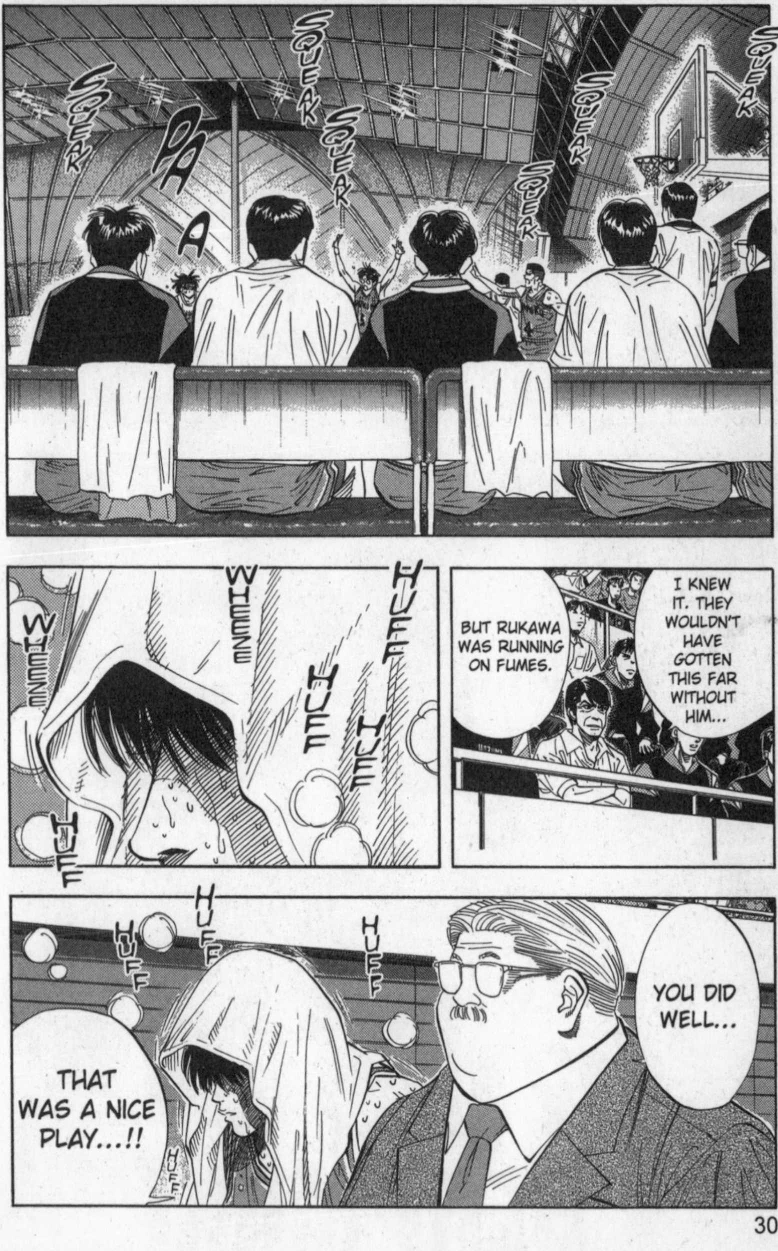
SQUEAK
SQUEAK
SQUEAK
SQUEAK
SQUEAK
SQUEAK
PA
A
I KNEW IT. THEY WOULDN'T HAVE GOTTEN THIS FAR WITHOUT HIM...
BUT RUKAWA WAS RUNNING ON FUMES.
HUFF
HUFF
HUFF
WHEEZE
WHEEZE
HUFF
HUFF
HUFF
YOU DID WELL...
HUFF
THAT WAS A NICE PLAY...!!
HUFF

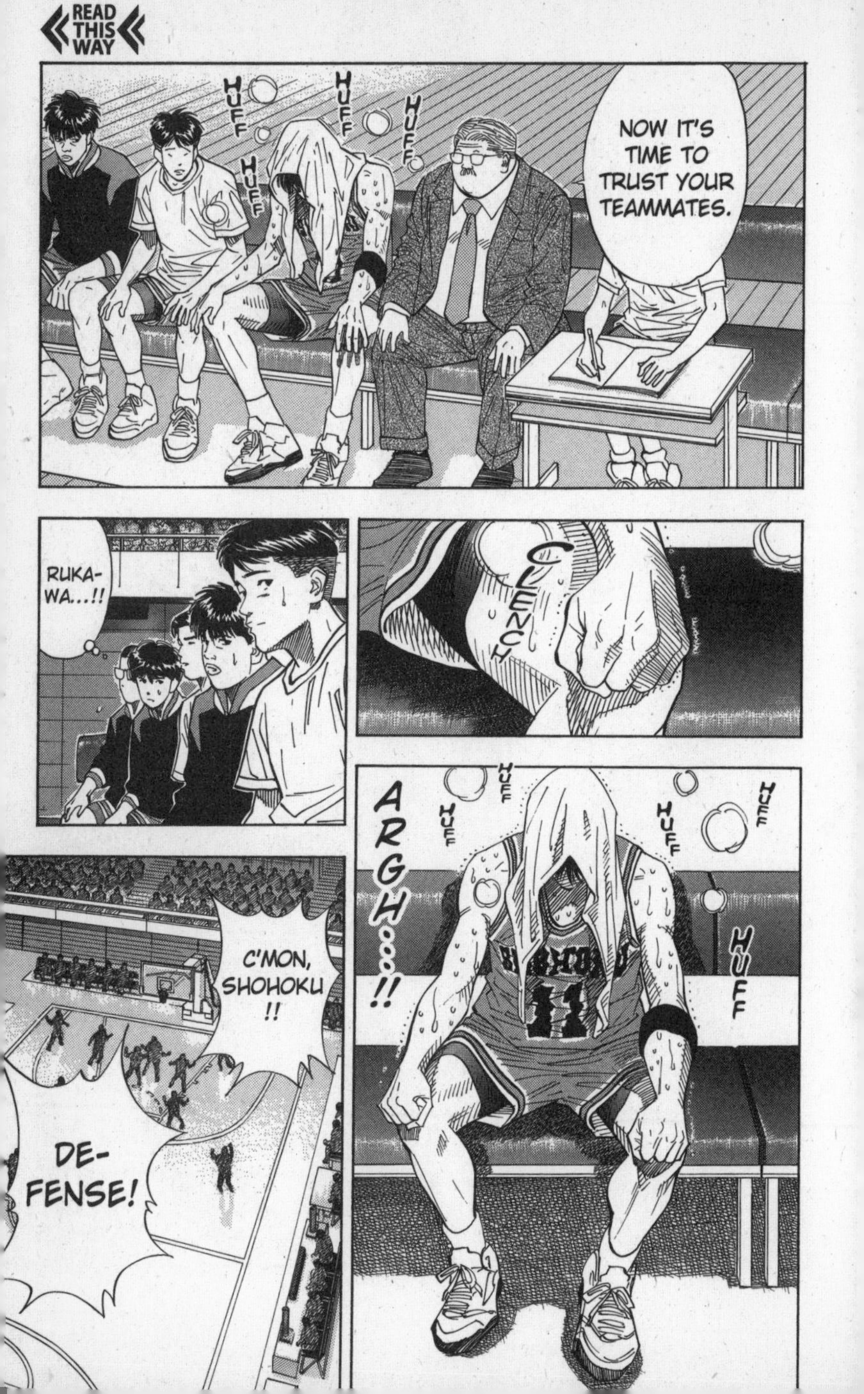
READ THIS WAY
NOW IT'S TIME TO TRUST YOUR TEAMMATES.
HUFF
HUFF
HUFF
HUFF
CLENCH
RUKAWA...!!
HUFF
HUFF
HUFF
HUFF
HUFF
ARGH...!!
C'MON, SHOHOKU!!
DEFENSE!

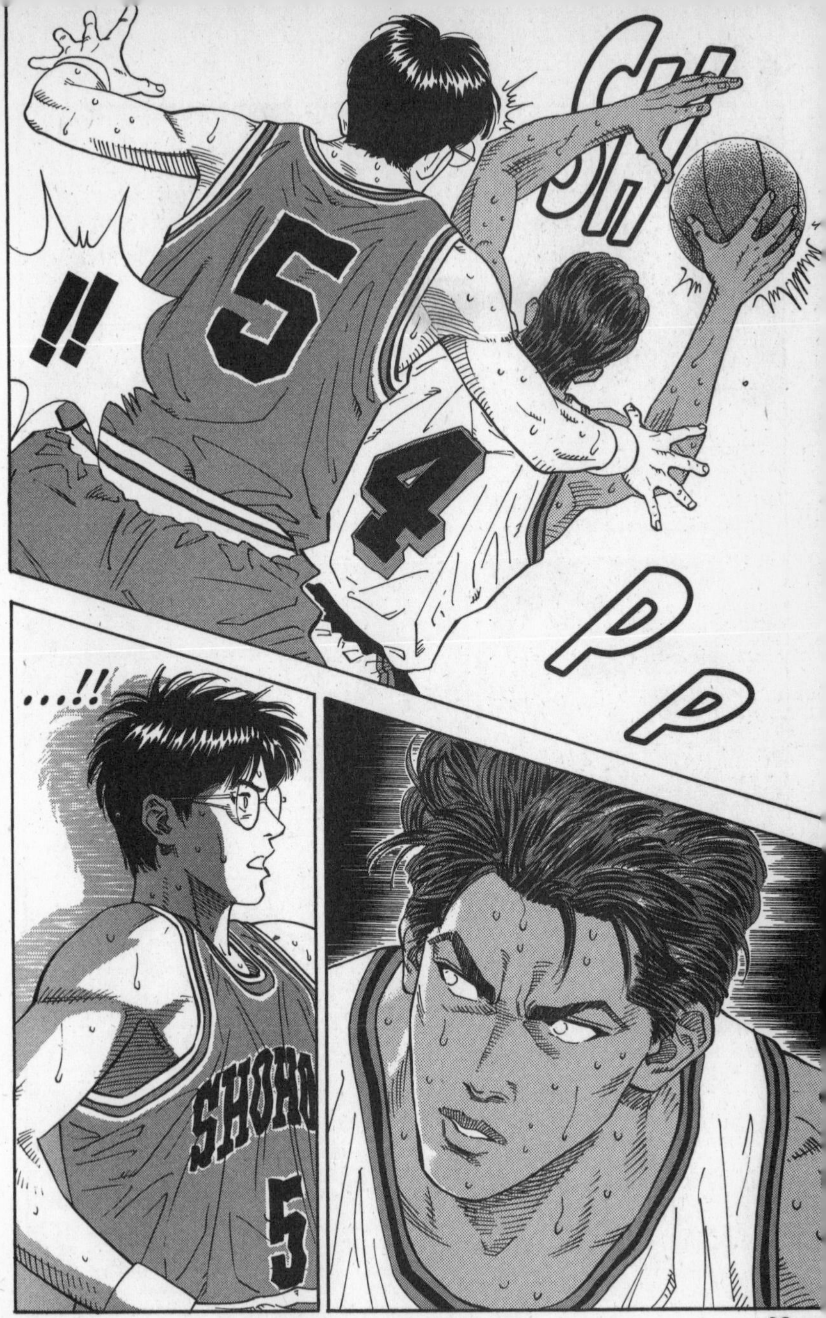
!!
SHH
PP
PP
...!!
SHOHO
5
5
4

READ THIS WAY

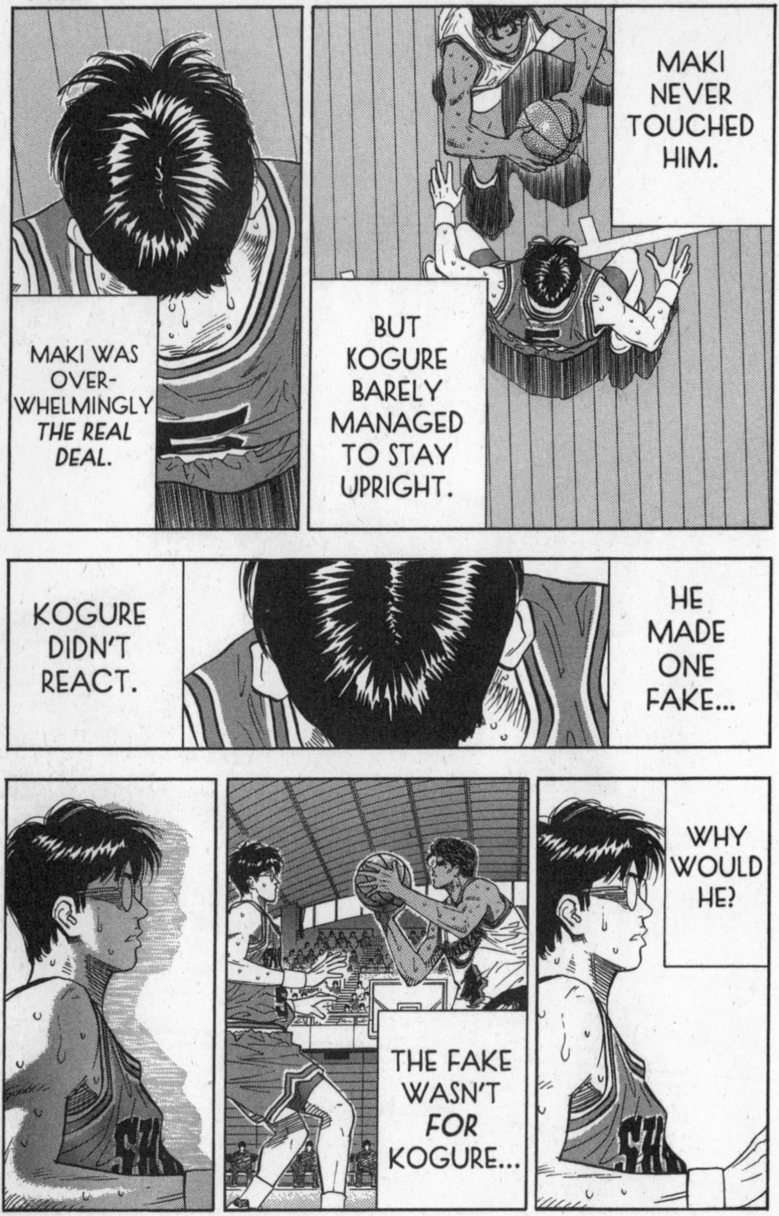
MAKI NEVER TOUCHED HIM.
BUT KOGURE BARELY MANAGED TO STAY UPRIGHT.
MAKI WAS OVER-WHELMINGLY *THE REAL DEAL*.
HE MADE ONE FAKE...
KOGURE DIDN'T REACT.
WHY WOULD HE?
THE FAKE WASN'T *FOR* KOGURE...

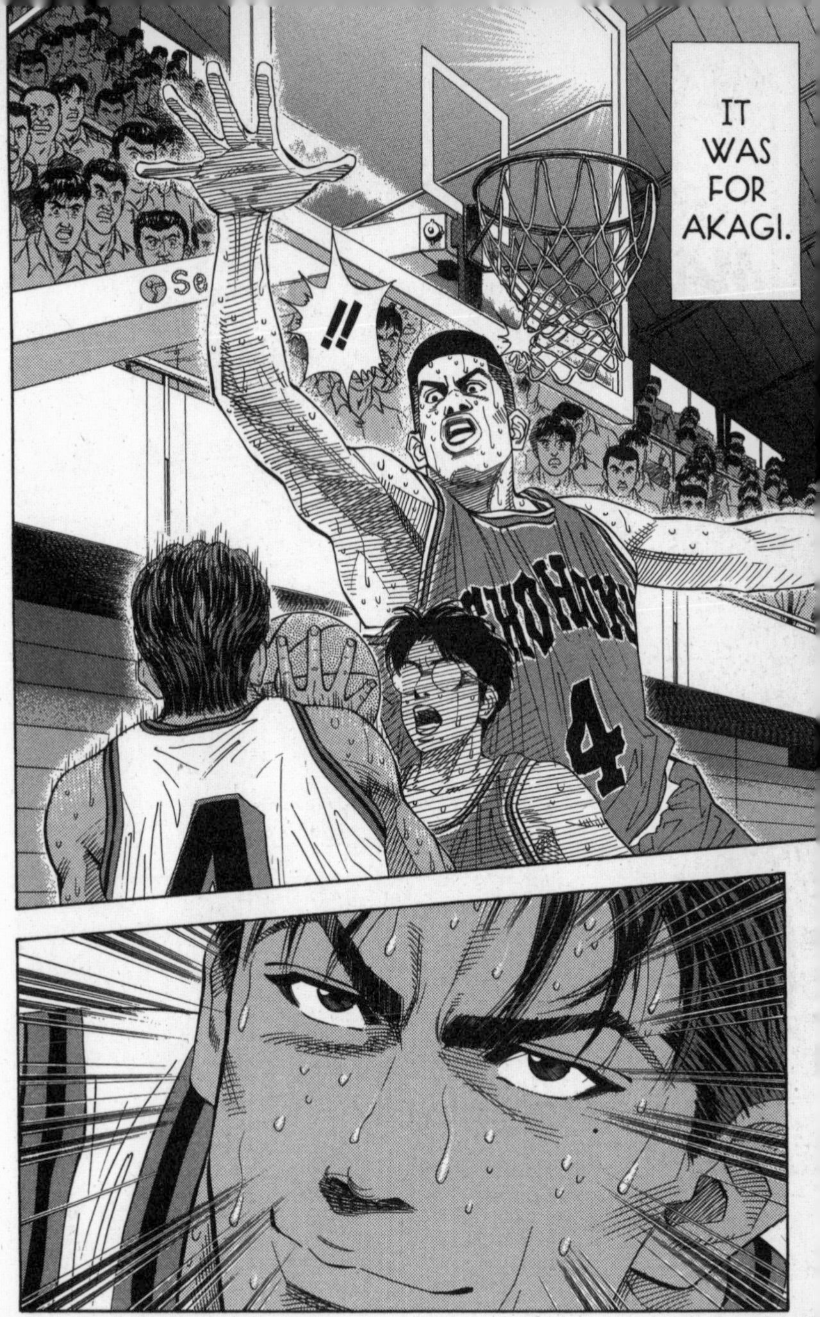
IT WAS FOR AKAGI.
!!
SHOHOKU
4

READ THIS WAY

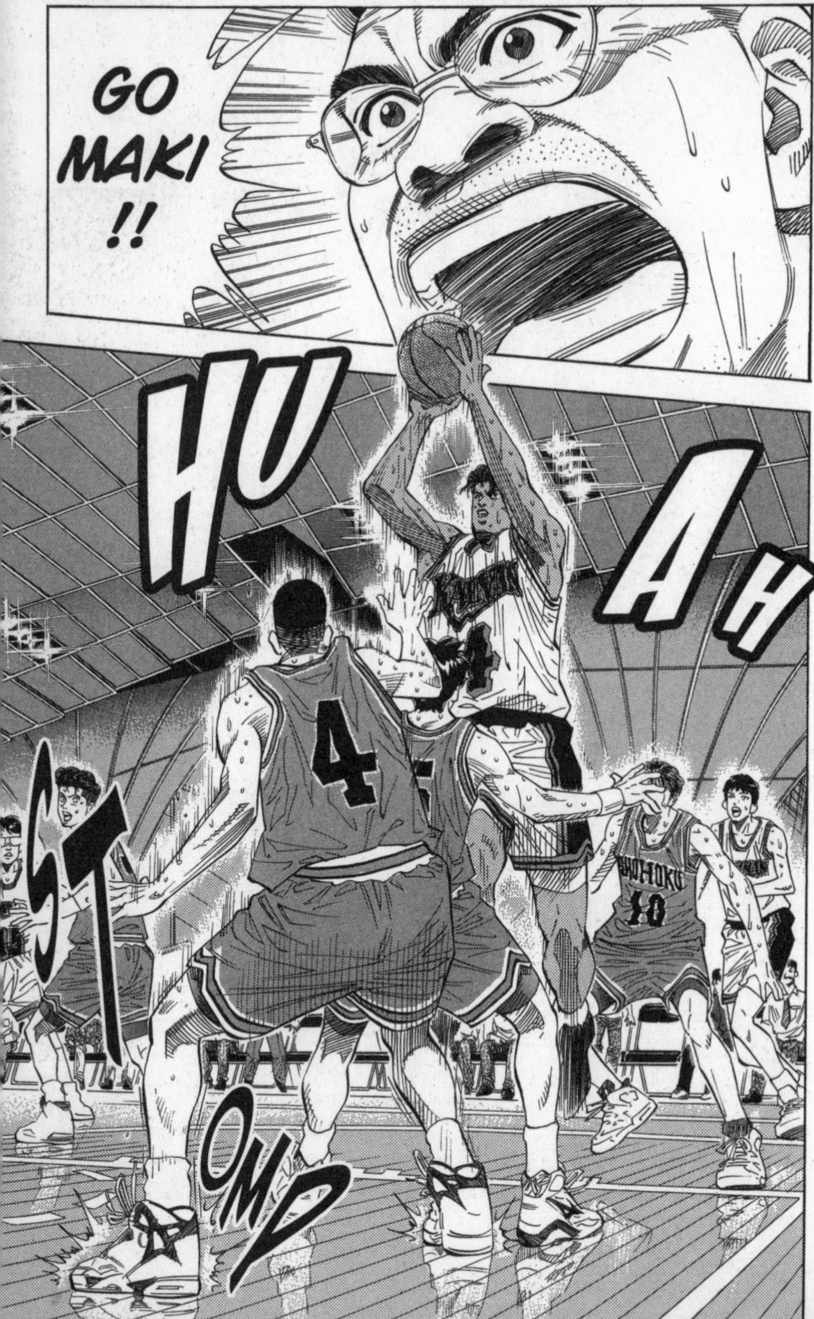
GO MAKI !!
HUAH
STOMP

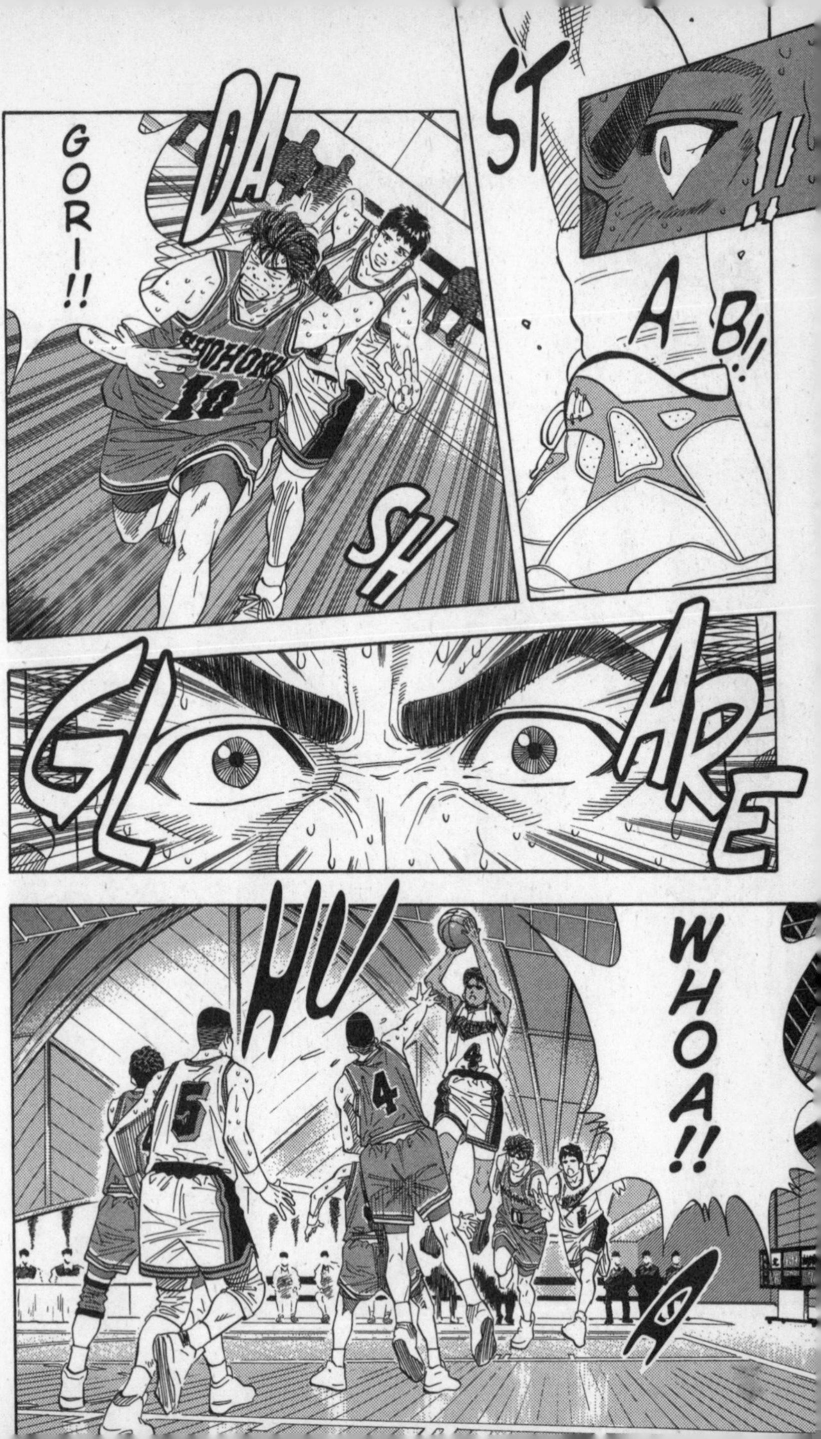
ST
!!
A B!!
DA
GORI!!
SH
GL ARE
WHOA!!
HU
A

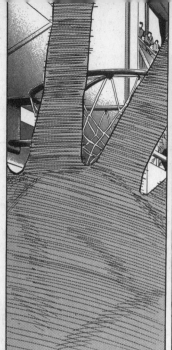

!!

NOOO!

THAT'S IT!!

FLICK

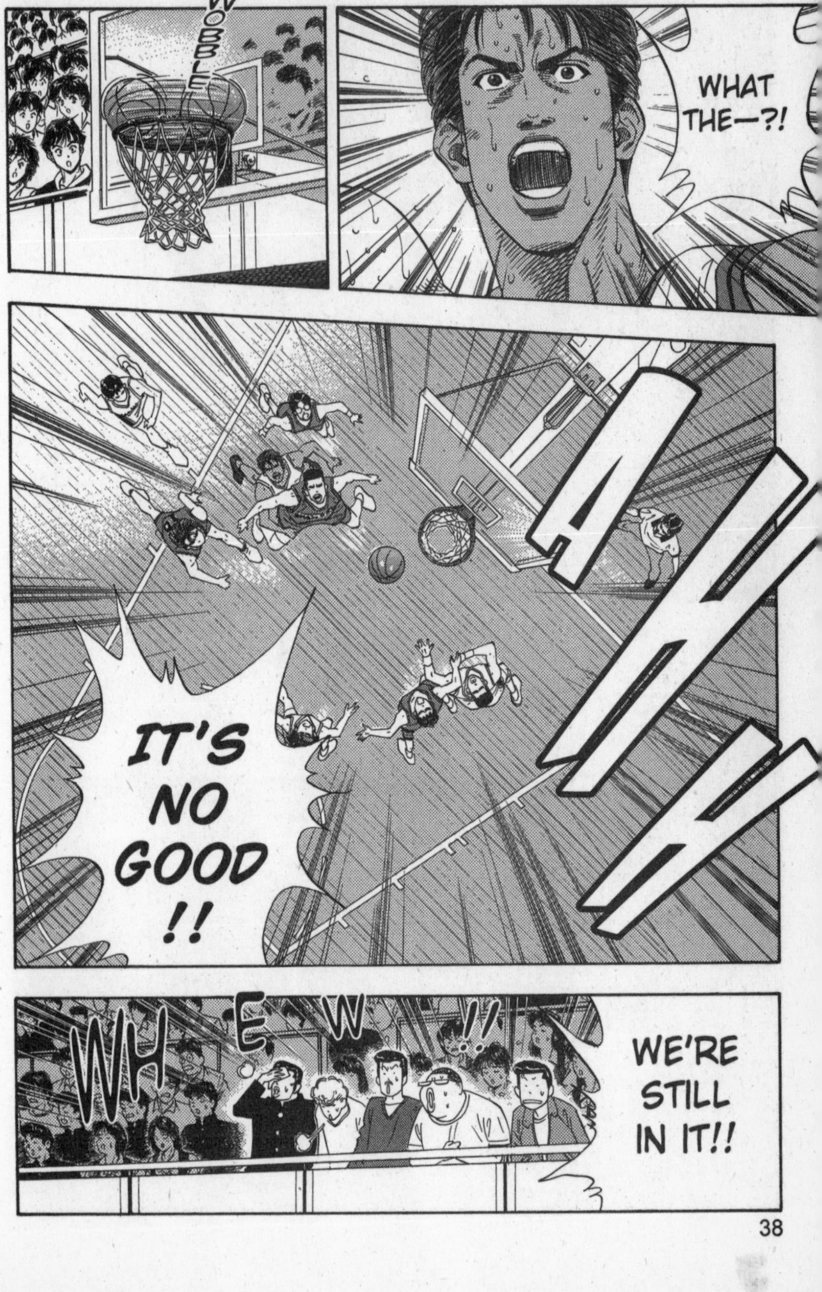
WHAT THE—?!
WOBBLE
IT'S NO GOOD!!
WE'RE STILL IN IT!!
WHEW!!

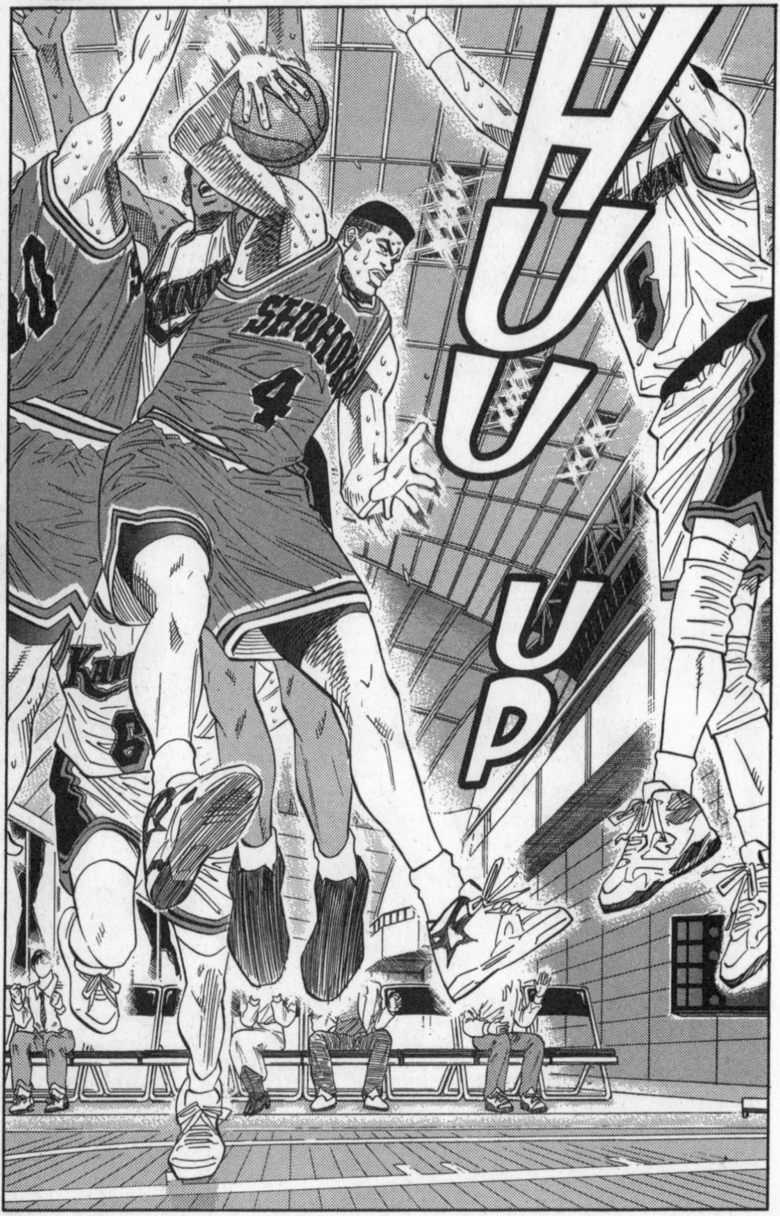
HUUUUP

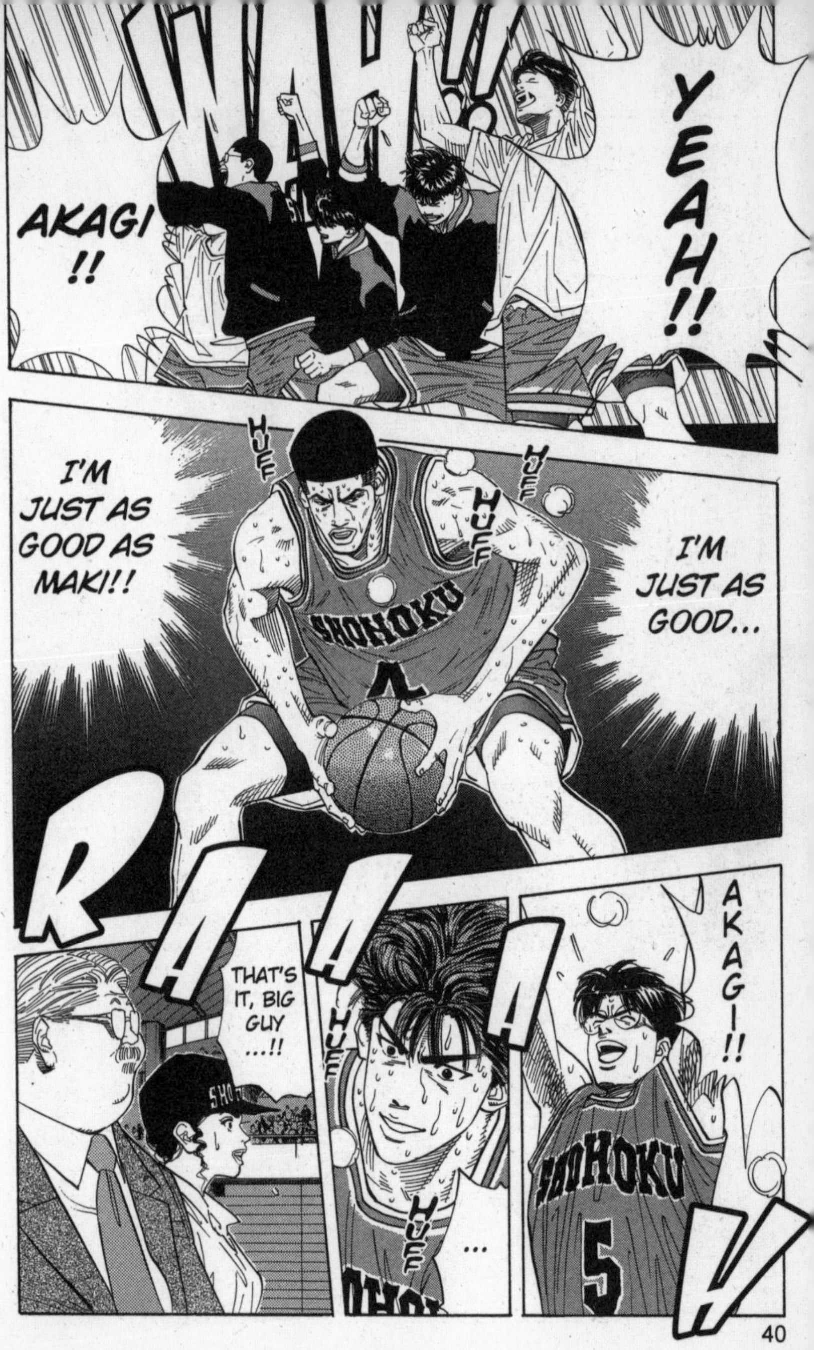
YEAH!!
AKAGI !!
I'M JUST AS GOOD...
HUFF
HUFF
HUFF
I'M JUST AS GOOD AS MAKI!!
SHOHOKU
RAAA
AKAGI!!
SHOHOKU
HUFF
...
HUFF
THAT'S IT, BIG GUY ...!!

READ THIS WAY

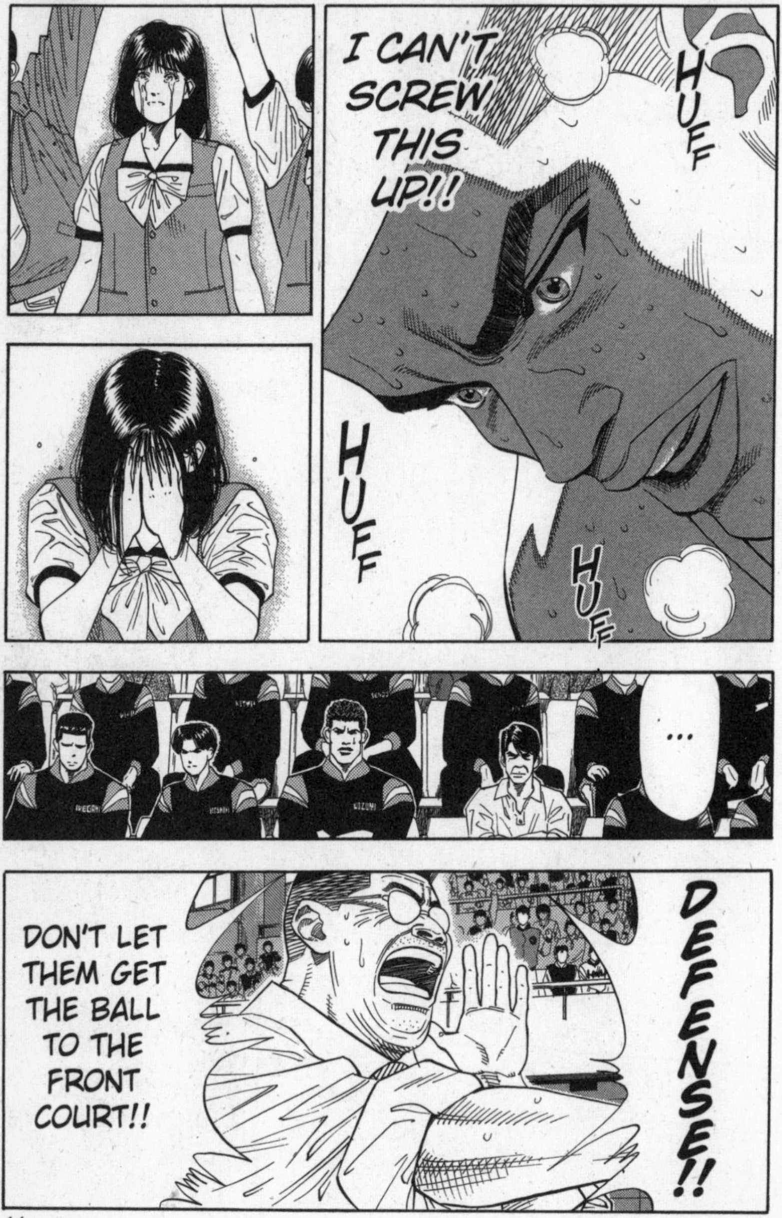
I CAN'T SCREW THIS UP!!
HUFF
HUFF
HUFF
...
DEFENSE!!
DON'T LET THEM GET THE BALL TO THE FRONT COURT!!

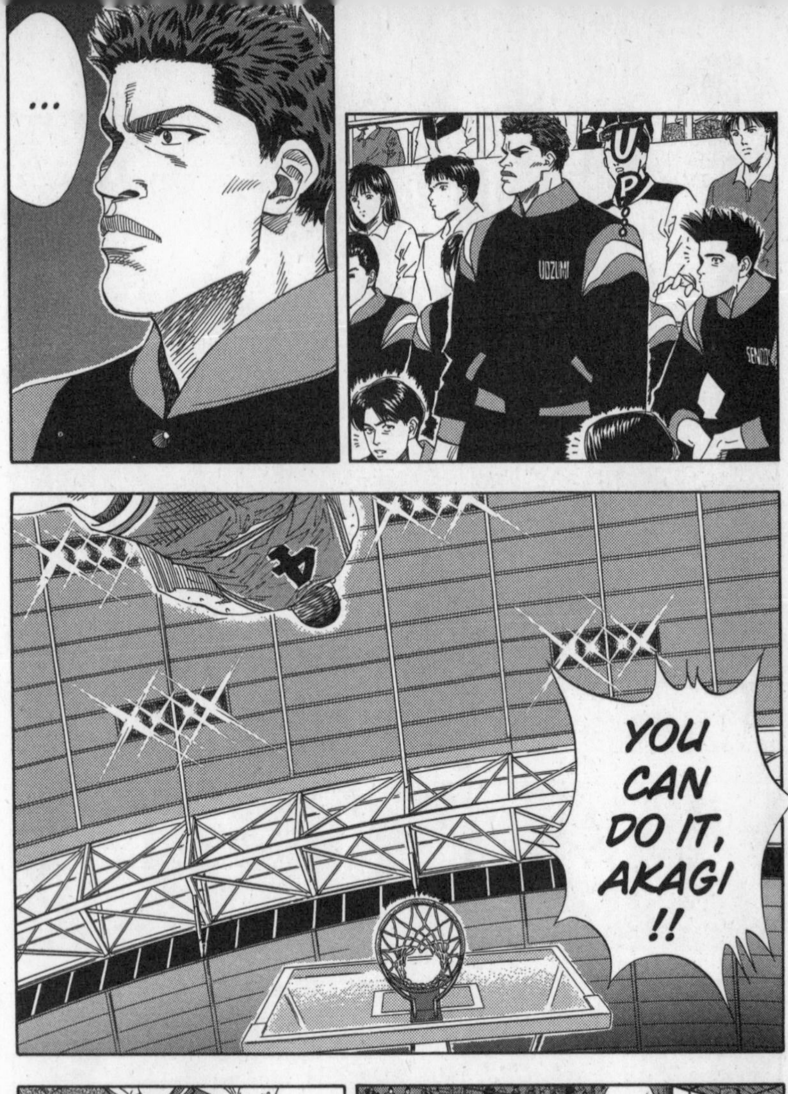
...
YOU CAN DO IT, AKAGI !!
!!
WHAT'S GOING ON?

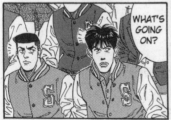

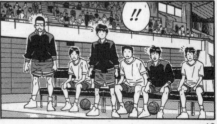

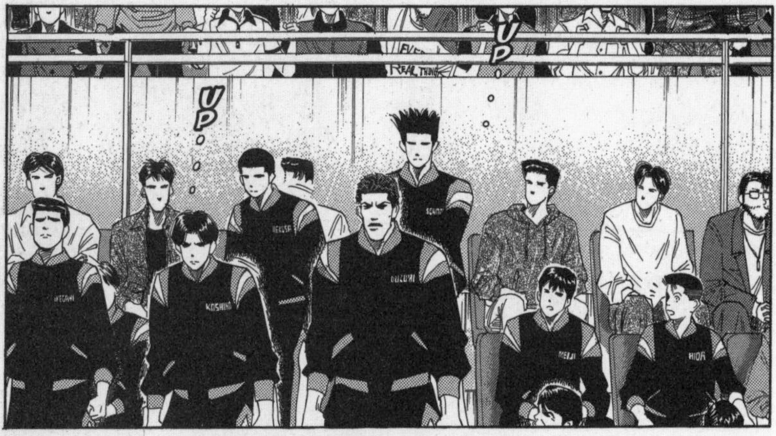
UP...
UP...

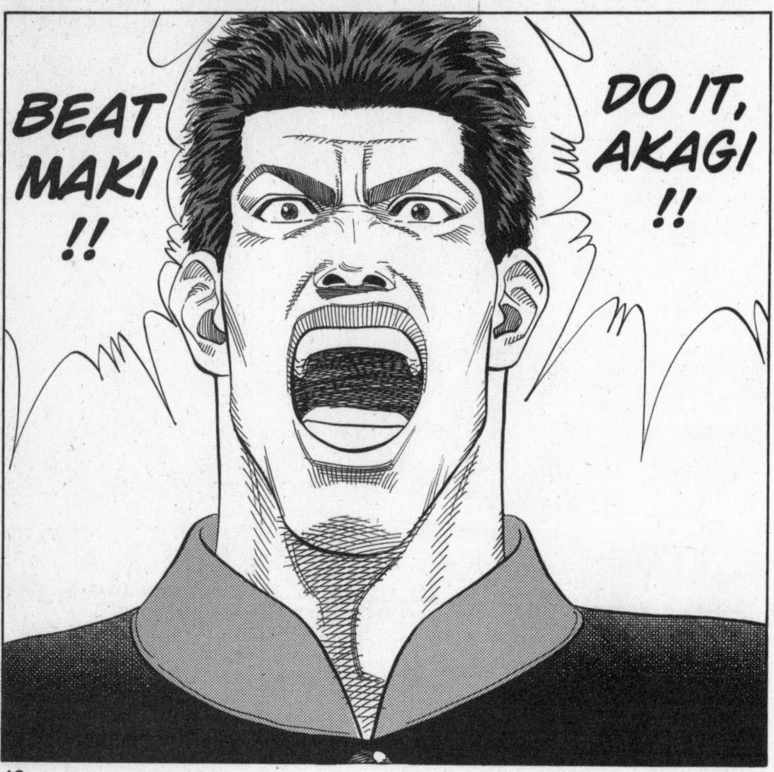
DO IT, AKAGI !!
BEAT MAKI !!

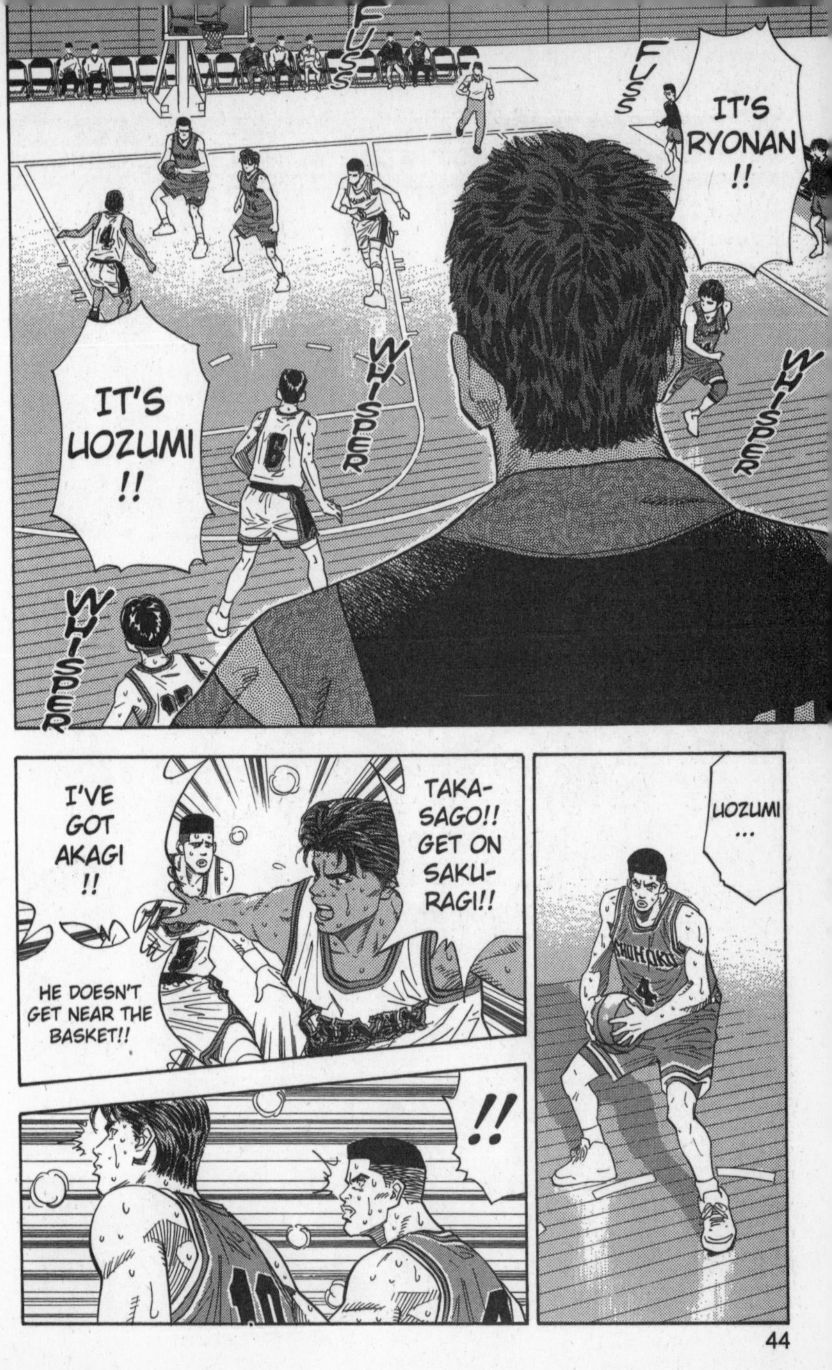
FUSS
FUSS
IT'S RYONAN!!
WHISPER
IT'S UOZUMI!!
WHISPER
WHISPER
UOZUMI...
TAKA-SAGO!! GET ON SAKU-RAGI!!
I'VE GOT AKAGI!!
HE DOESN'T GET NEAR THE BASKET!!
!!

READ THIS WAY

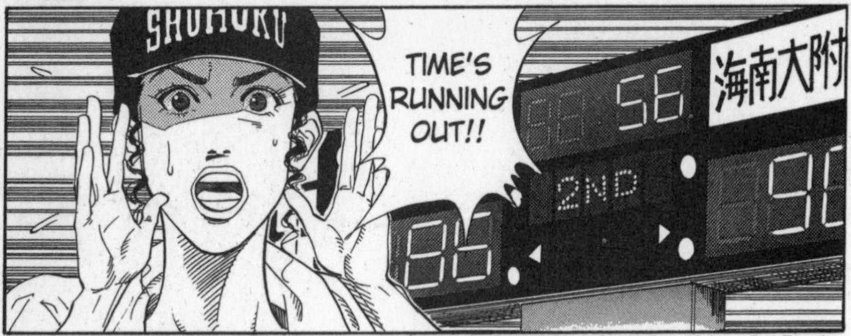
SHOHOKU
TIME'S RUNNING OUT!!
海南大附
56
2ND

Scoreboard: Shohoku   Kainan Dai Fuzoku

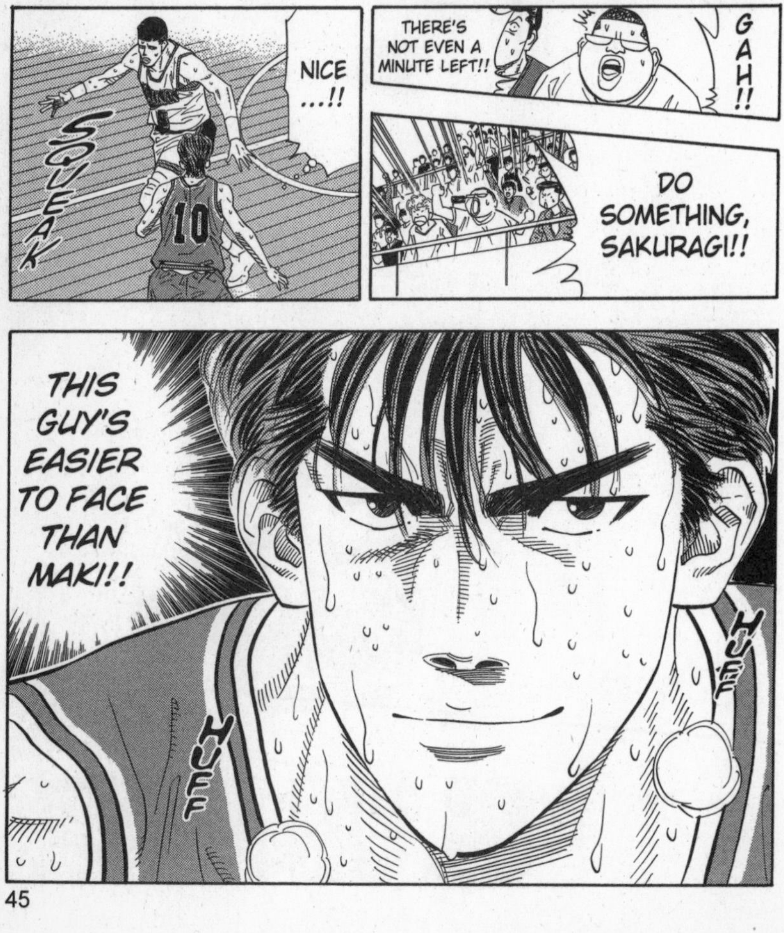
GAH!!
THERE'S NOT EVEN A MINUTE LEFT!!
DO SOMETHING, SAKURAGI!!
NICE ...!!
SQUEAK
10
THIS GUY'S EASIER TO FACE THAN MAKI!!
HUFF
HUFF

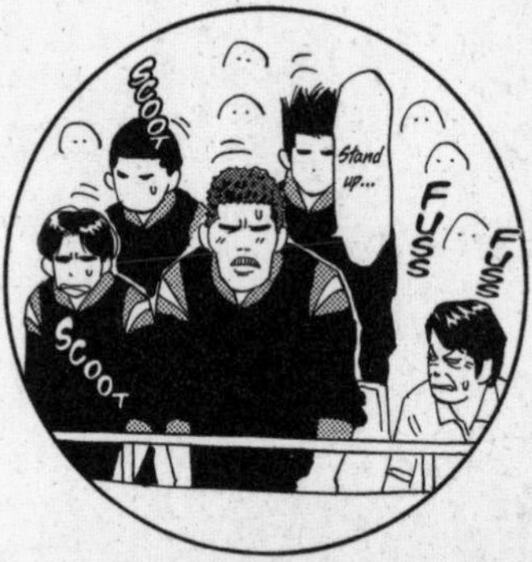
SCOOT
Stand up...
FUSS
FUSS
SCOOT

SLAM DUNK

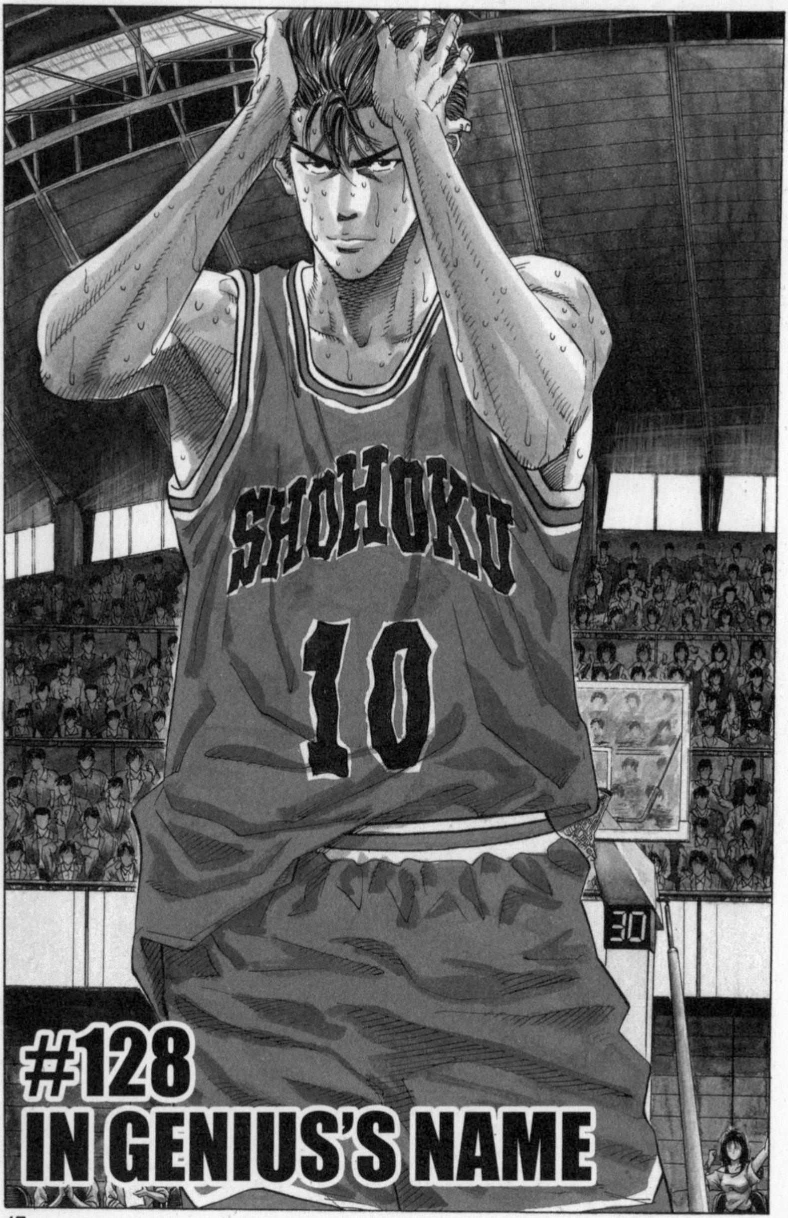
SHOHOKU
10
30
#128
IN GENIUS'S NAME

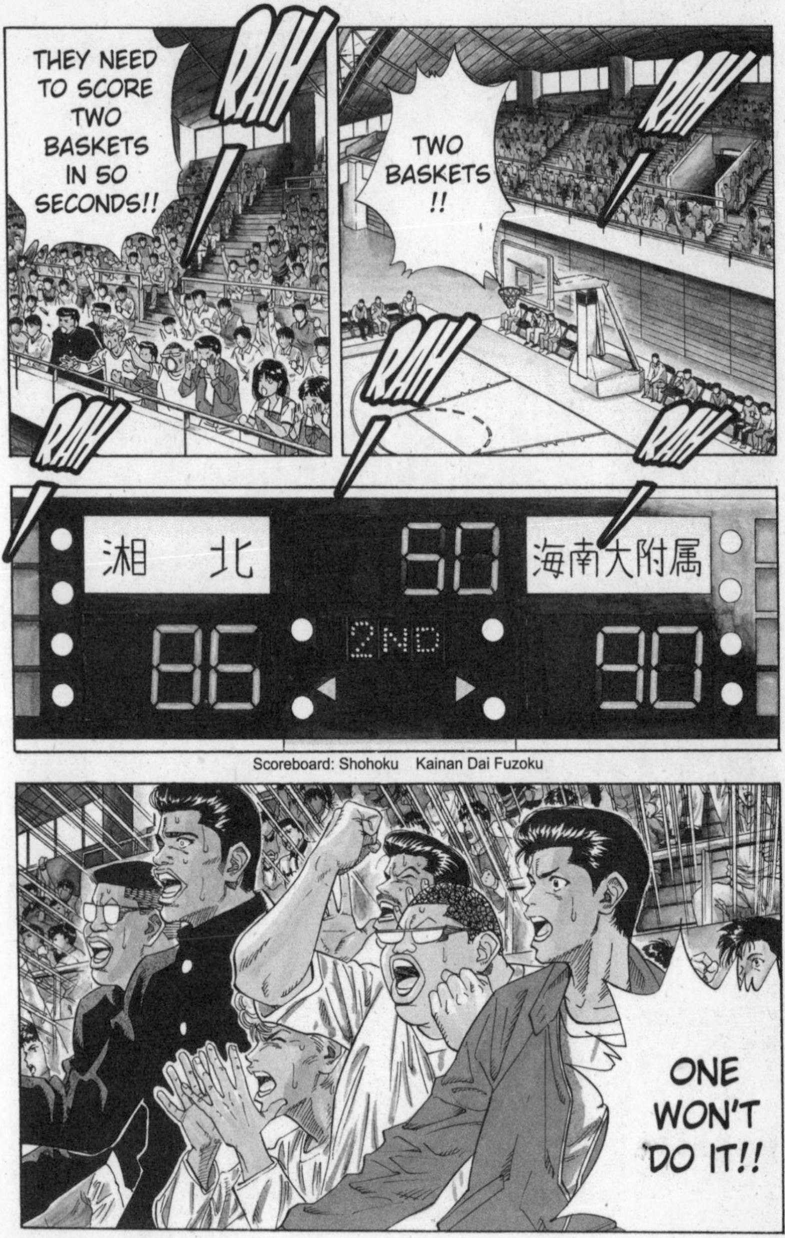

RAH
TWO BASKETS !!
RAH
RAH
THEY NEED TO SCORE TWO BASKETS IN 50 SECONDS!!
RAH
RAH
湘北
50
海南大附属
86
2ND
90
ONE WON'T DO IT!!

Scoreboard: Shohoku Kainan Dai Fuzoku

READ THIS WAY

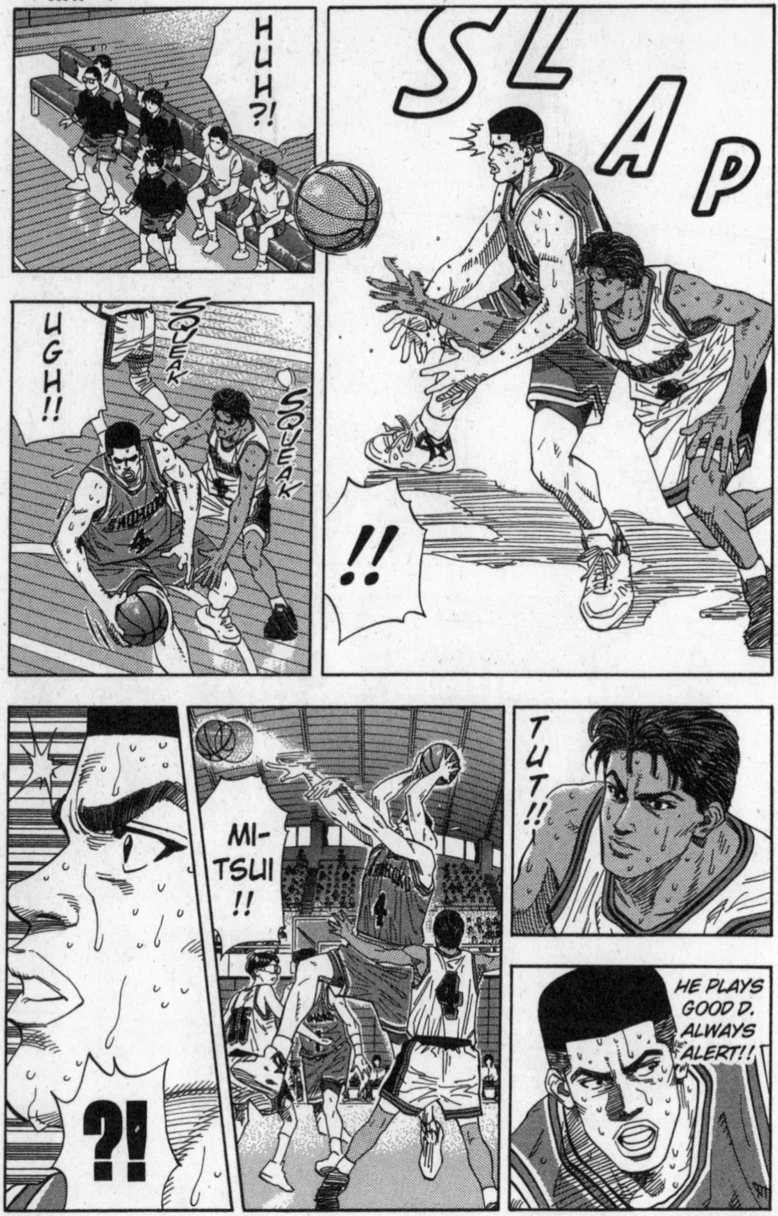

SLAP
!!
HUH?!
UGH!!
SQUEAK
SQUEAK
TUT!!
HE PLAYS GOOD D. ALWAYS ALERT!!
MI-TSUI!!
?!

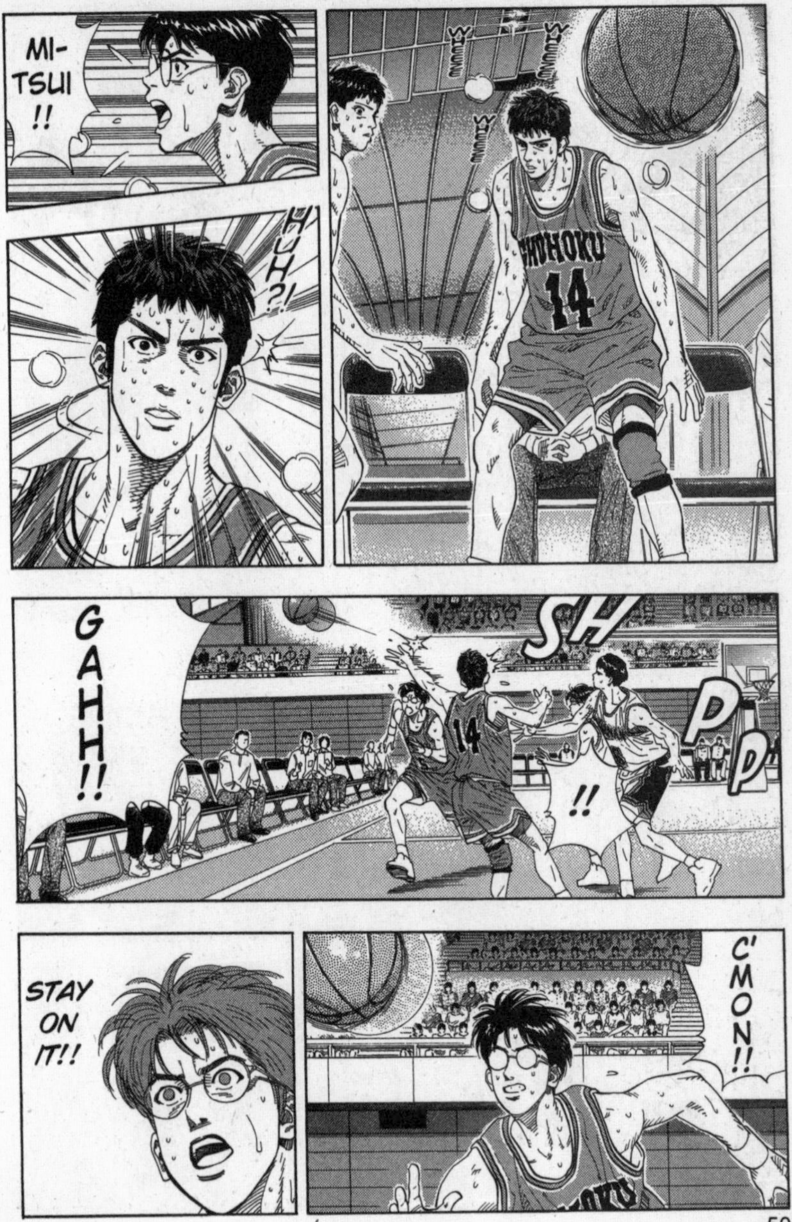
WHEEZE
WHEEZE
WHEEZE
MI-
TSUI
!!
HUH?!
SH
P
P
!!
GAHH!!
C'MON!!
STAY
ON
IT!!

READ THIS WAY

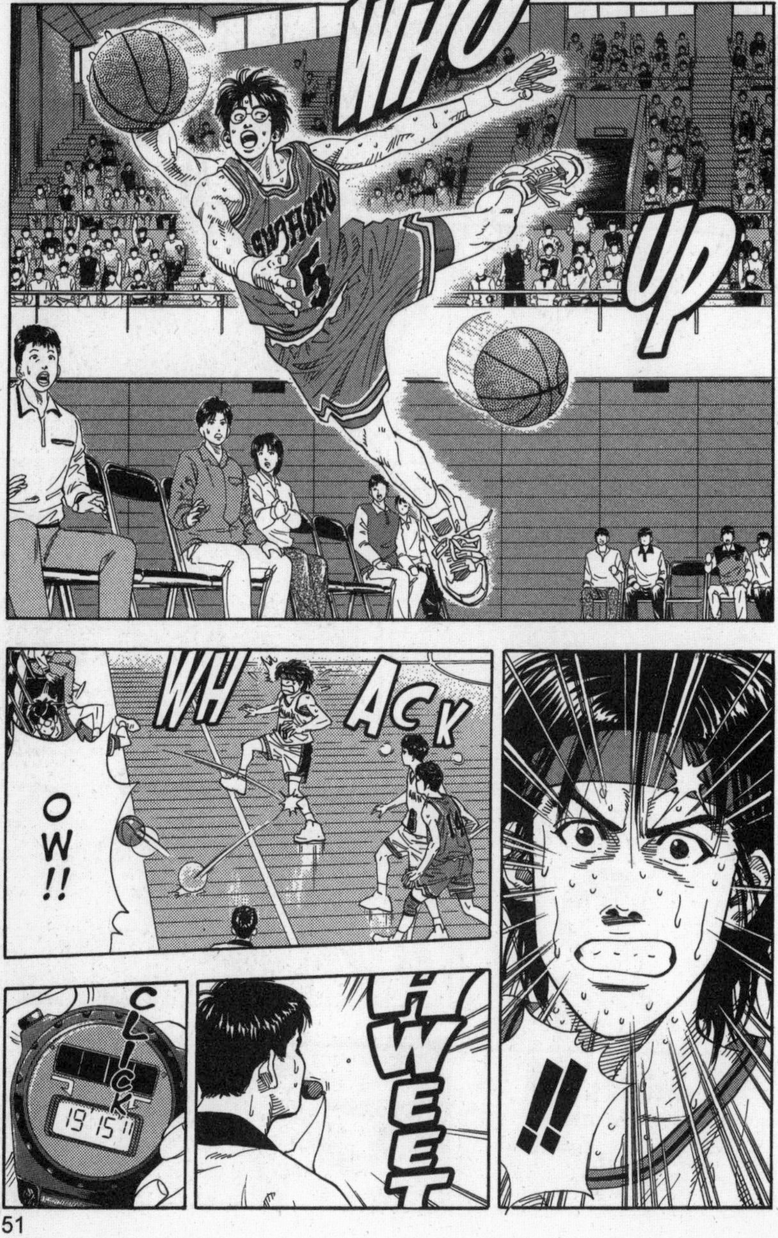
WHU
UP
!!
WH
ACK
OW!!
HWEET
CLICK

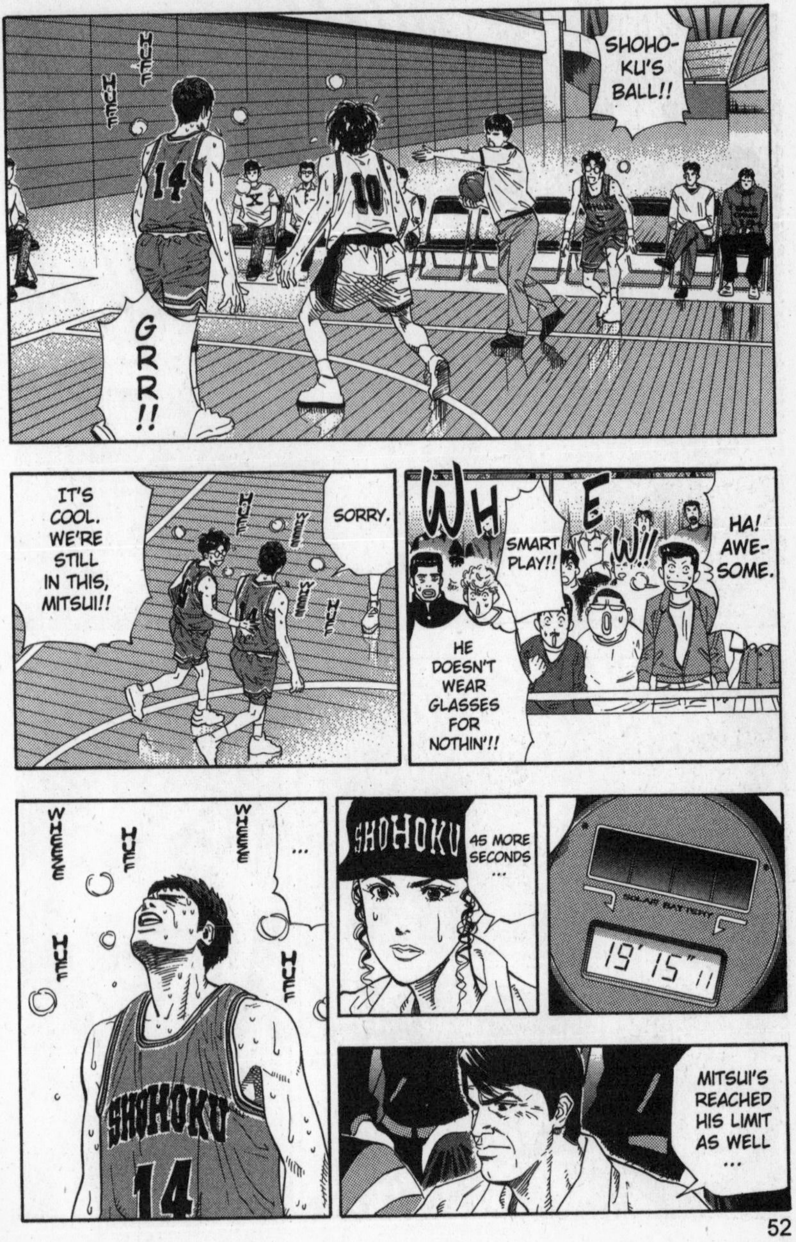
SHOHOKU'S BALL!!
HUFF
HUFF
GRR!!
WHEEW!!
HA! AWESOME.
SMART PLAY!!
HE DOESN'T WEAR GLASSES FOR NOTHIN'!!
SORRY.
HUFF
WHEEZE
WHEEZE
HUFF
IT'S COOL. WE'RE STILL IN THIS, MITSUI!!
SOLAR BATTERY
19'15"11
45 MORE SECONDS ...
MITSUI'S REACHED HIS LIMIT AS WELL ...
WHEEZE
...
HUFF
WHEEZE
HUFF
HUFF

READ THIS WAY

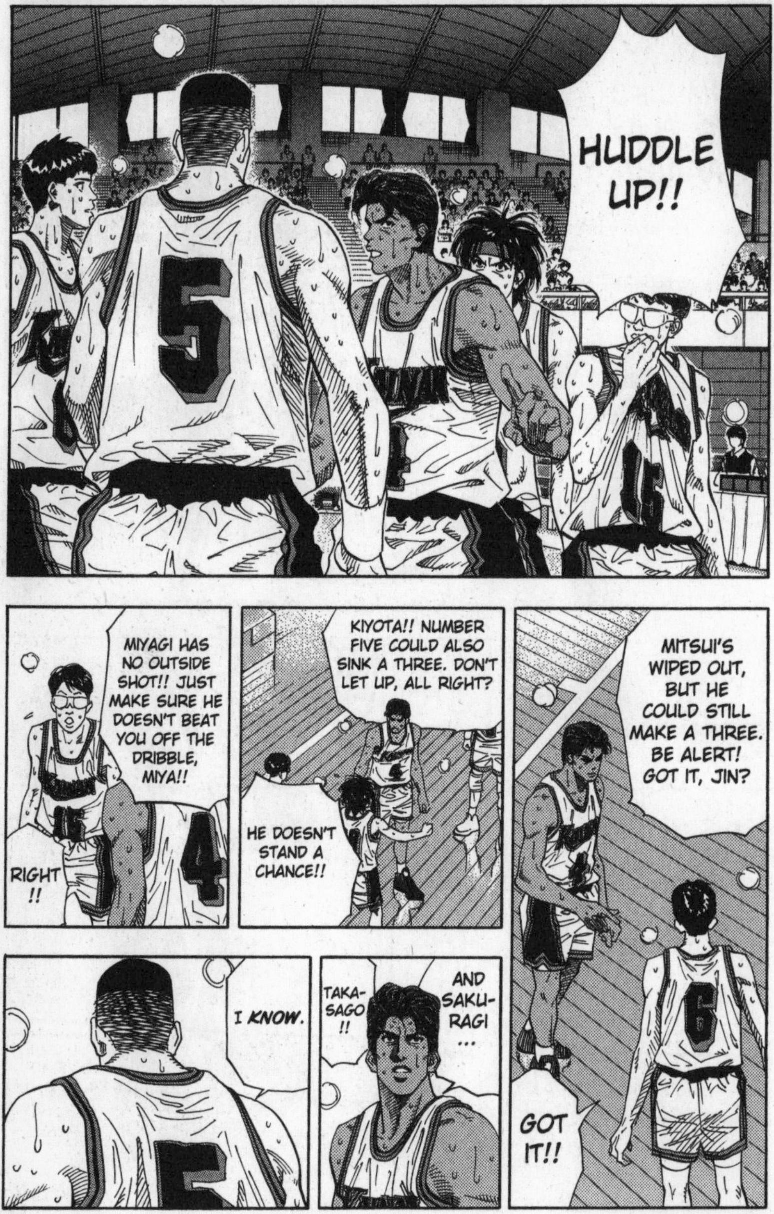
HUDDLE UP!!
MITSUI'S WIPED OUT, BUT HE COULD STILL MAKE A THREE. BE ALERT! GOT IT, JIN?
GOT IT!!
KIYOTA!! NUMBER FIVE COULD ALSO SINK A THREE. DON'T LET UP, ALL RIGHT?
HE DOESN'T STAND A CHANCE!!
MIYAGI HAS NO OUTSIDE SHOT!! JUST MAKE SURE HE DOESN'T BEAT YOU OFF THE DRIBBLE, MIYA!!
RIGHT!!
TAKA-SAGO!!
AND SAKU-RAGI...
I *KNOW*.

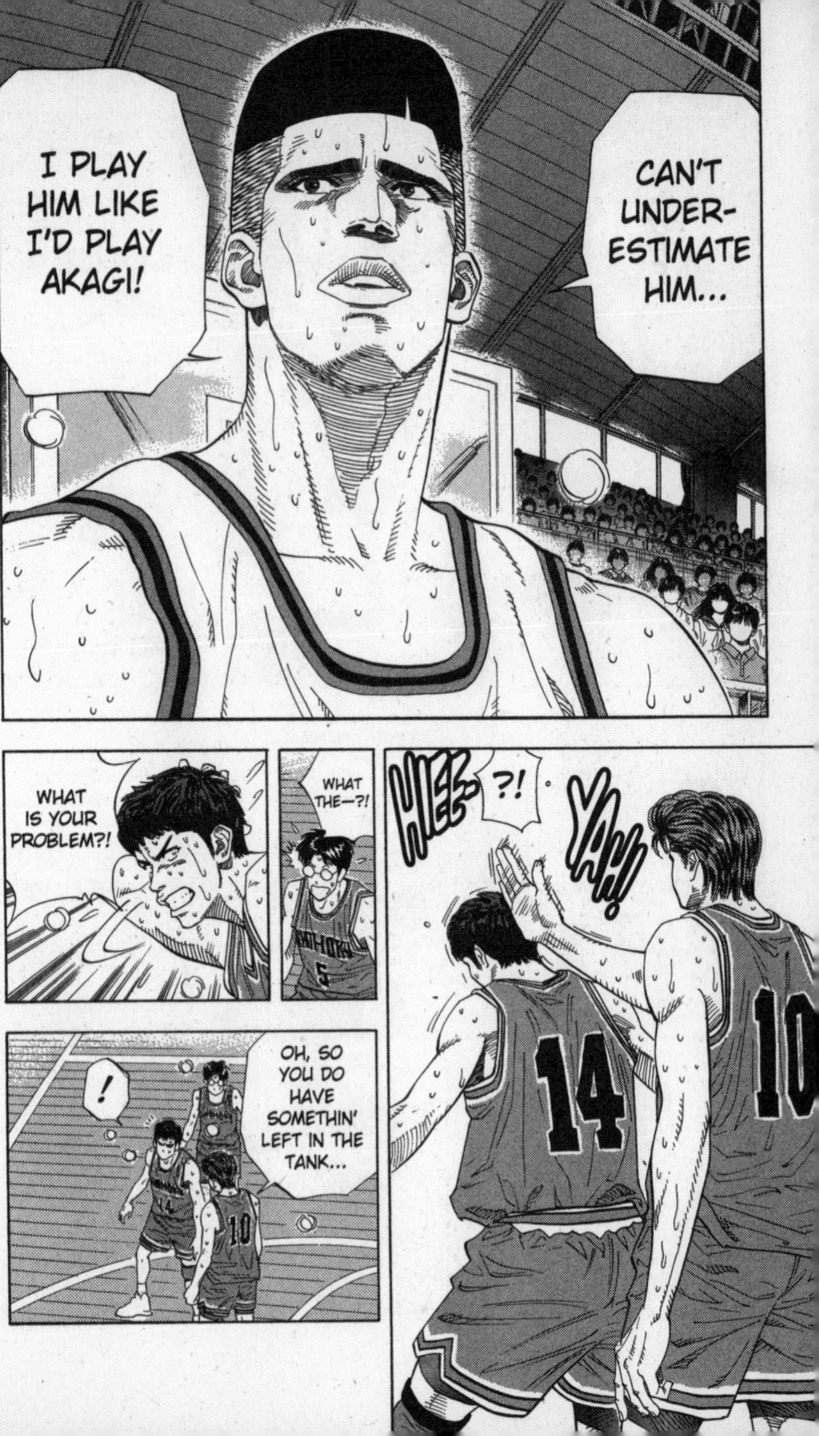
CAN'T UNDER-ESTIMATE HIM...
I PLAY HIM LIKE I'D PLAY AKAGI!
HIEE-
?!
YAH!
WHAT THE—?!
WHAT IS YOUR PROBLEM?!
OH, SO YOU DO HAVE SOMETHIN' LEFT IN THE TANK...
!

READ THIS WAY

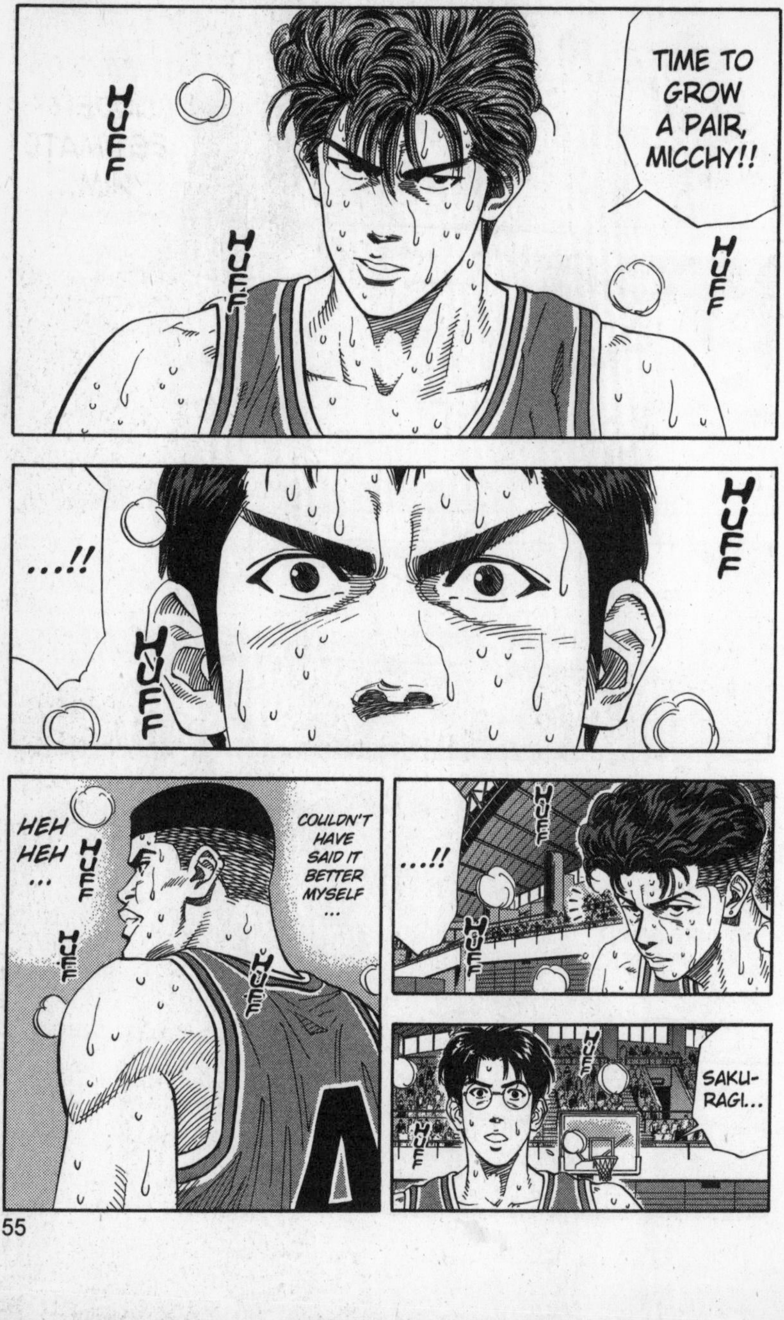
TIME TO GROW A PAIR, MICCHY!!
HUFF
HUFF
HUFF
HUFF
...!!
HUFF
...!!
HUFF
HUFF
SAKU-RAGI...
HUFF
HUFF
COULDN'T HAVE SAID IT BETTER MYSELF ...
HEH HEH ...
HUFF
HUFF
HUFF

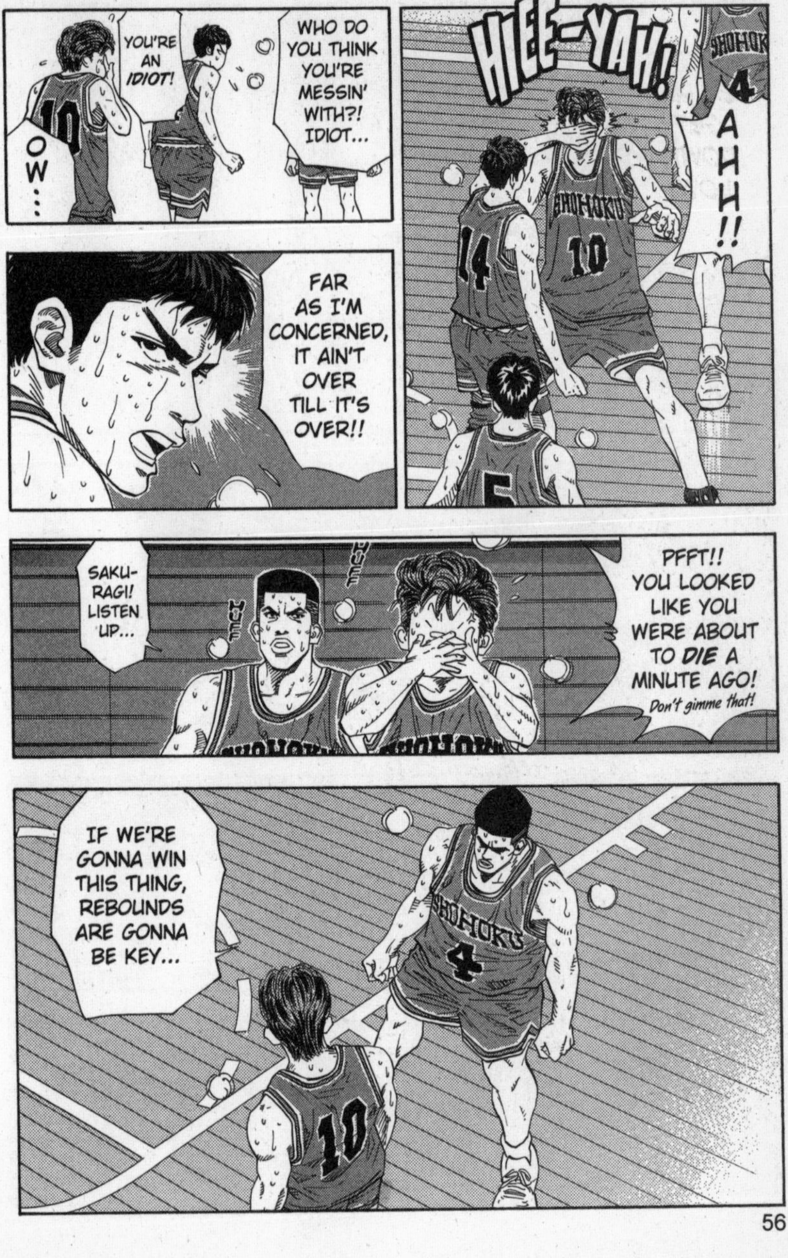
HIEE-YAH!
AHH!!
WHO DO YOU THINK YOU'RE MESSIN' WITH?! IDIOT...
YOU'RE AN *IDIOT!*
OW...
FAR AS I'M CONCERNED, IT AIN'T OVER TILL IT'S OVER!!
PFFT!! YOU LOOKED LIKE YOU WERE ABOUT TO *DIE* A MINUTE AGO!
Don't gimme that!
HUFF
SAKURAGI! LISTEN UP...
HUFF
IF WE'RE GONNA WIN THIS THING, REBOUNDS ARE GONNA BE KEY...

READ THIS WAY

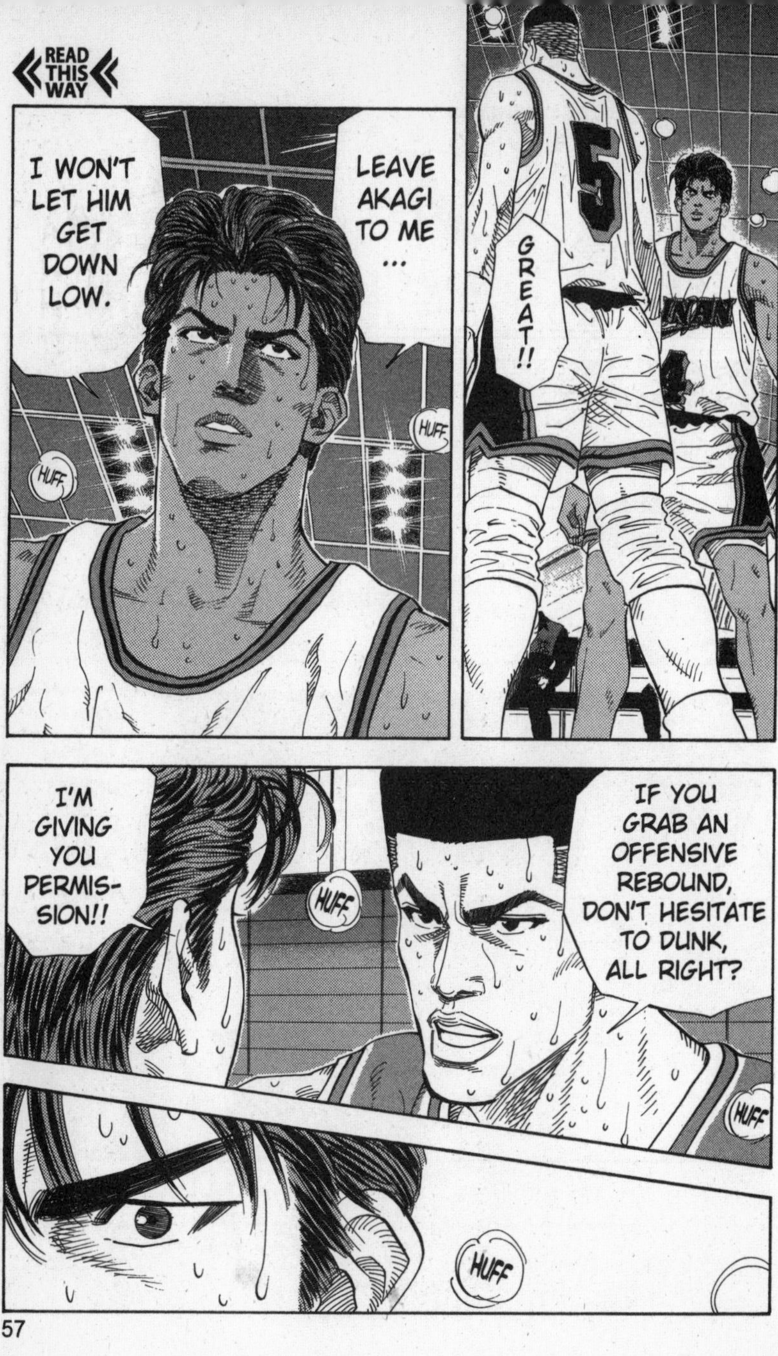

GREAT!!
LEAVE AKAGI TO ME...
I WON'T LET HIM GET DOWN LOW.
HUFF
HUFF
IF YOU GRAB AN OFFENSIVE REBOUND, DON'T HESITATE TO DUNK, ALL RIGHT?
HUFF
I'M GIVING YOU PERMIS-SION!!
HUFF
HUFF

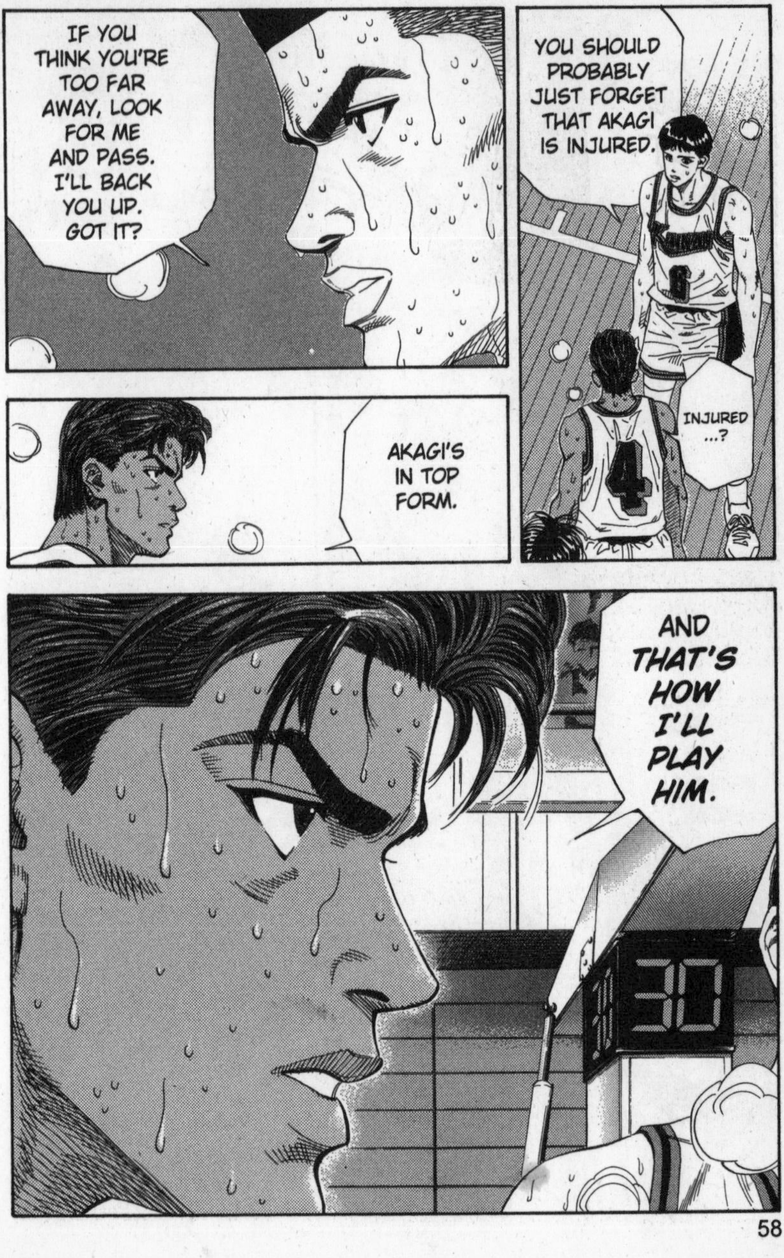
YOU SHOULD PROBABLY JUST FORGET THAT AKAGI IS INJURED.
INJURED ...?
IF YOU THINK YOU'RE TOO FAR AWAY, LOOK FOR ME AND PASS. I'LL BACK YOU UP. GOT IT?
AKAGI'S IN TOP FORM.
AND *THAT'S HOW I'LL PLAY HIM.*

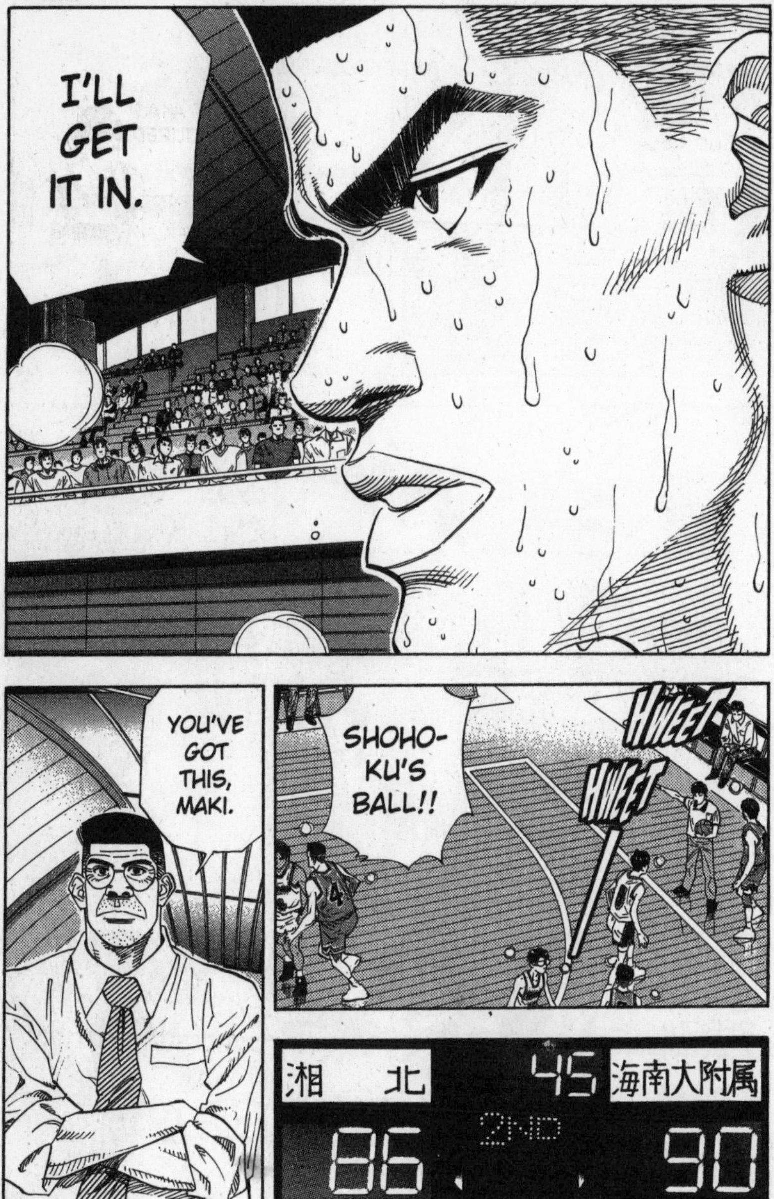
I'LL GET IT IN.
SHOHO-KU'S BALL!!
HWEET
HWEET
YOU'VE GOT THIS, MAKI.
湘　北
45
海南大附属
2ND
86
90

Scoreboard: Shohoku Kainan Dai Fuzoku

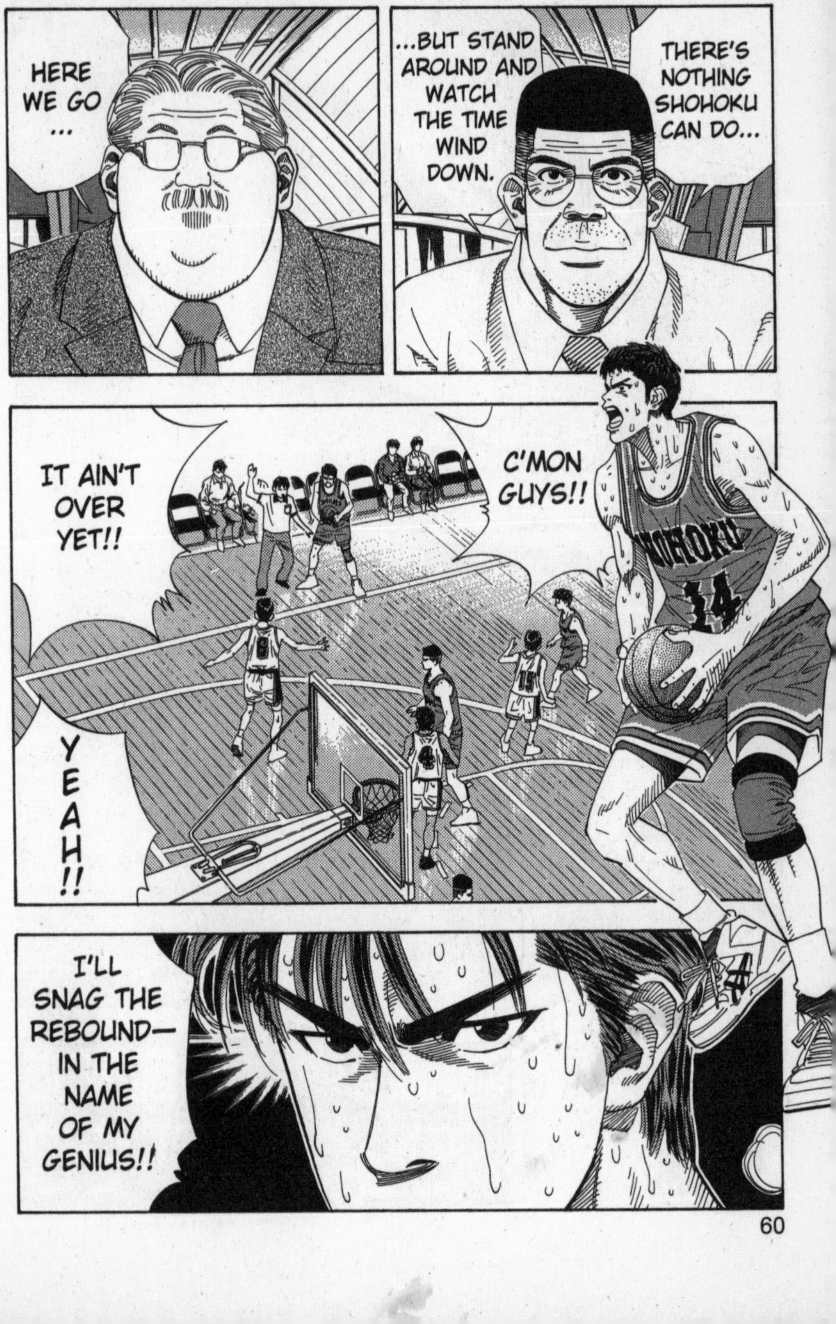
THERE'S NOTHING SHOHOKU CAN DO...
...BUT STAND AROUND AND WATCH THE TIME WIND DOWN.
HERE WE GO ...
C'MON GUYS!!
IT AIN'T OVER YET!!
YEAH!!
I'LL SNAG THE REBOUND— IN THE NAME OF MY GENIUS!!

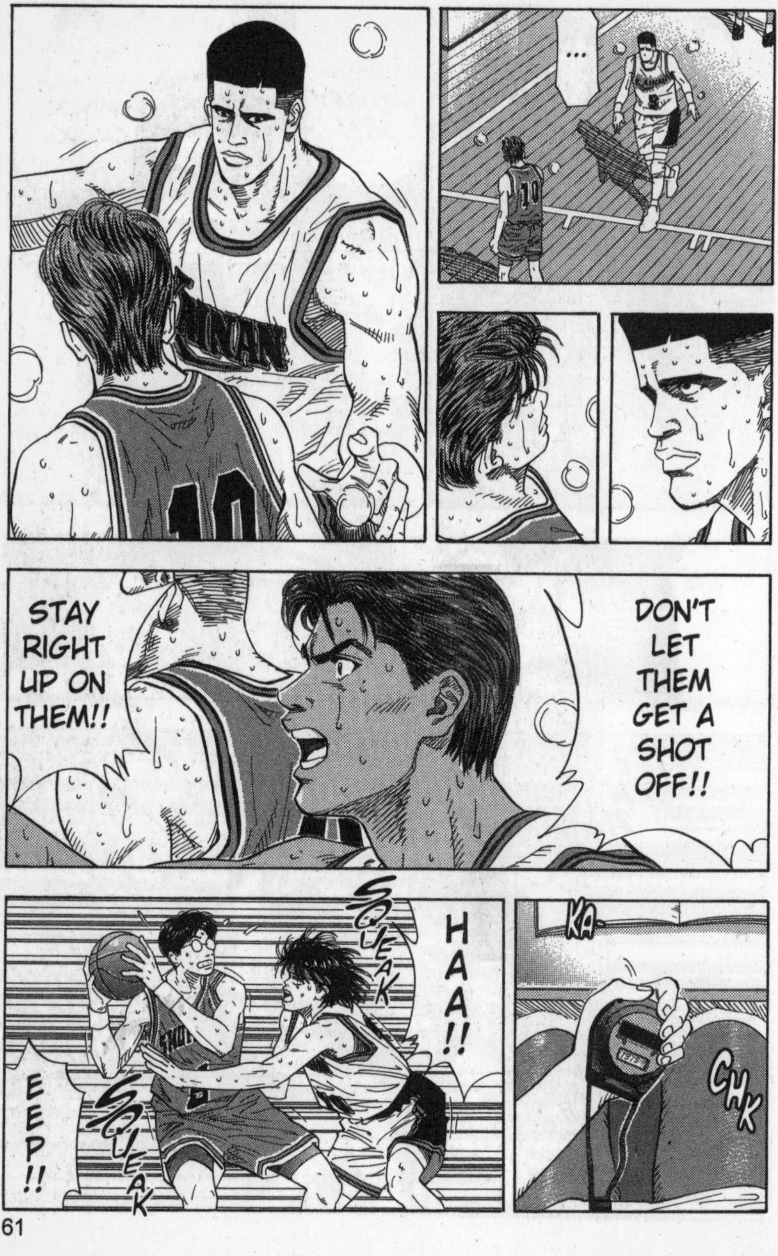
...
DON'T LET THEM GET A SHOT OFF!!
STAY RIGHT UP ON THEM!!
KA-
CHK
SQUEAK
HAAA!!
EEP!!
SQUEAK

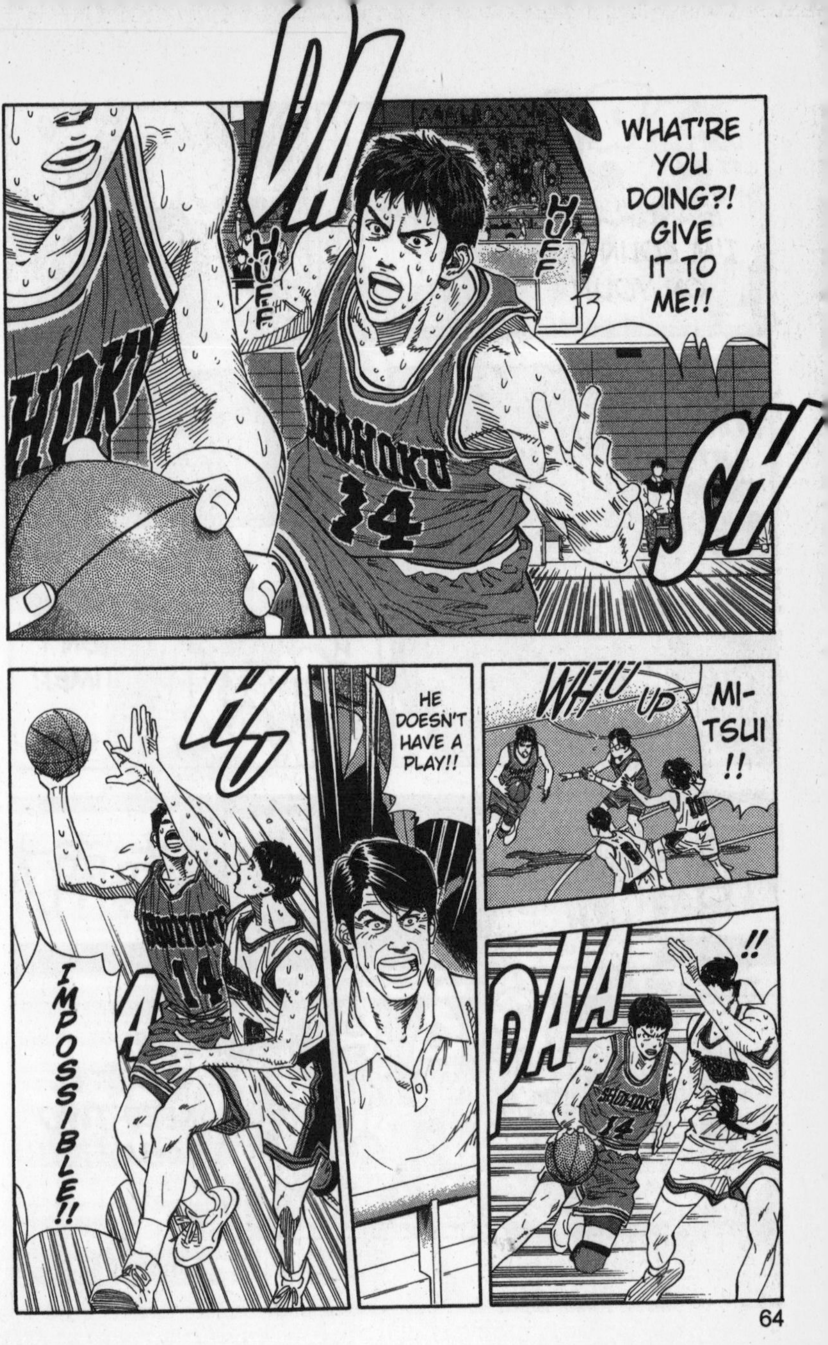
WHAT'RE YOU DOING?! GIVE IT TO ME!!
HUFF
HUFF
DA
SH
MI-TSUI!!
WHUP
!!
DAA
HE DOESN'T HAVE A PLAY!!
IMPOSSIBLE!!

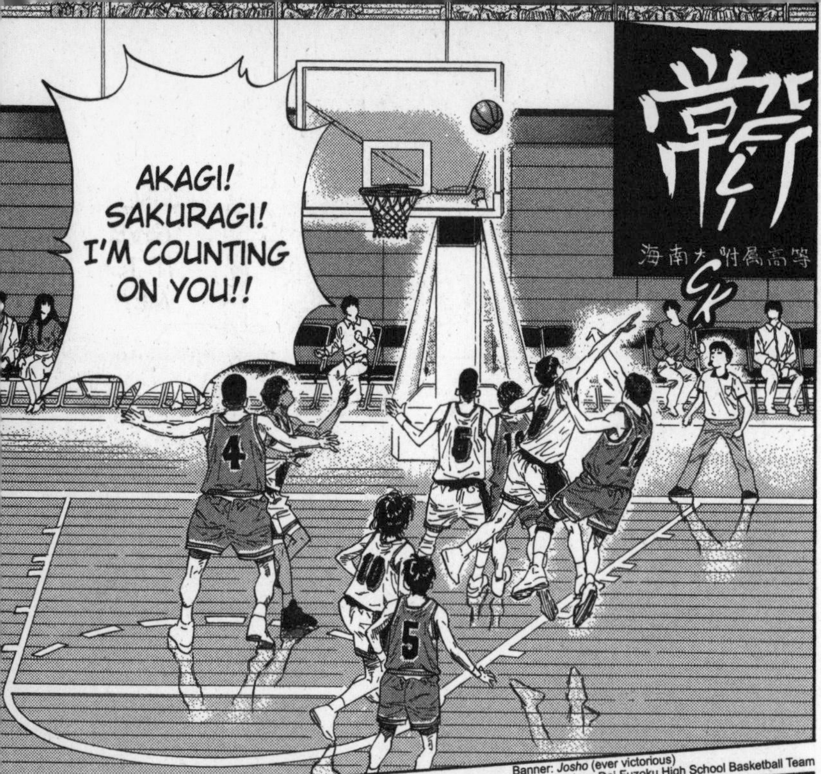
AKAGI! SAKURAGI! I'M COUNTING ON YOU!!
常勝
海南大附属高等
GK
Banner: *Josho* (ever victorious)
Kainan Dai Fuzoku High School Basketball Team

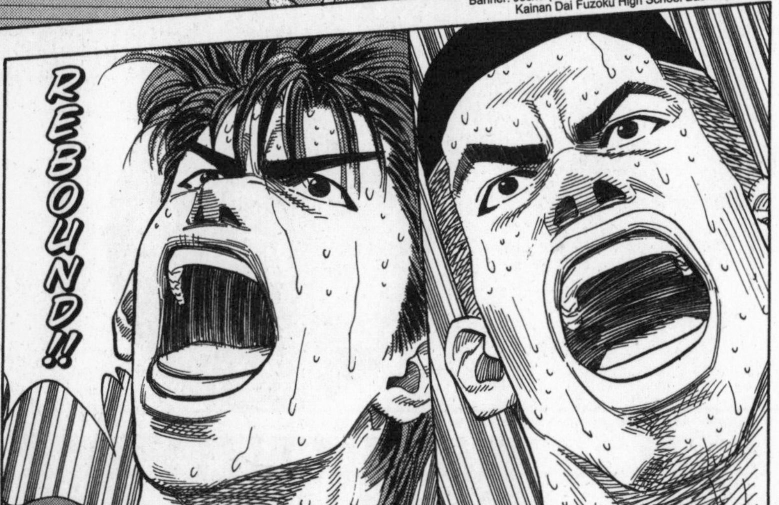
REBOUND!!

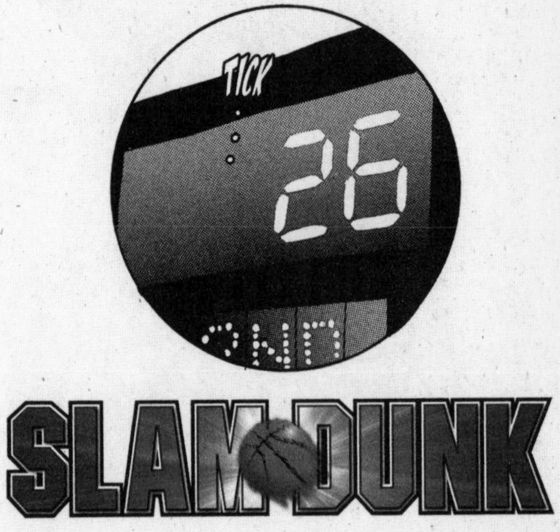
TICK
26

SLAM DUNK

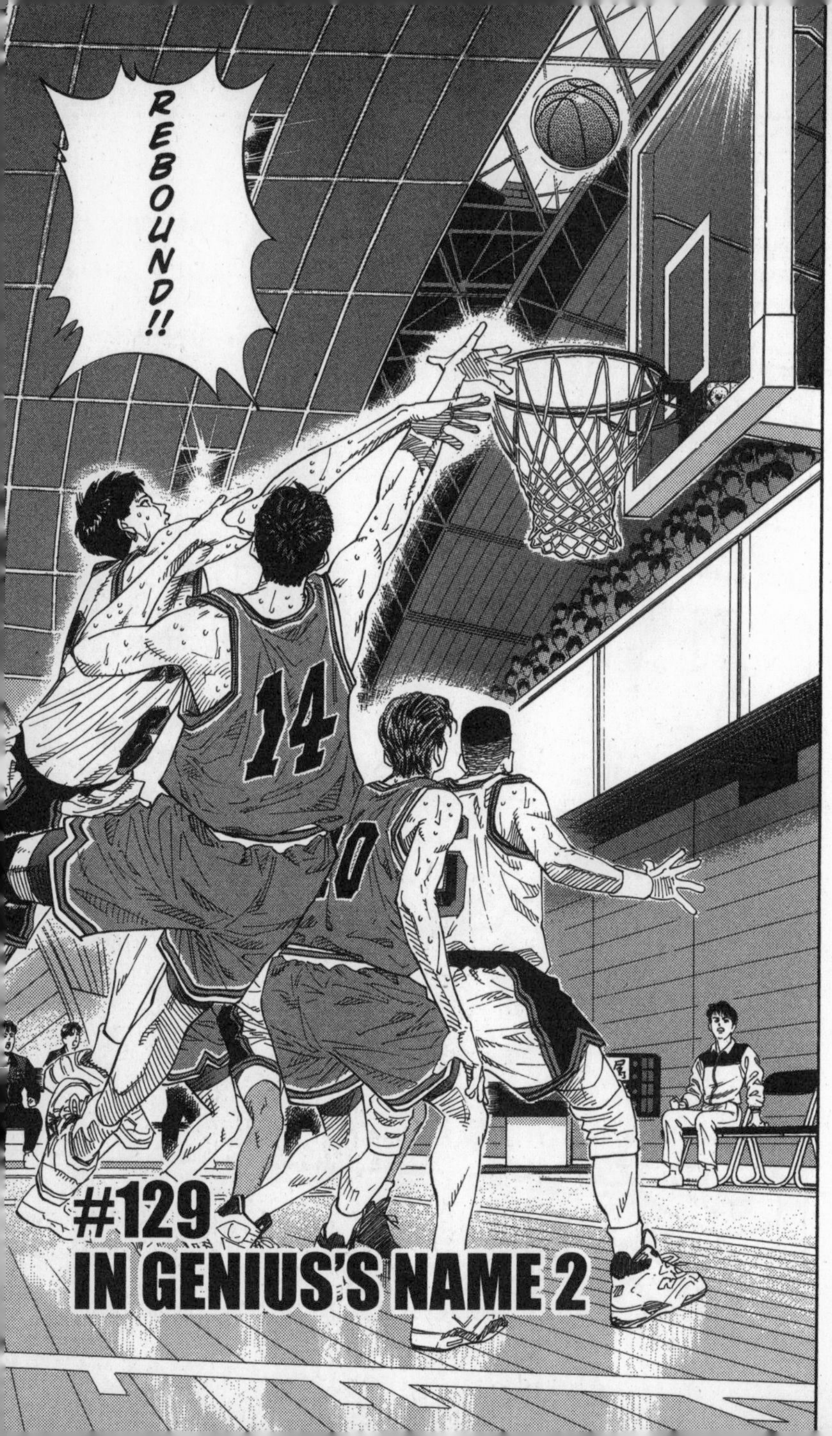
REBOUND!!
14
#129
IN GENIUS'S NAME 2

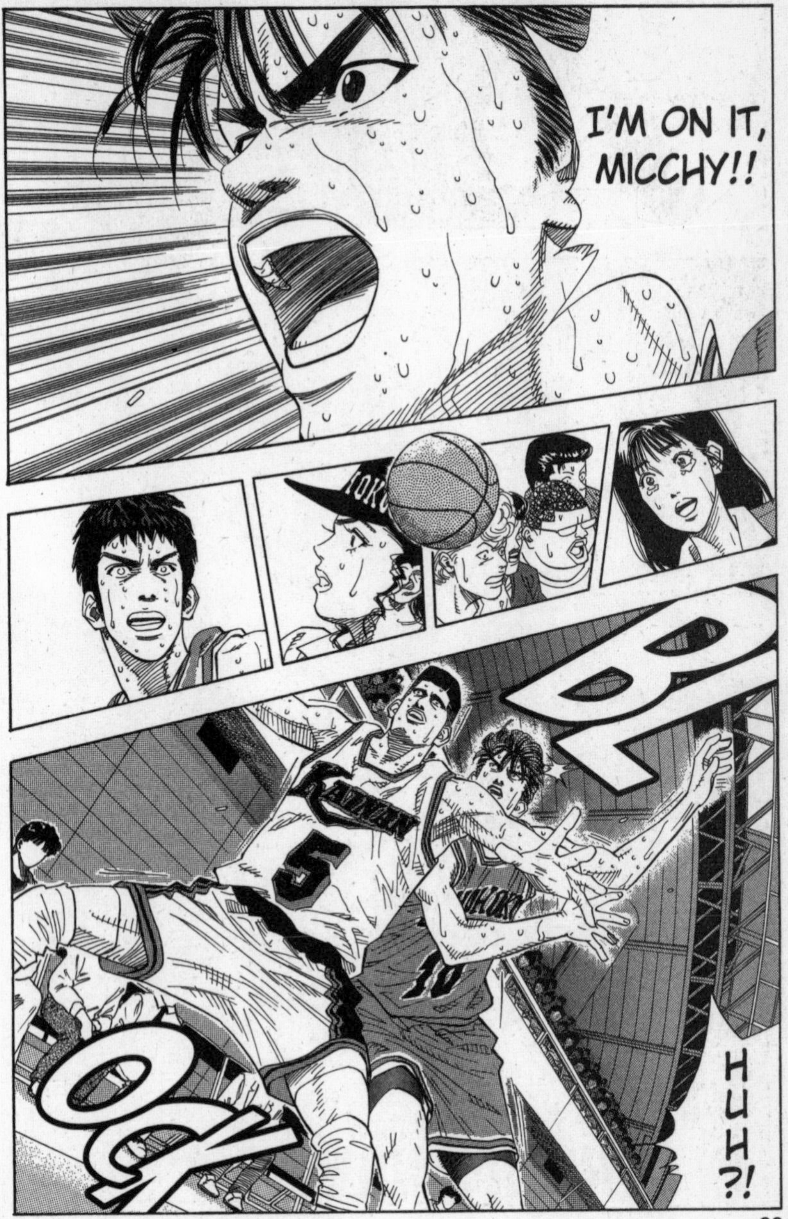
I'M ON IT, MICCHY!!
HUH?!

READ THIS WAY

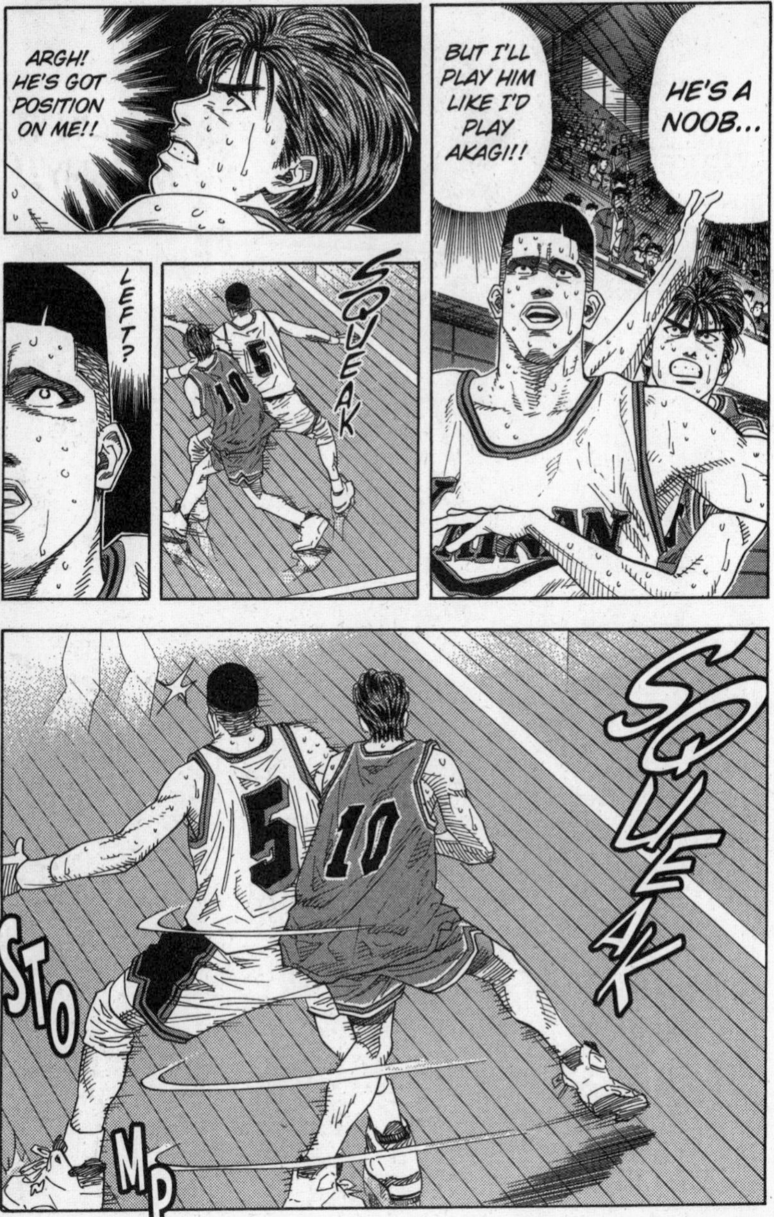

HE'S A NOOB...
BUT I'LL PLAY HIM LIKE I'D PLAY AKAGI!!
ARGH! HE'S GOT POSITION ON ME!!
SQUEAK
LEFT?
SQUEAK
STOMP

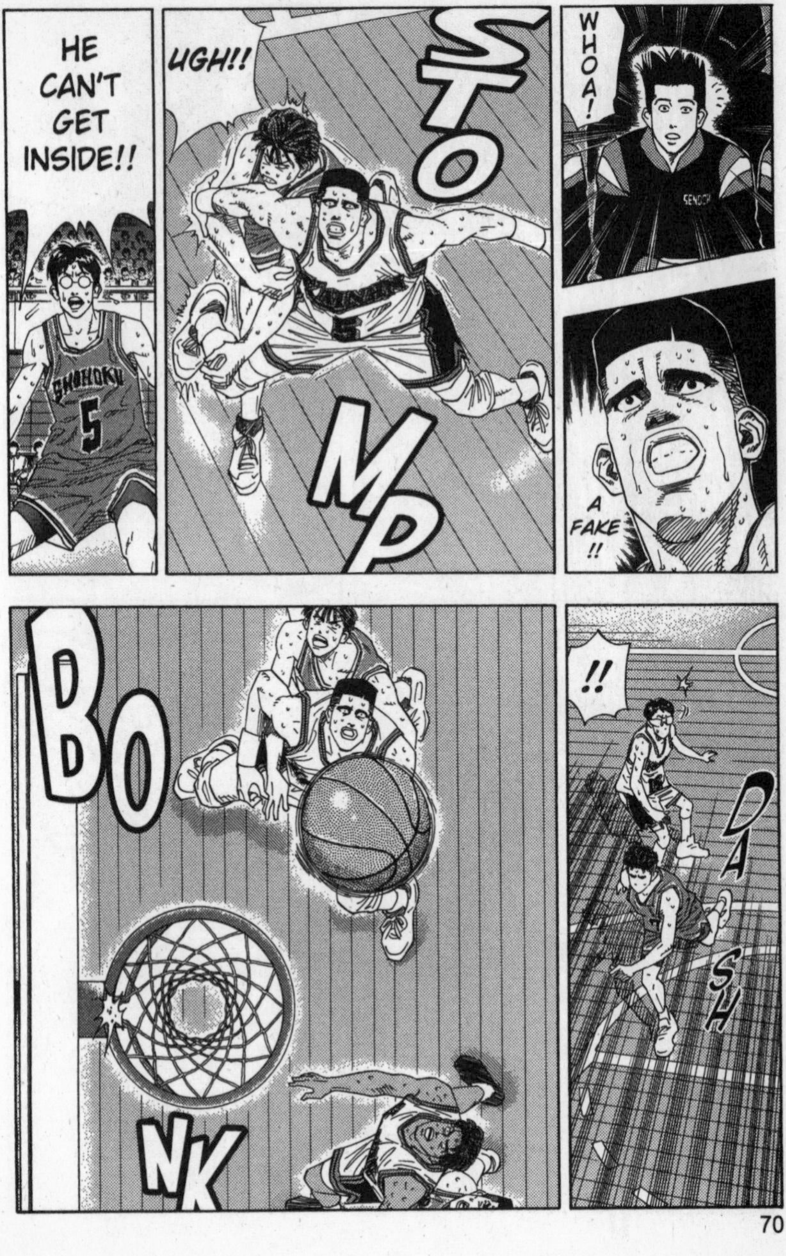
WHOA!
A FAKE!!
UGH!!
STOMP
HE CAN'T GET INSIDE!!
!!
DASH
BONK

IT'S OFF!

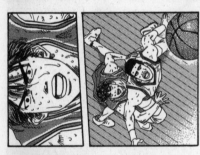

I'VE GOT THIS!!

71

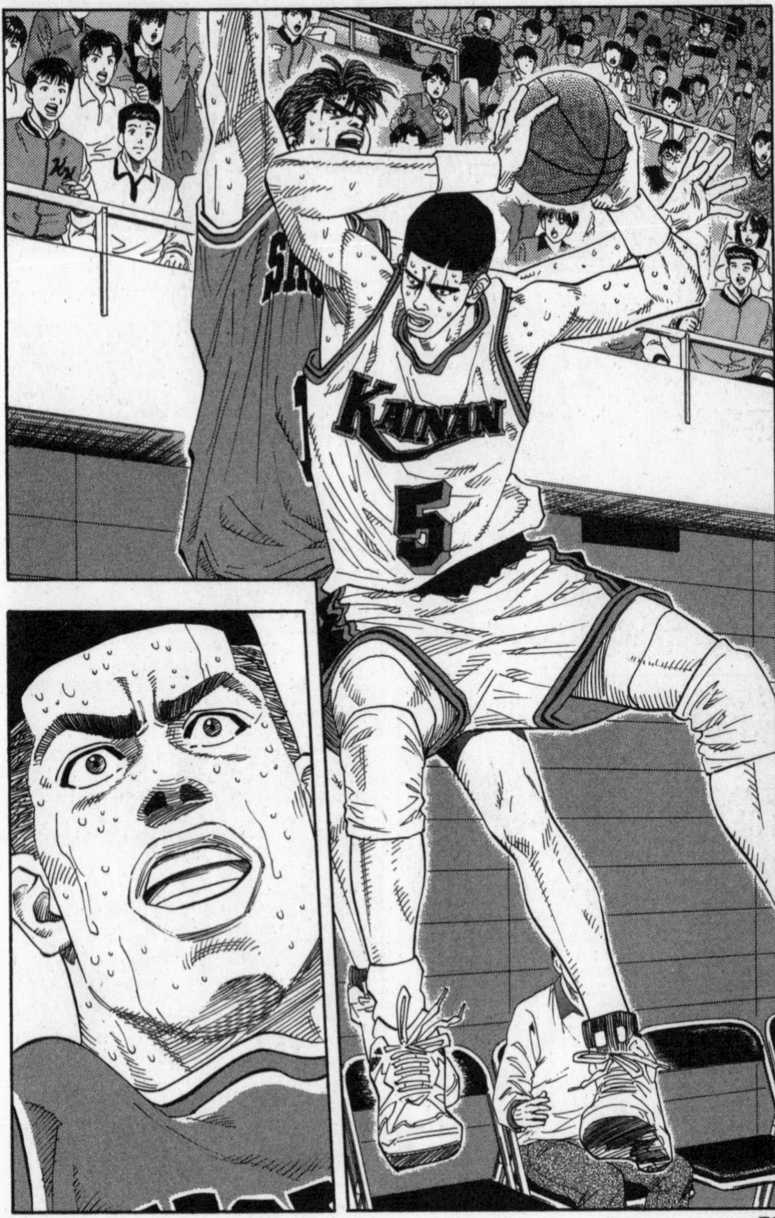
KAINAN
5

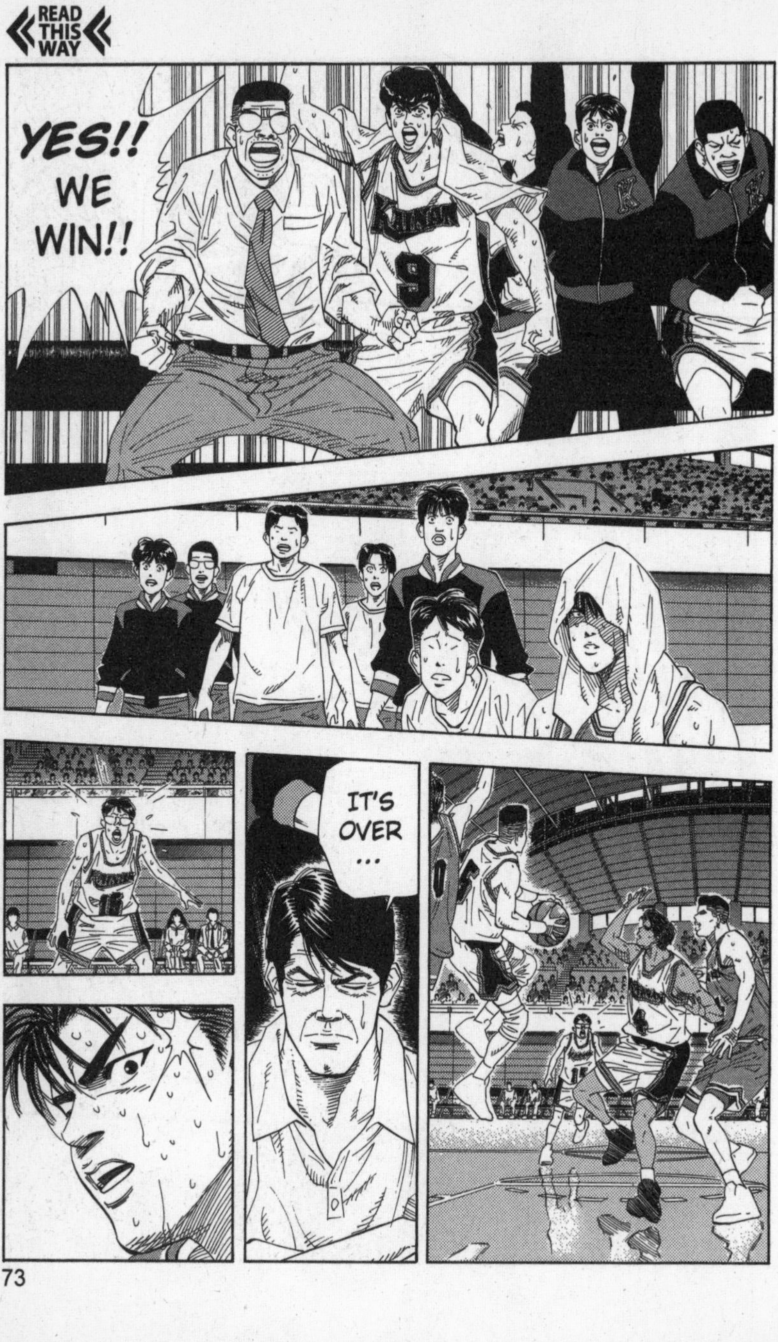
READ THIS WAY
YES!! WE WIN!!
IT'S OVER ...

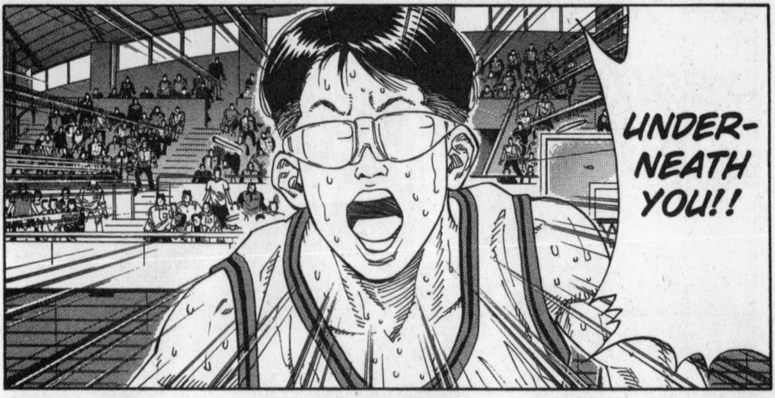
UNDER-
NEATH
YOU!!
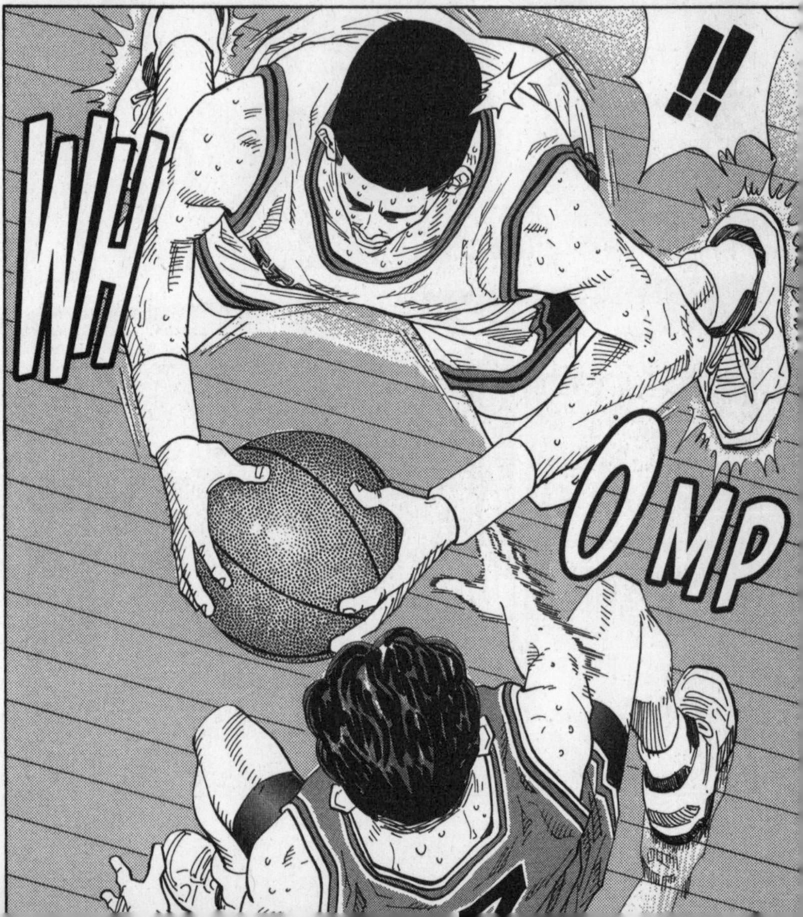
!!
WH
OMP

HUH
?!

SMACK

海

HOW
THE—?!

!!

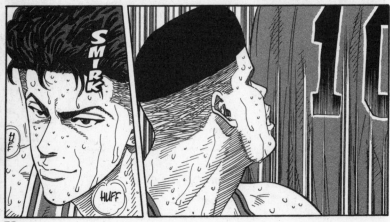

SMIRK

HUFF

HUFF

75

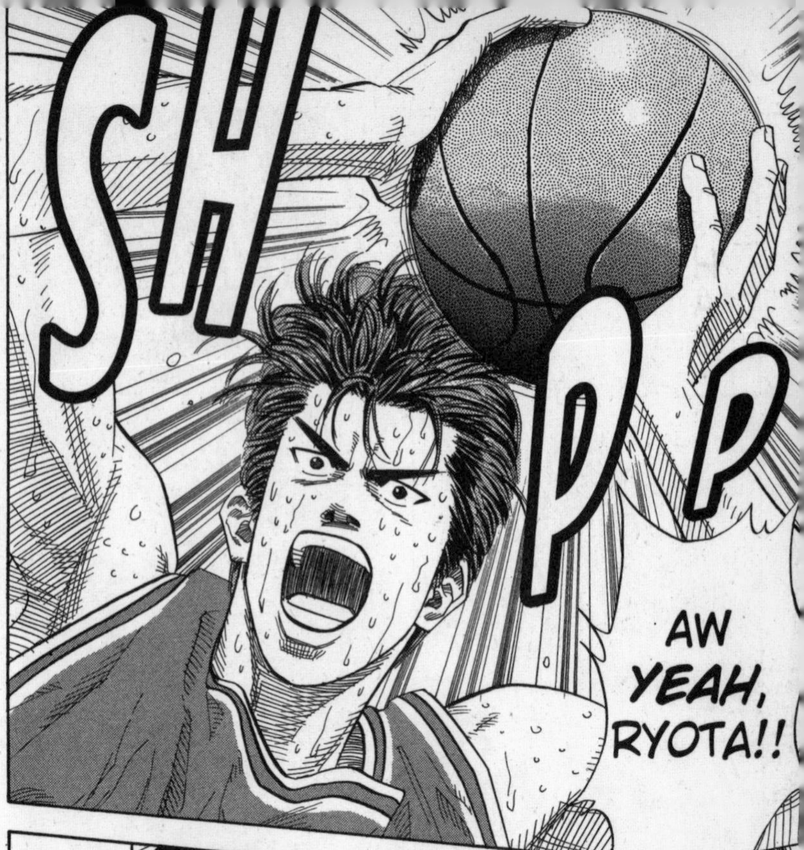
SHPPP
AW YEAH, RYOTA!!
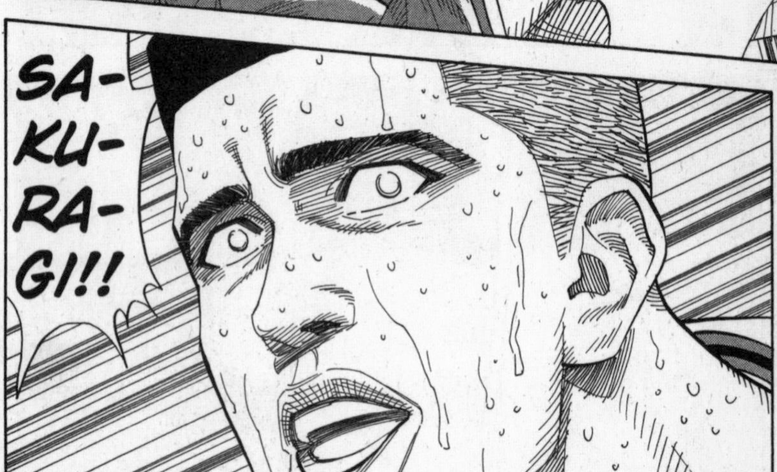
SA-KU-RA-GI!!

READ THIS WAY

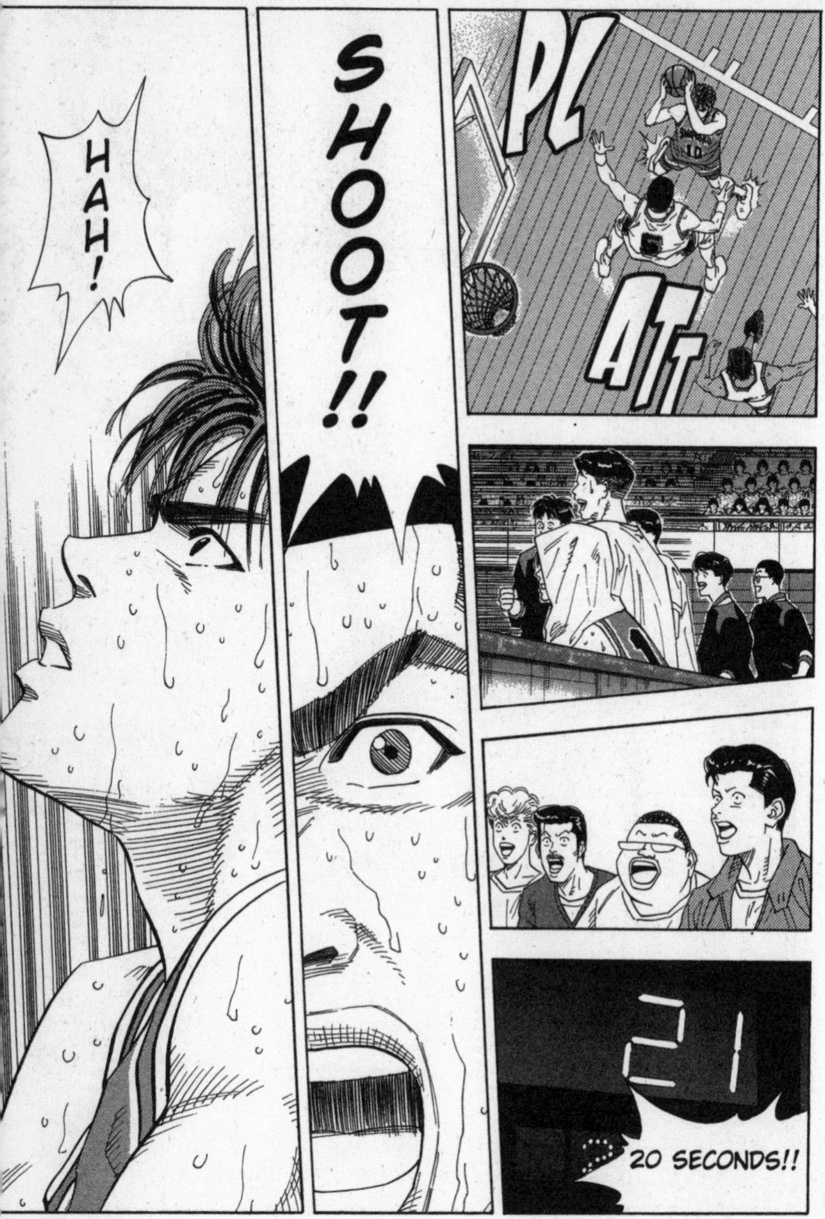
PL
ATT
20 SECONDS!!
SHOOT!!
HAH!

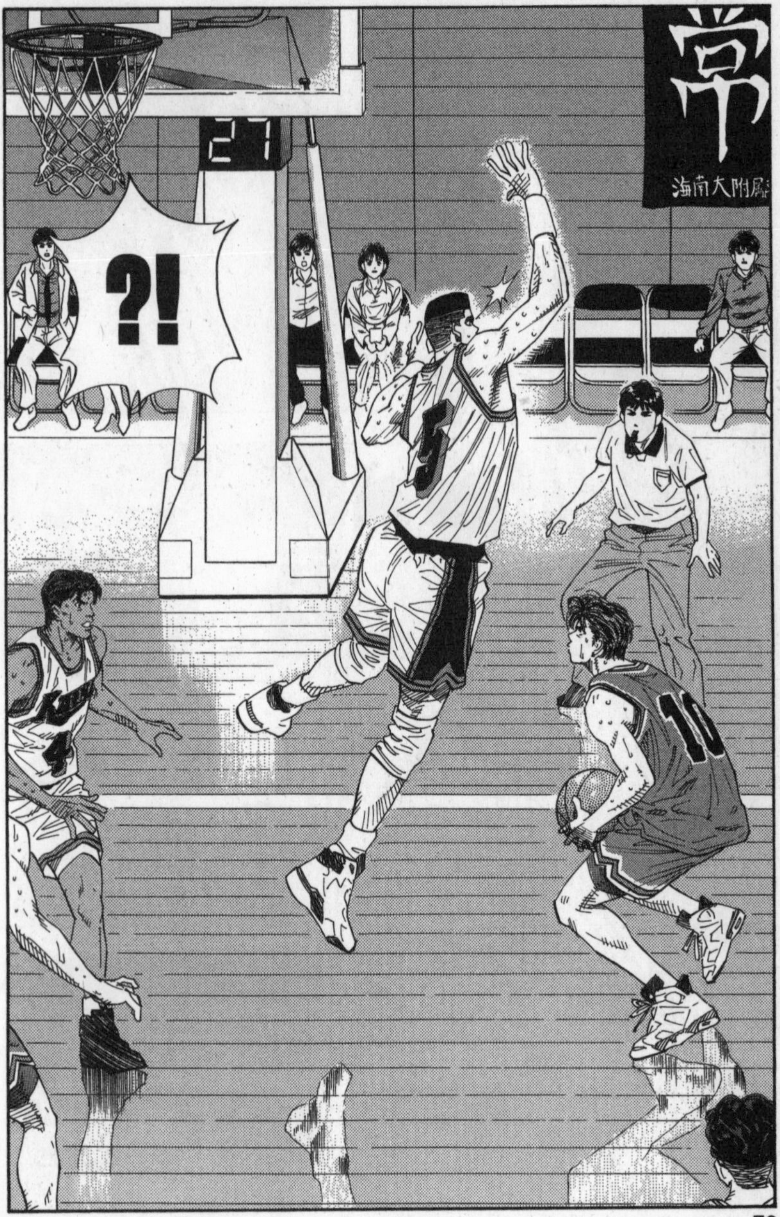
?!
常
海南大附属

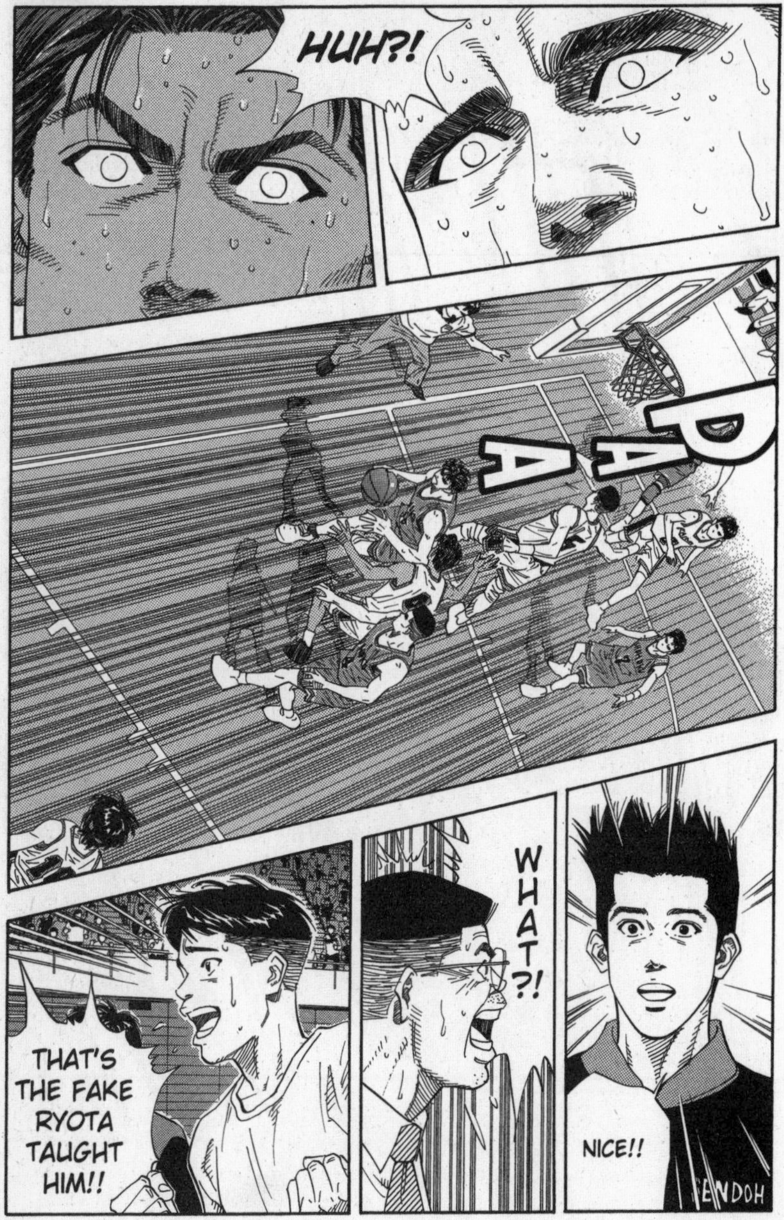
HUH?!
PA
NICE!!
SENDOH
WHAT?!
THAT'S THE FAKE RYOTA TAUGHT HIM!!

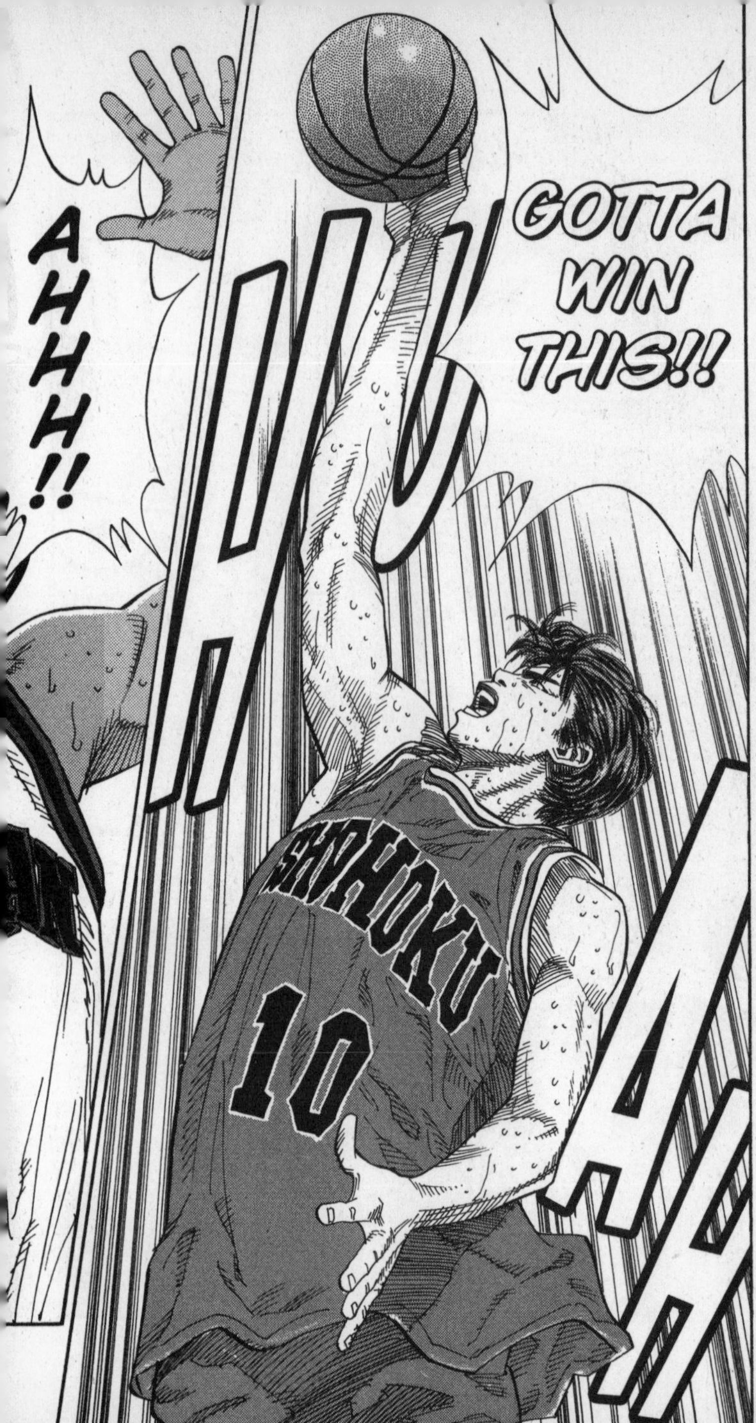
GOTTA WIN THIS!!
AHHHH!!
SHOHOKU
10

READ THIS WAY

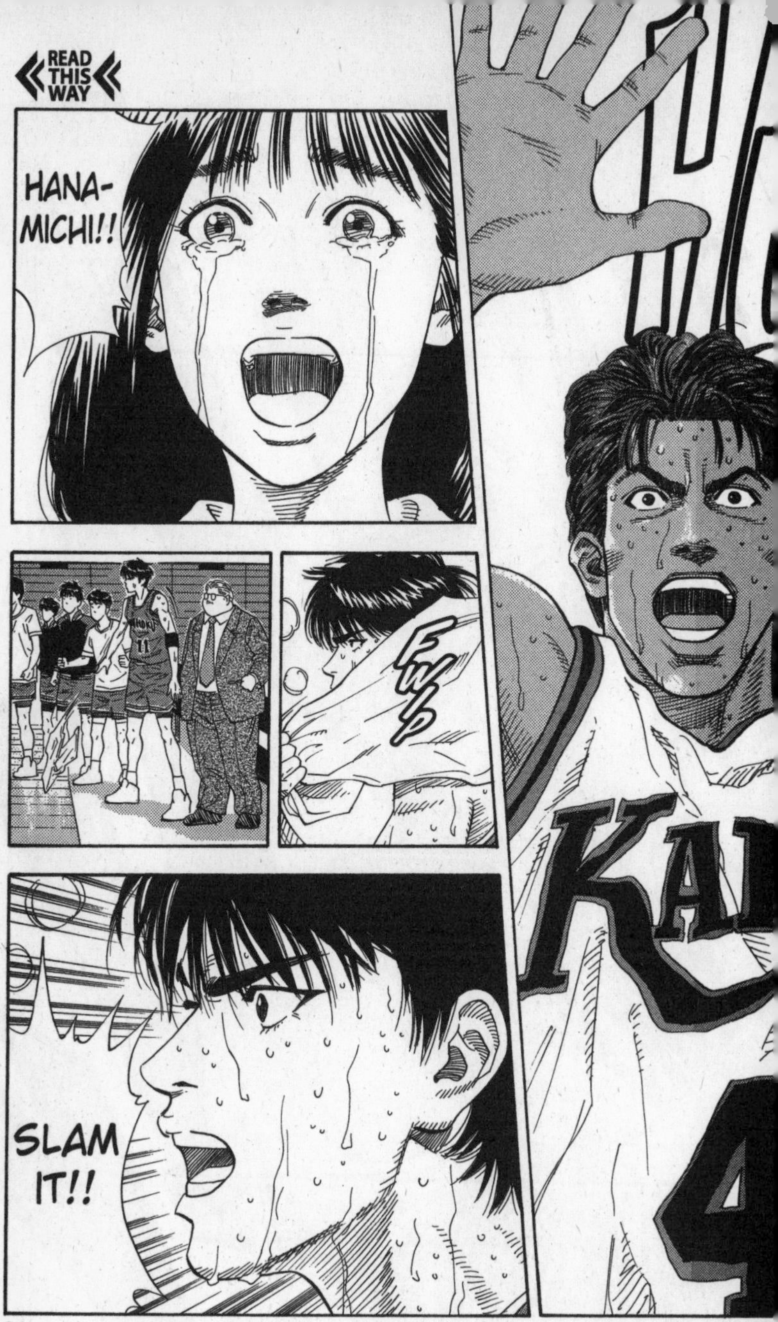
HANA-
MICHI!!
FWIP
SLAM IT!!

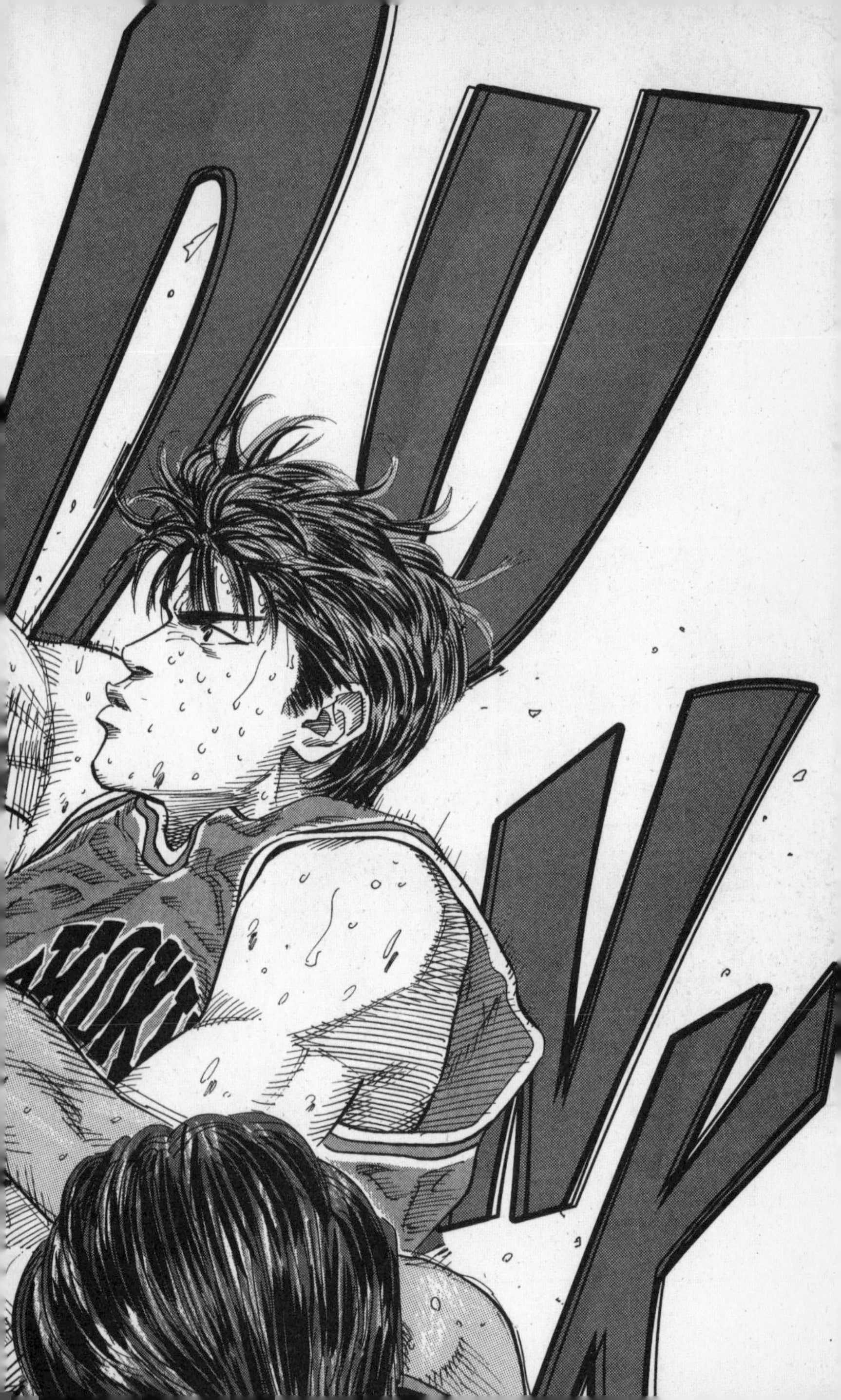
DUNK

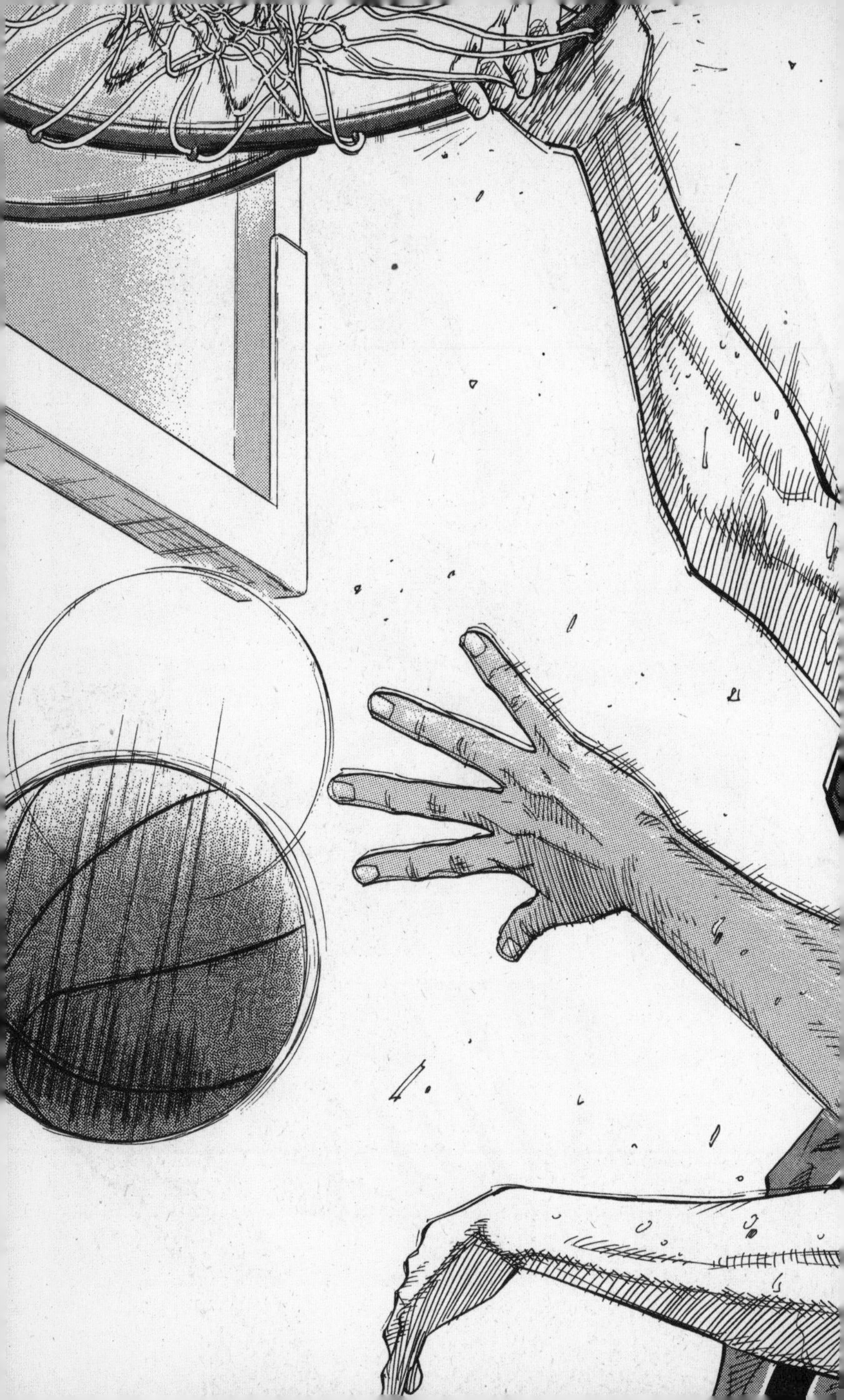

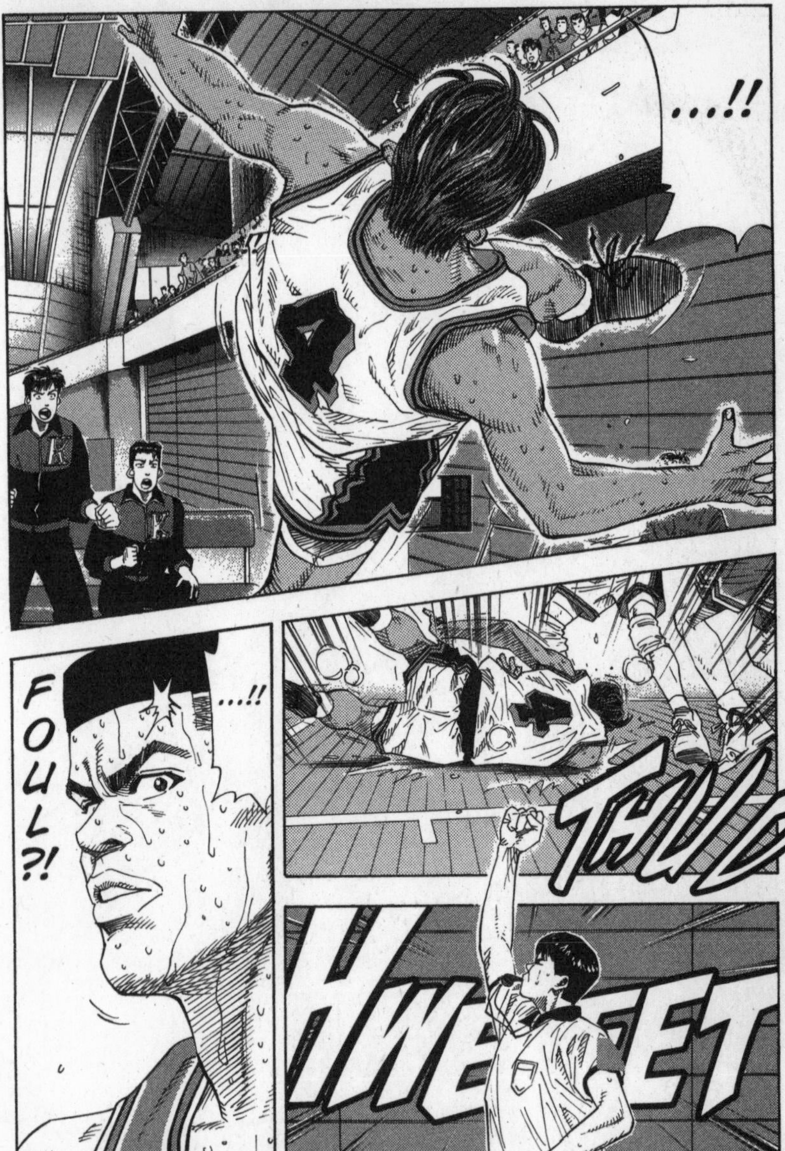
...!!
THUD
...!!
FOUL?!
HWEEET

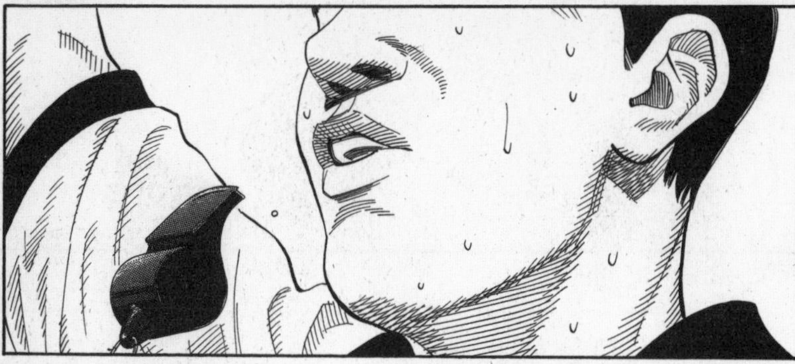

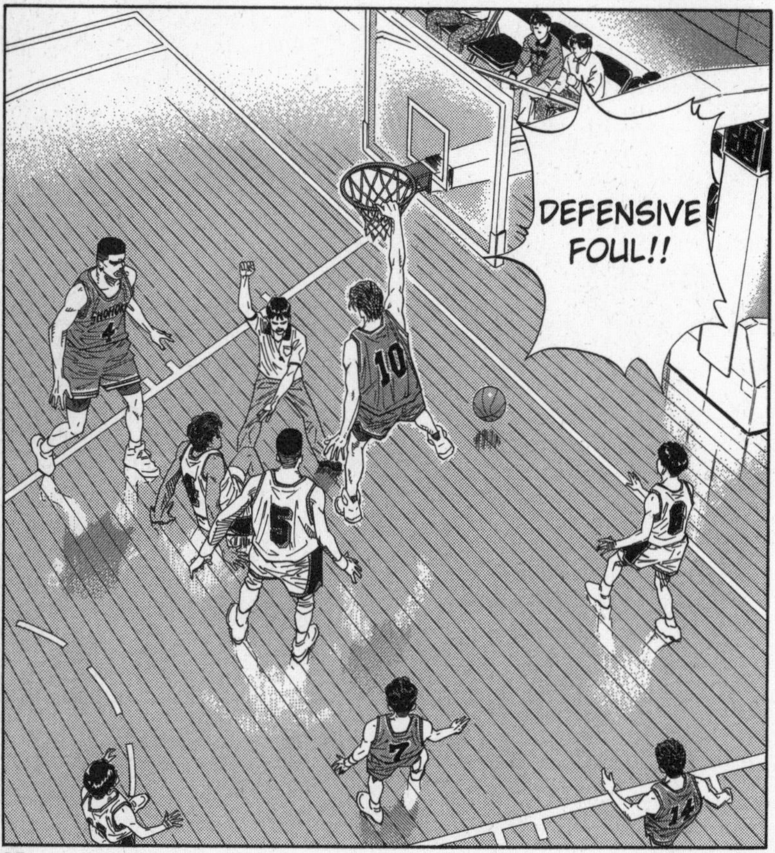
DEFENSIVE FOUL!!
SHOHOKU

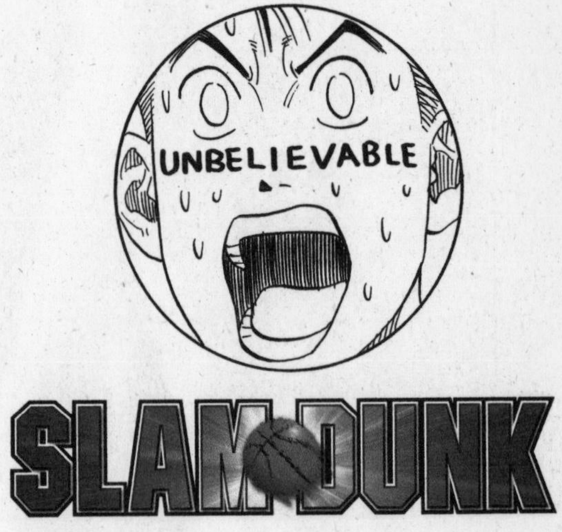
UNBELIEVABLE

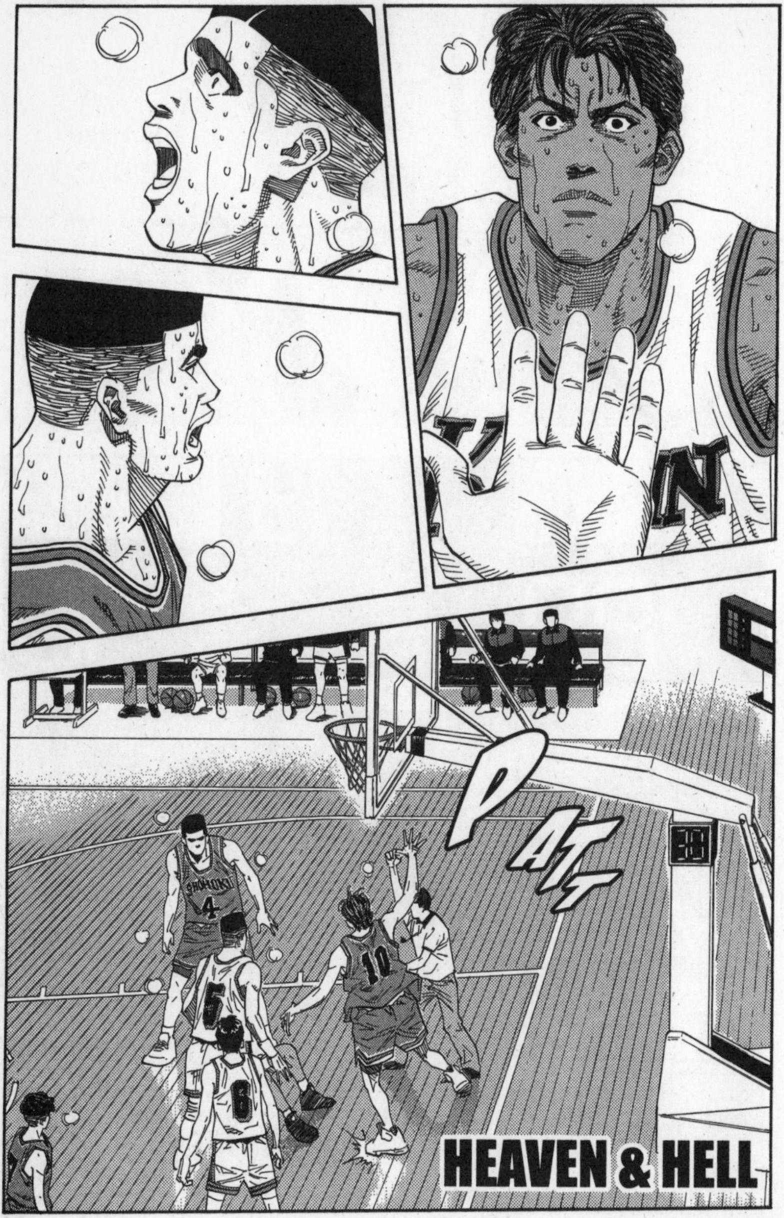
PAT
HEAVEN & HELL

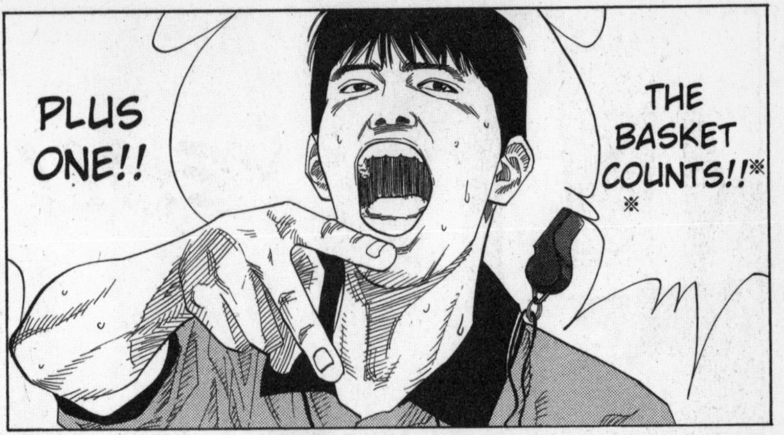
THE BASKET COUNTS!!※
※
PLUS ONE!!

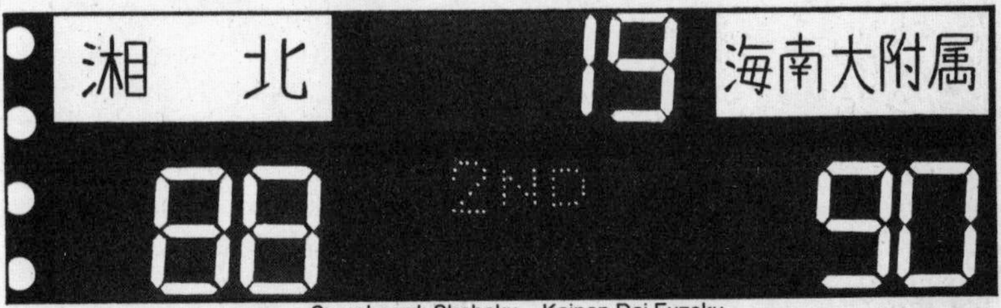
湘北
19
海南大附属
88
2ND
90

Scoreboard: Shohoku Kainan Dai Fuzoku

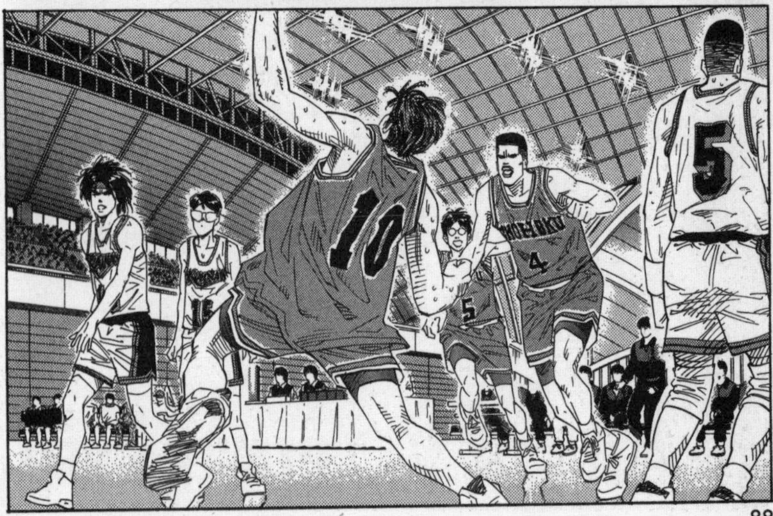

※WHEN A PLAYER MAKES A SHOT WHILE BEING FOULED, POINTS FROM THE SHOT ARE AWARDED IN ADDITION TO ONE FREE THROW ATTEMPT.

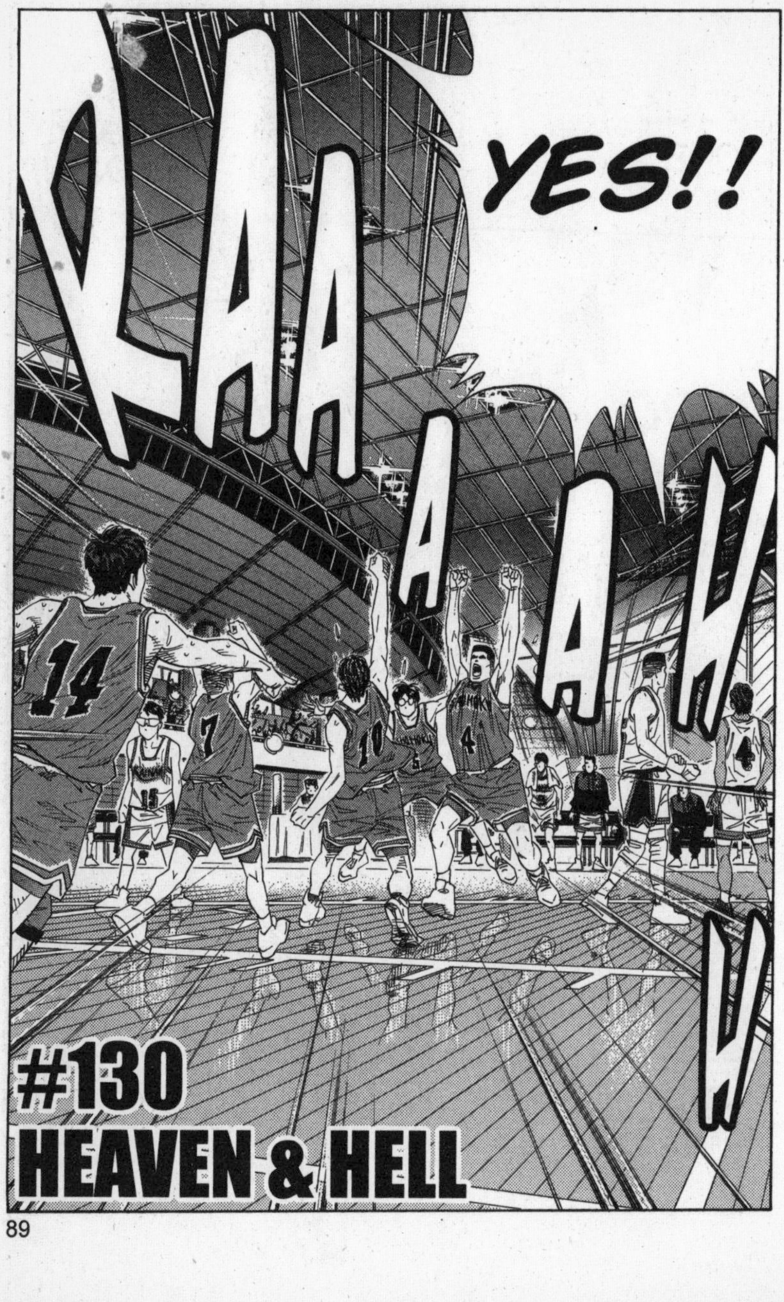
YES!!

#130 HEAVEN & HELL

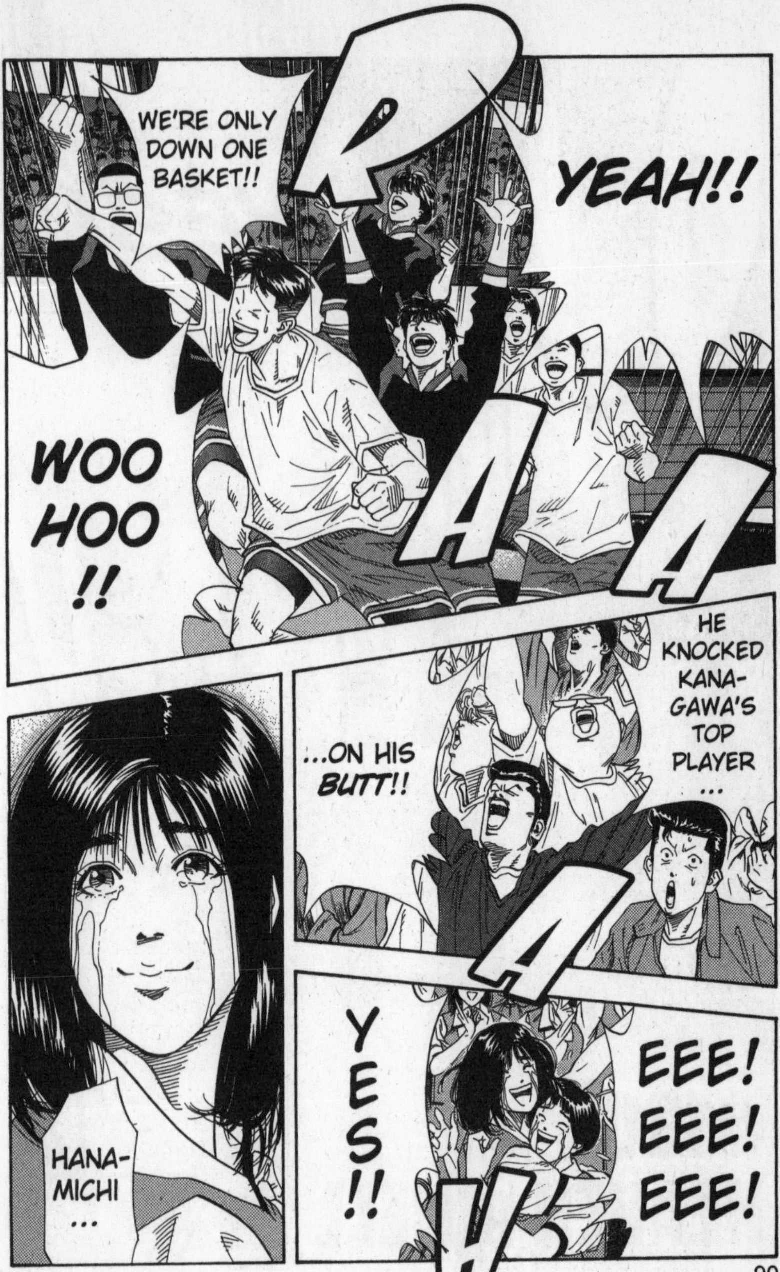
R
YEAH!!
WE'RE ONLY DOWN ONE BASKET!!
WOO HOO !!
A
A
HE KNOCKED KANA-GAWA'S TOP PLAYER ...
...ON HIS BUTT!!
A
EEE! EEE! EEE!
YES!!
H
HANA-MICHI ...

READ THIS WAY

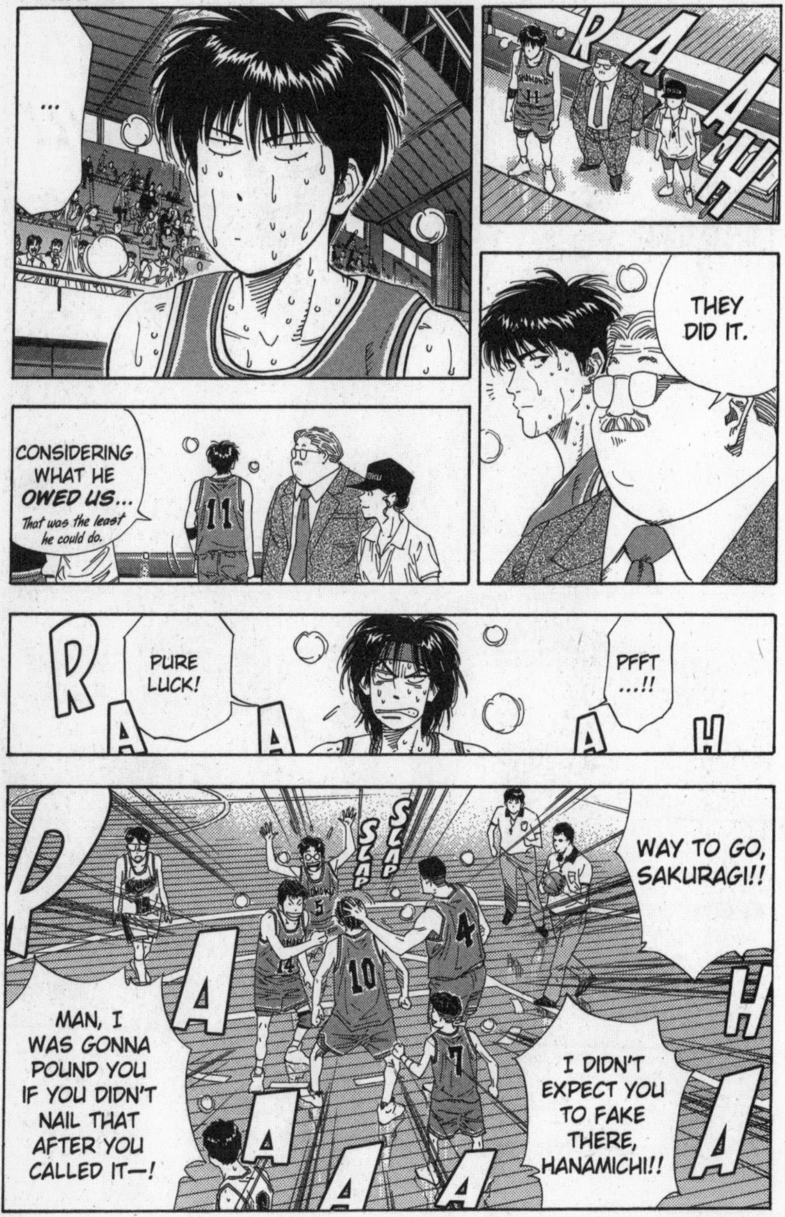
RAAAHH
...
THEY DID IT.
CONSIDERING WHAT HE OWED US... That was the least he could do.
PFFT ...!!
PURE LUCK!
RAAAH
WAY TO GO, SAKURAGI!!
SLAP SLAP
I DIDN'T EXPECT YOU TO FAKE THERE, HANAMICHI!!
MAN, I WAS GONNA POUND YOU IF YOU DIDN'T NAIL THAT AFTER YOU CALLED IT—!
RAAAAAAH

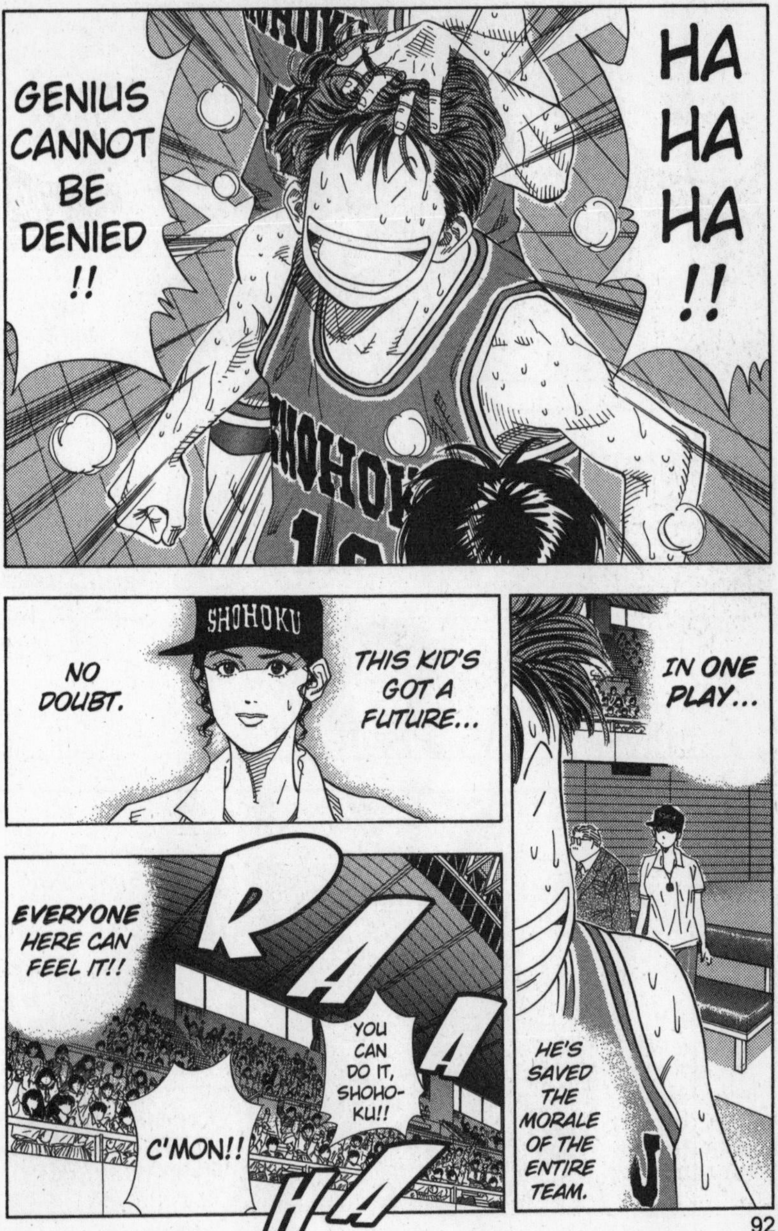

HA HA HA!!
GENIUS CANNOT BE DENIED!!
IN ONE PLAY...
HE'S SAVED THE MORALE OF THE ENTIRE TEAM.
THIS KID'S GOT A FUTURE...
NO DOUBT.
SHOHOKU
EVERYONE HERE CAN FEEL IT!!
RAA
YOU CAN DO IT, SHOHO-KU!!
C'MON!!
HA

READ THIS WAY

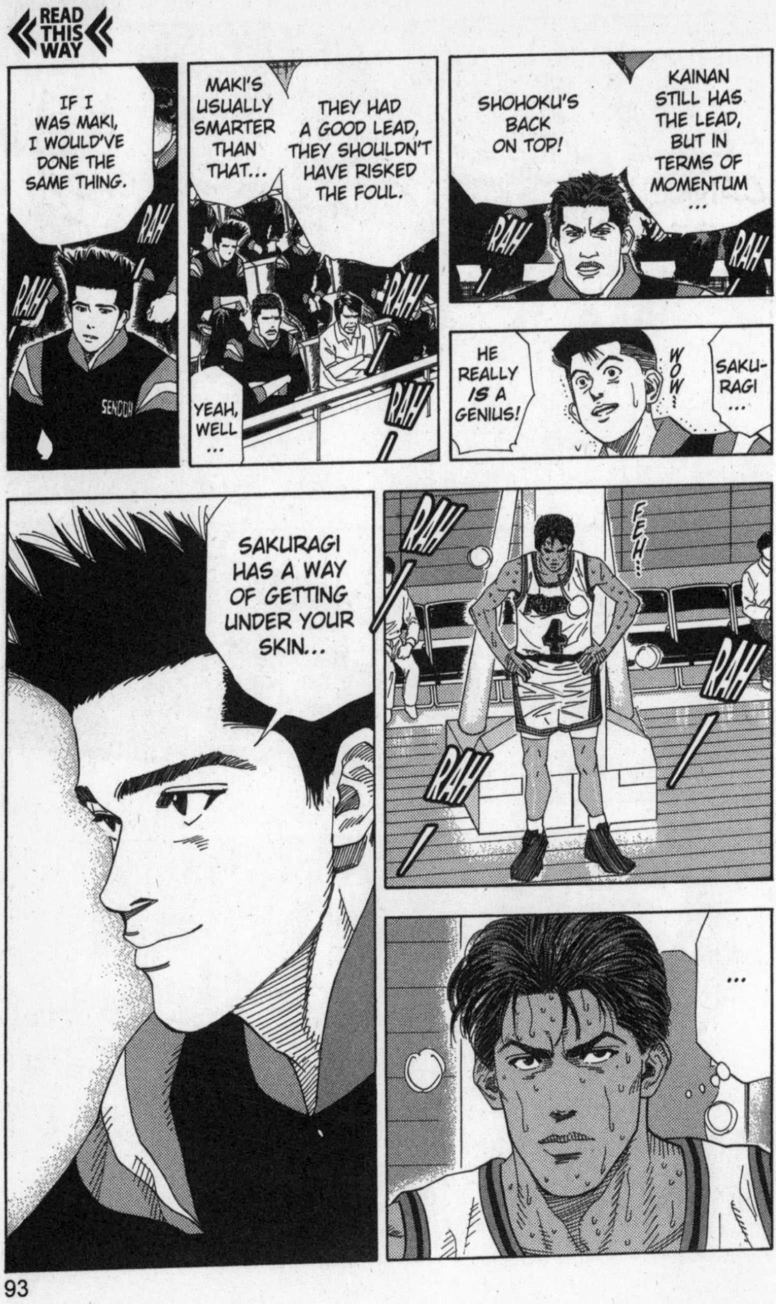
KAINAN STILL HAS THE LEAD, BUT IN TERMS OF MOMENTUM ...
SHOHOKU'S BACK ON TOP!
RAH
RAH
SAKU-RAGI ...
WOW...
HE REALLY IS A GENIUS!
THEY HAD A GOOD LEAD, THEY SHOULDN'T HAVE RISKED THE FOUL.
MAKI'S USUALLY SMARTER THAN THAT...
YEAH, WELL ...
RAH
RAH
IF I WAS MAKI, I WOULD'VE DONE THE SAME THING.
RAH
RAH
FEH...
RAH
RAH
RAH
...
SAKURAGI HAS A WAY OF GETTING UNDER YOUR SKIN...

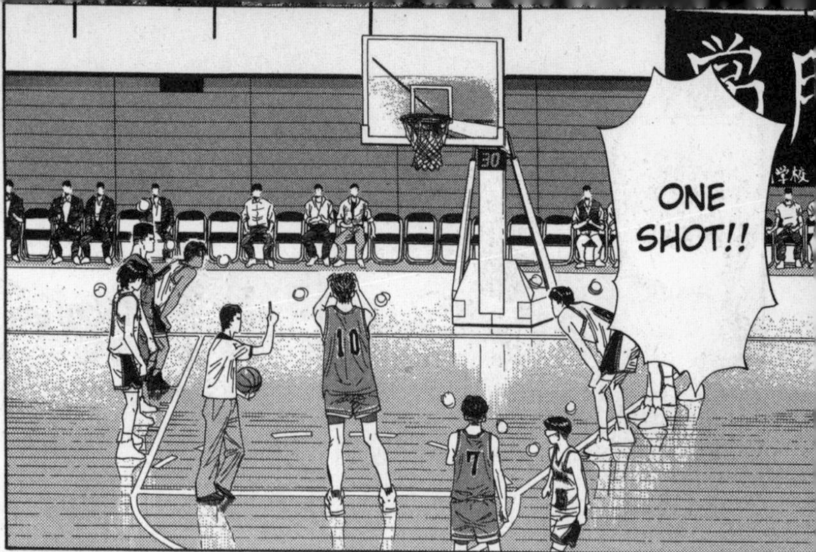
ONE SHOT!!
Banner: *Josho* (ever victorious)
Kainan Dai Fuzoku High School Basketball Team

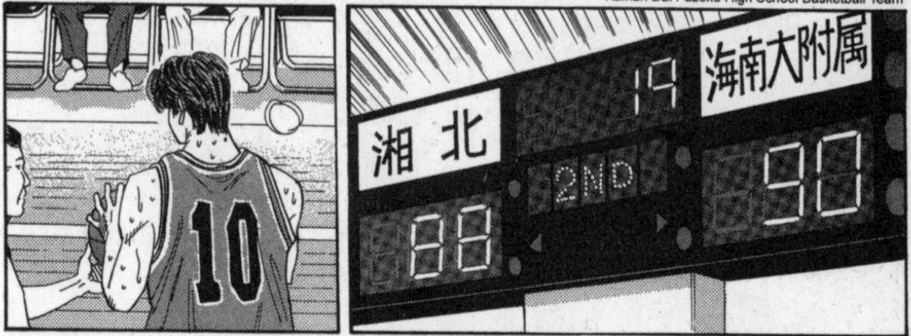
海南大附属
19
湘北
2ND
88
90
Scoreboard: Shohoku Kainan Dai Fuzoku

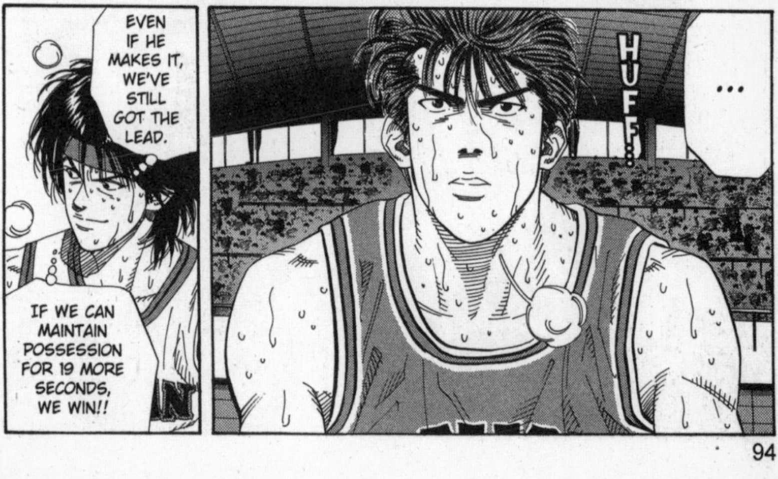
...
HUFF...
EVEN IF HE MAKES IT, WE'VE STILL GOT THE LEAD.
IF WE CAN MAINTAIN POSSESSION FOR 19 MORE SECONDS, WE WIN!!

READ THIS WAY

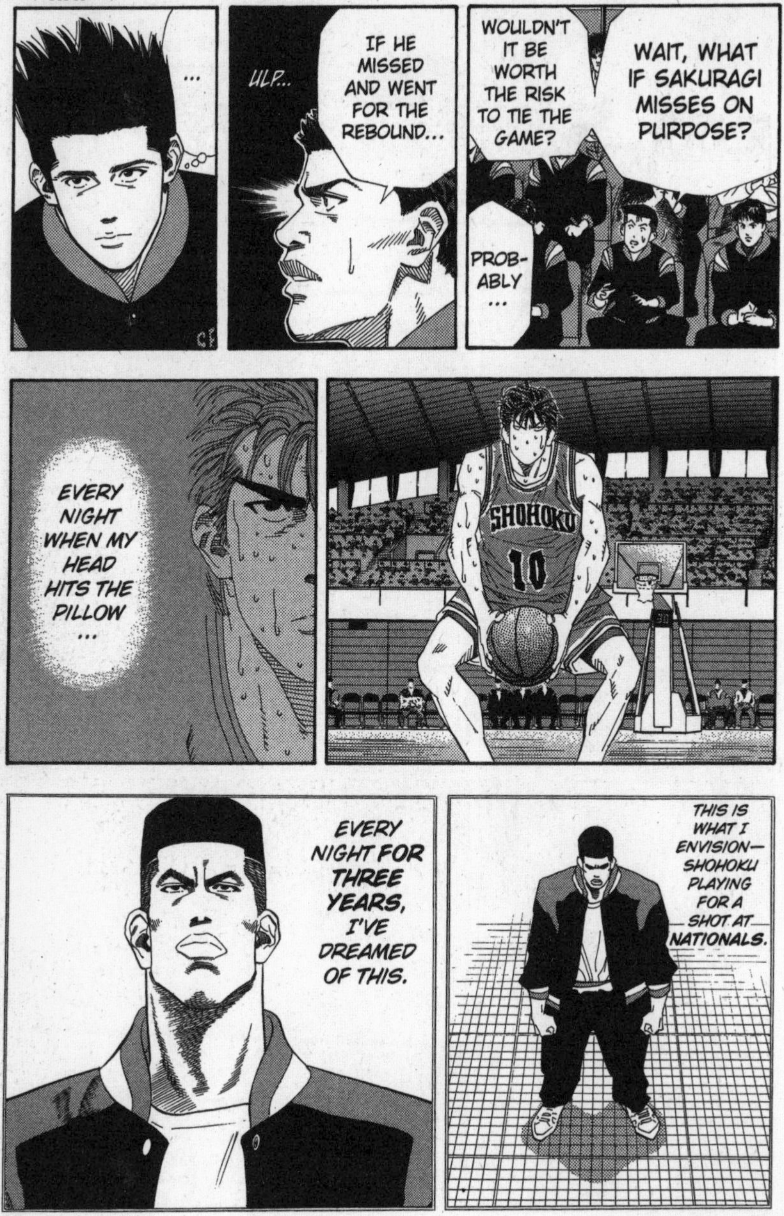

WAIT, WHAT IF SAKURAGI MISSES ON PURPOSE?
WOULDN'T IT BE WORTH THE RISK TO TIE THE GAME?
PROBABLY...
IF HE MISSED AND WENT FOR THE REBOUND...
ULP...
...
SHOHOKU
10
EVERY NIGHT WHEN MY HEAD HITS THE PILLOW...
THIS IS WHAT I ENVISION—SHOHOKU PLAYING FOR A SHOT AT NATIONALS.
EVERY NIGHT FOR THREE YEARS, I'VE DREAMED OF THIS.

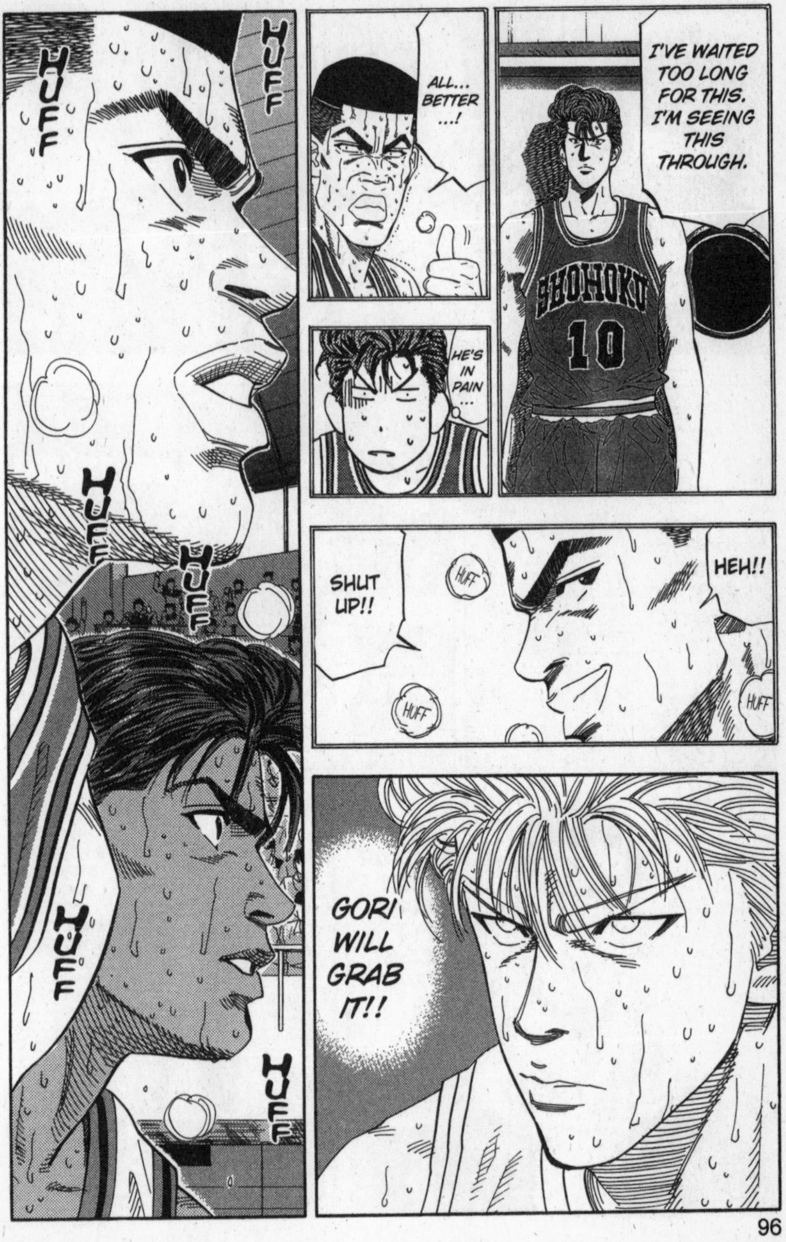
I'VE WAITED TOO LONG FOR THIS. I'M SEEING THIS THROUGH.
ALL... BETTER ...!
HE'S IN PAIN ...
HEH!!
HUFF
HUFF
SHUT UP!!
HUFF
GORI WILL GRAB IT!!
HUFF
HUFF
HUFF
HUFF
HUFF
HUFF

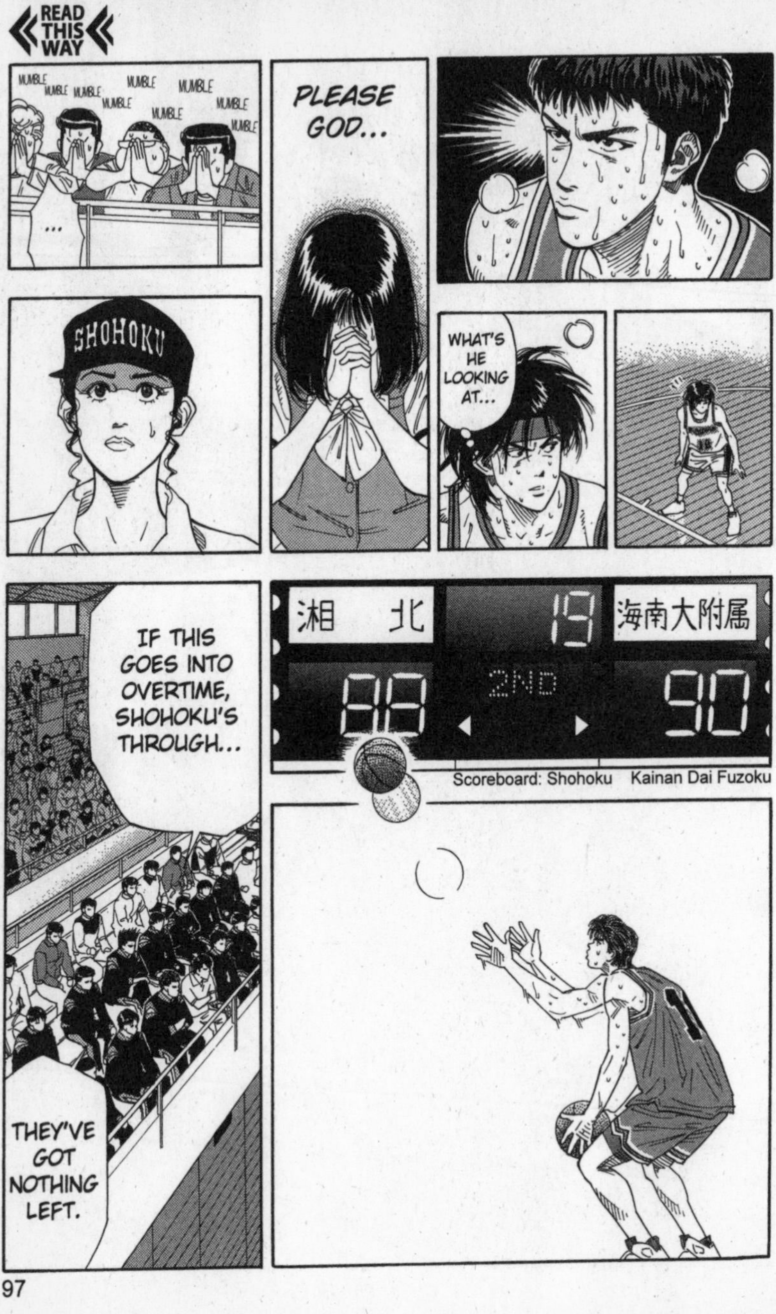
READ THIS WAY
WHAT'S HE LOOKING AT...
PLEASE GOD...
MUMBLE MUMBLE MUMBLE MUMBLE MUMBLE MUMBLE MUMBLE MUMBLE MUMBLE
...
湘 北
19
海南大附属
88
2ND
90
Scoreboard: Shohoku Kainan Dai Fuzoku
IF THIS GOES INTO OVERTIME, SHOHOKU'S THROUGH...
THEY'VE GOT NOTHING LEFT.

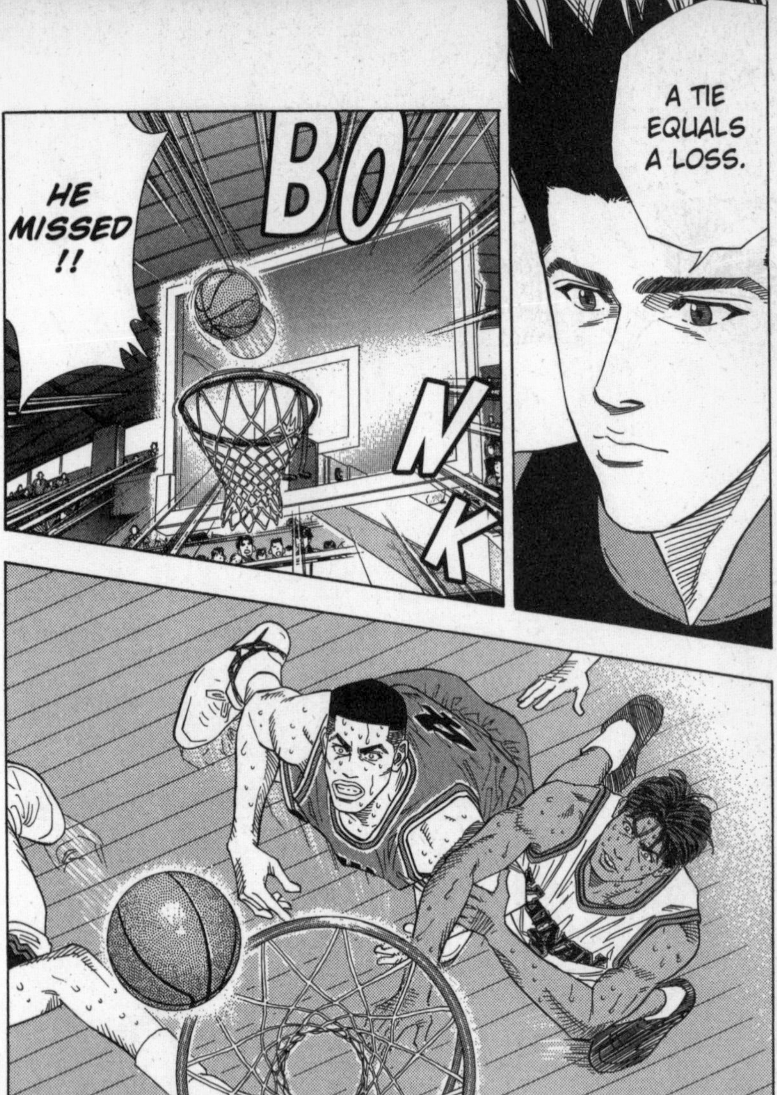
A TIE EQUALS A LOSS.
BONK
HE MISSED!!

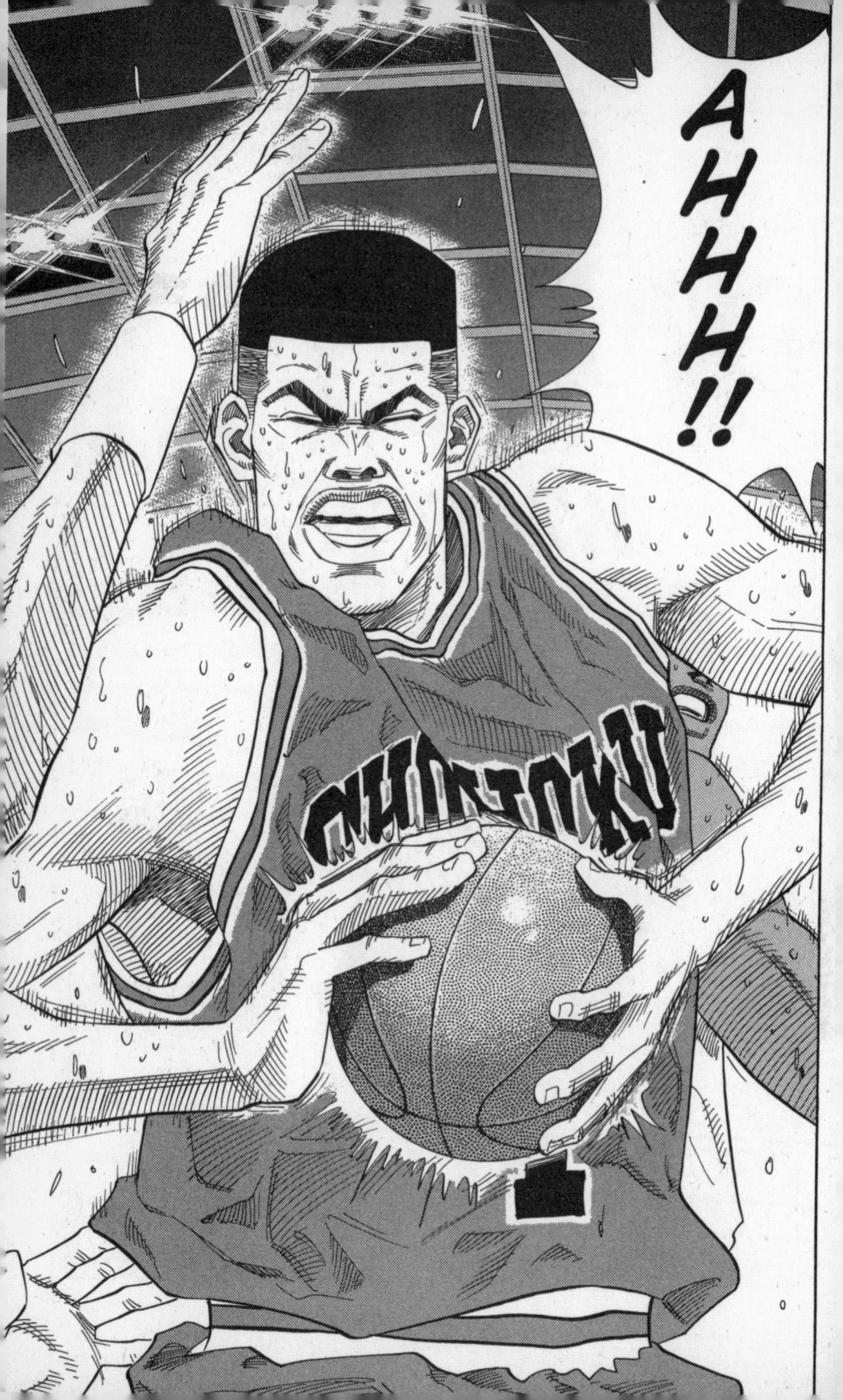
AHHHH!!

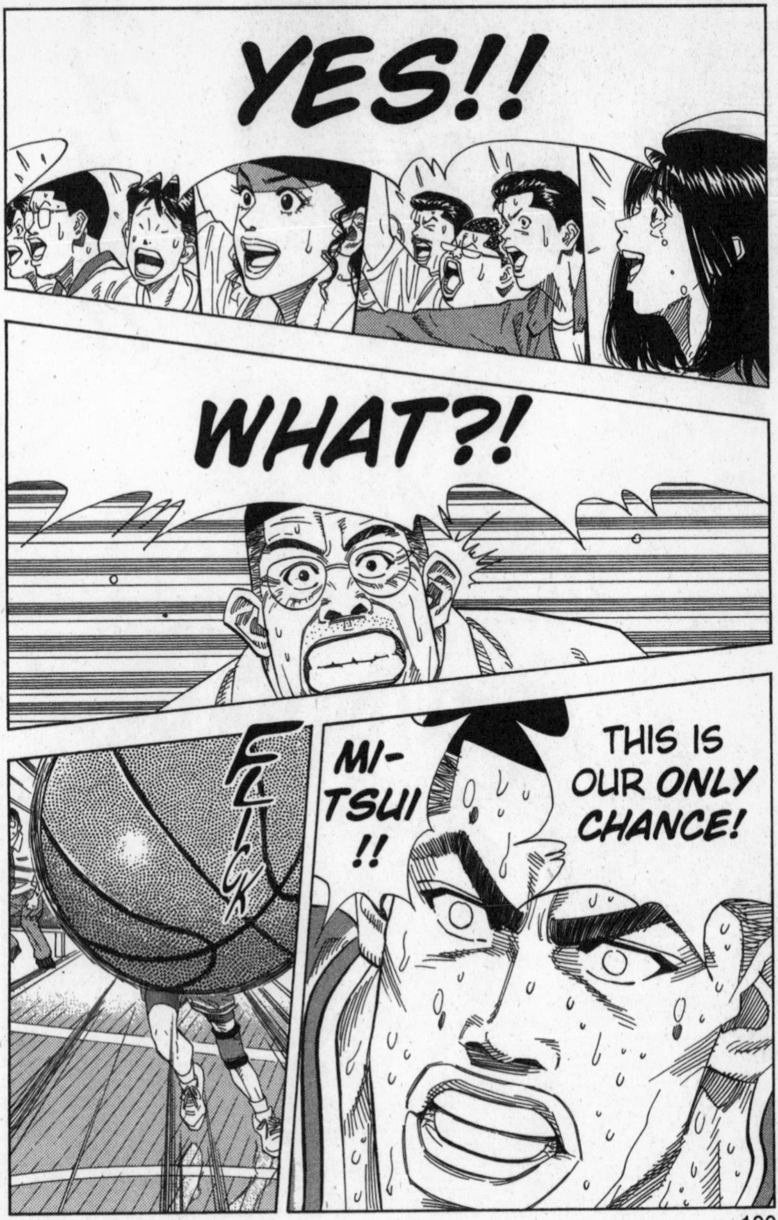
YES!!
WHAT?!
THIS IS OUR ONLY CHANCE!
MI-TSUI!!
FLICK

HUH?!

SHPP

SHOHOKU

AHH!!

HU

PP

HE'S GOING FOR THREE!!

SHOHOKU 14

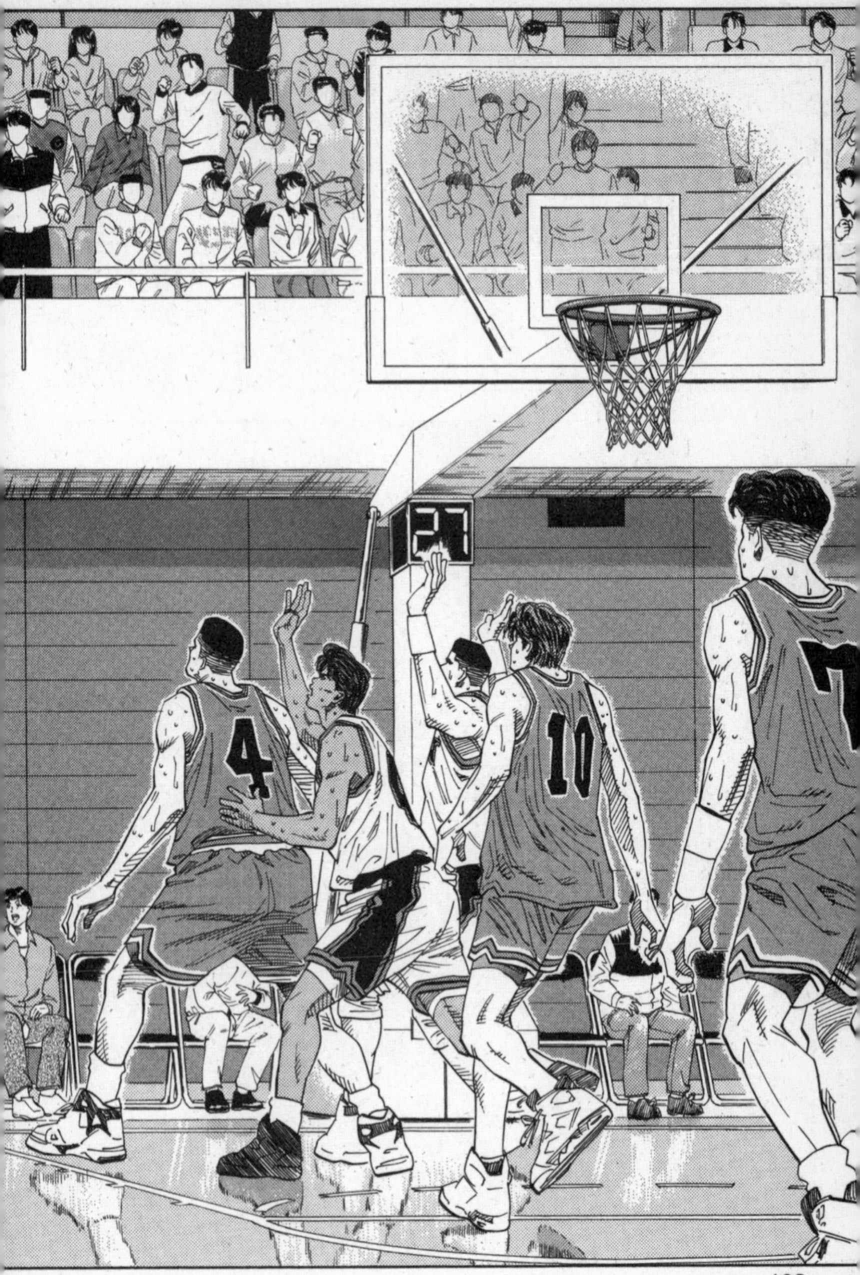

READ THIS WAY

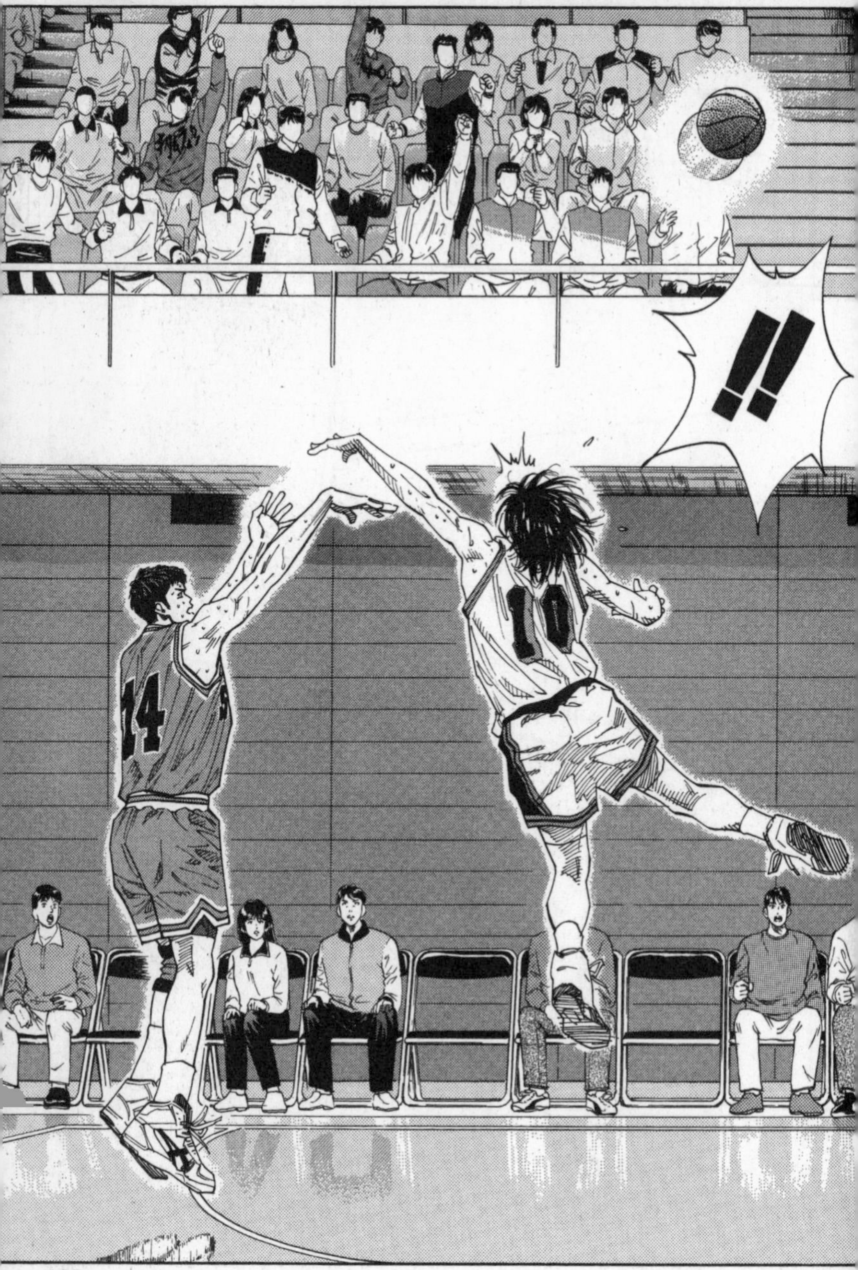
!!

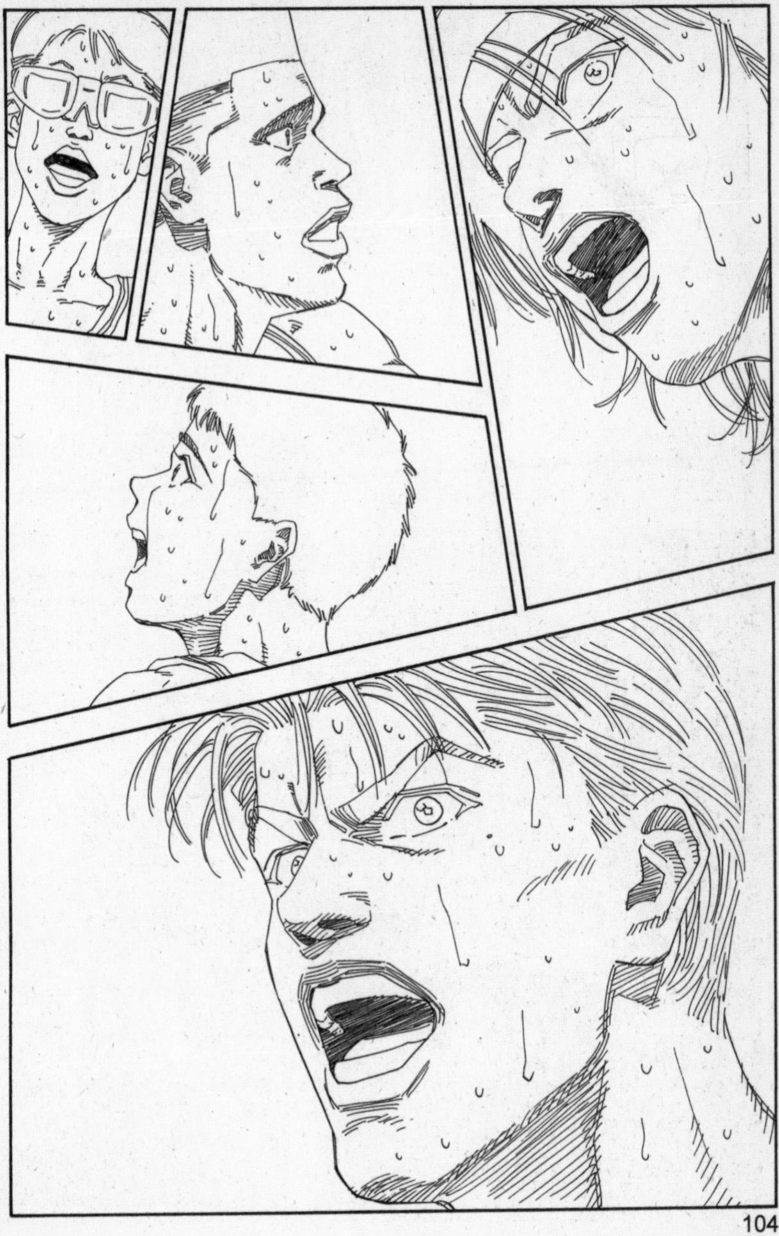

READ THIS WAY

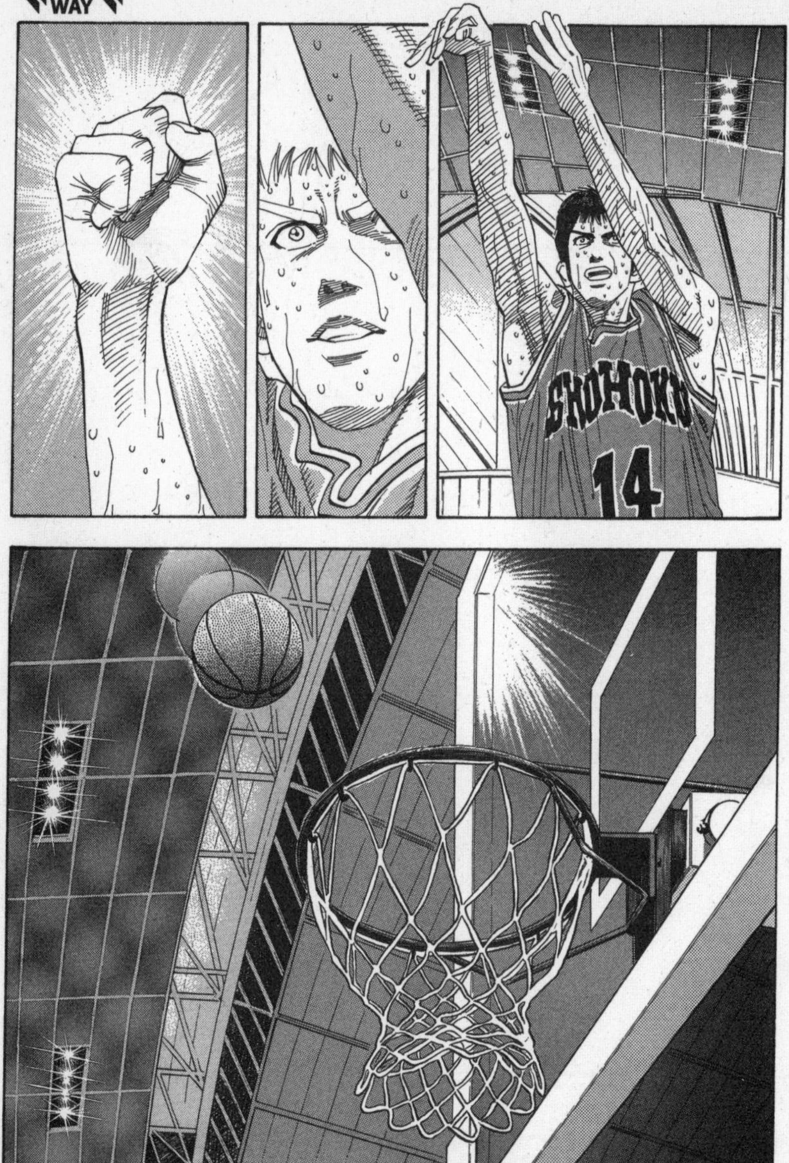
SHOHOKU
14

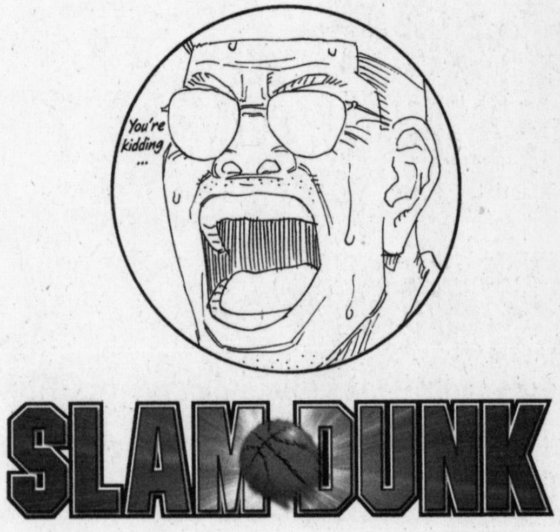
You're kidding ...

SLAM DUNK

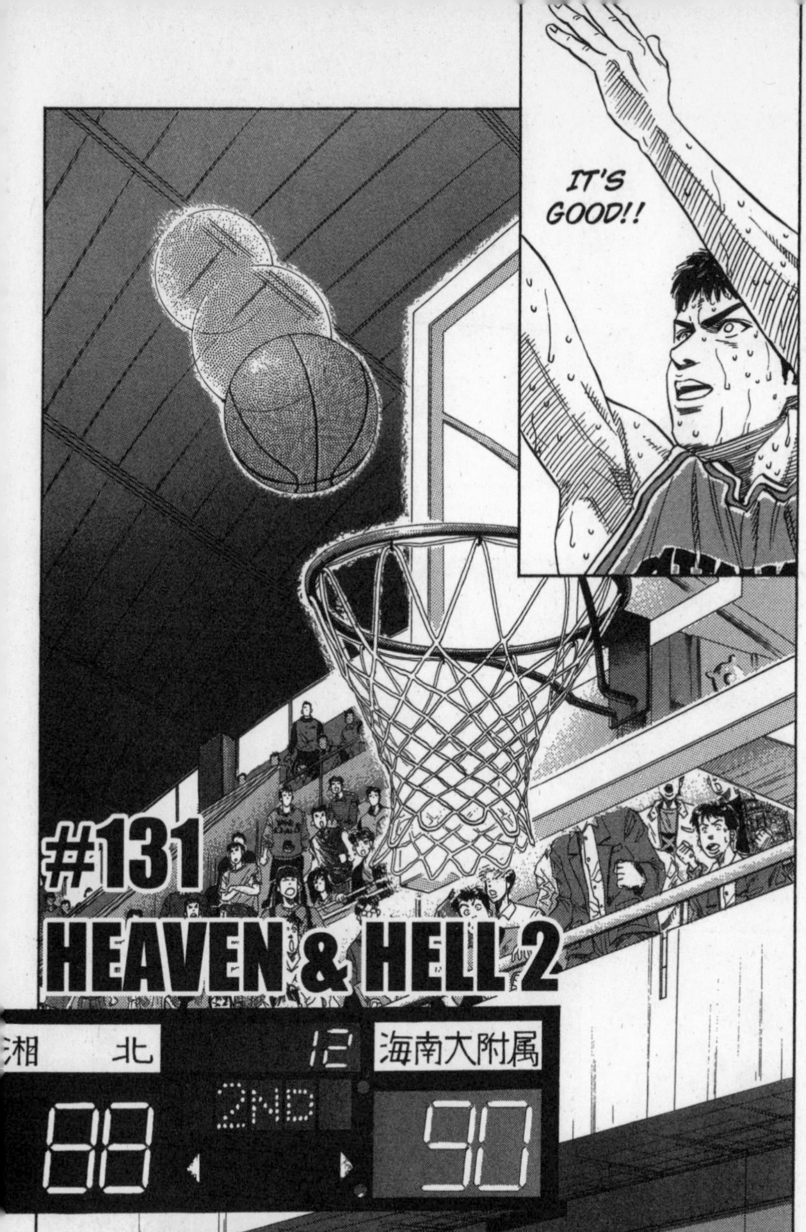
IT'S GOOD!!
#131
HEAVEN & HELL 2
湘 北
12
海南大附属
2ND
88
90

Scoreboard: Shohoku Kainan Dai Fuzoku

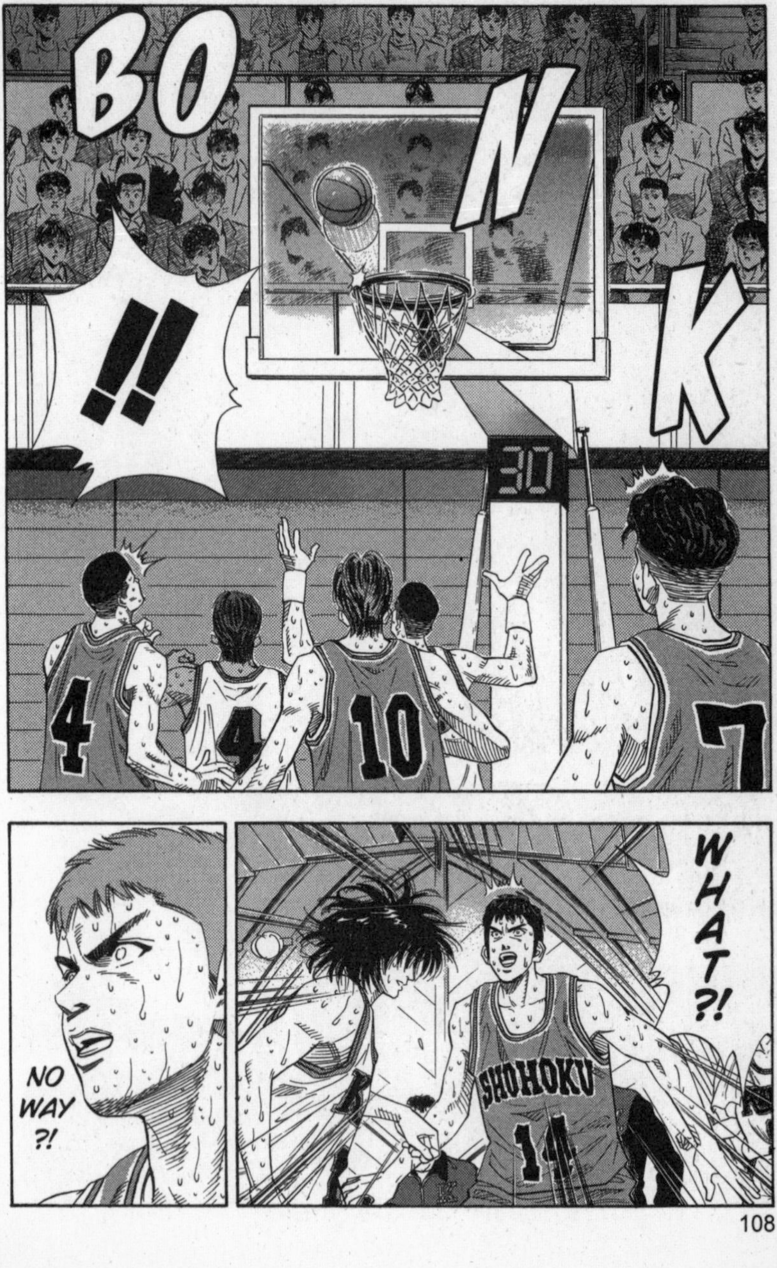
BONK
!!
WHAT?!
NO WAY?!

READ THIS WAY

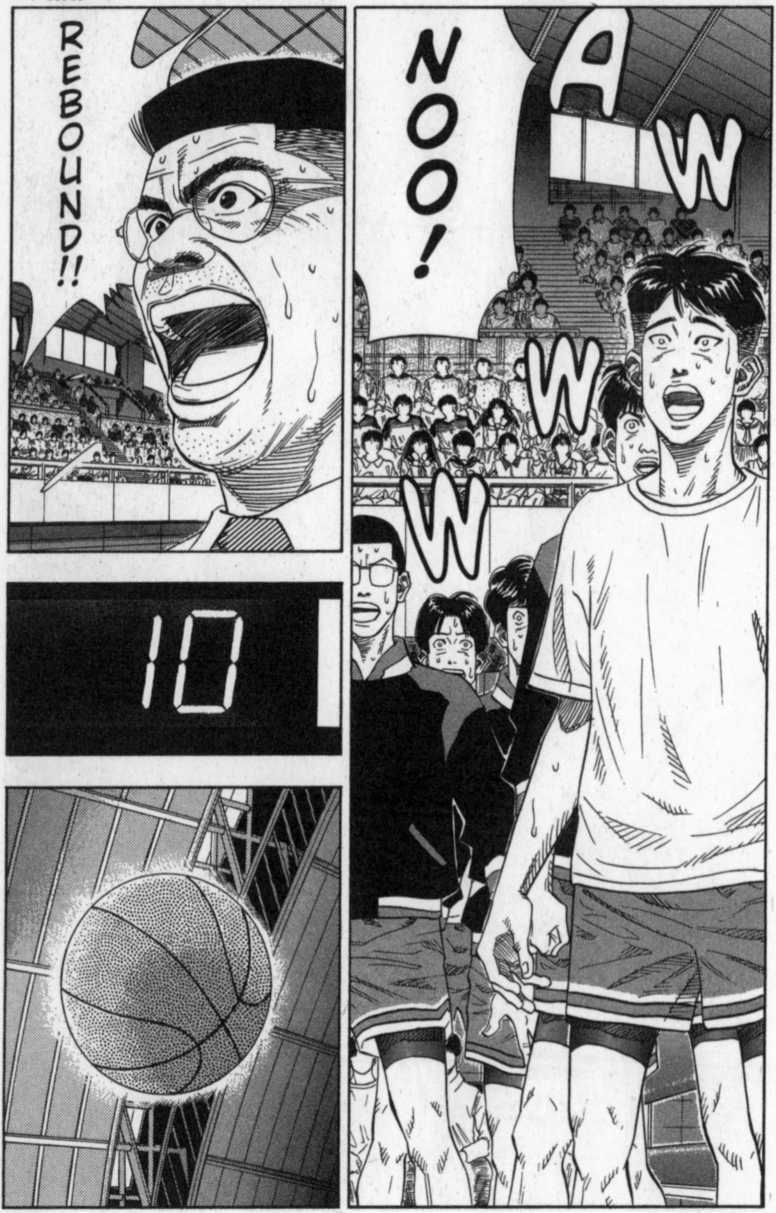
AWWW
NOO!
REBOUND!!
10

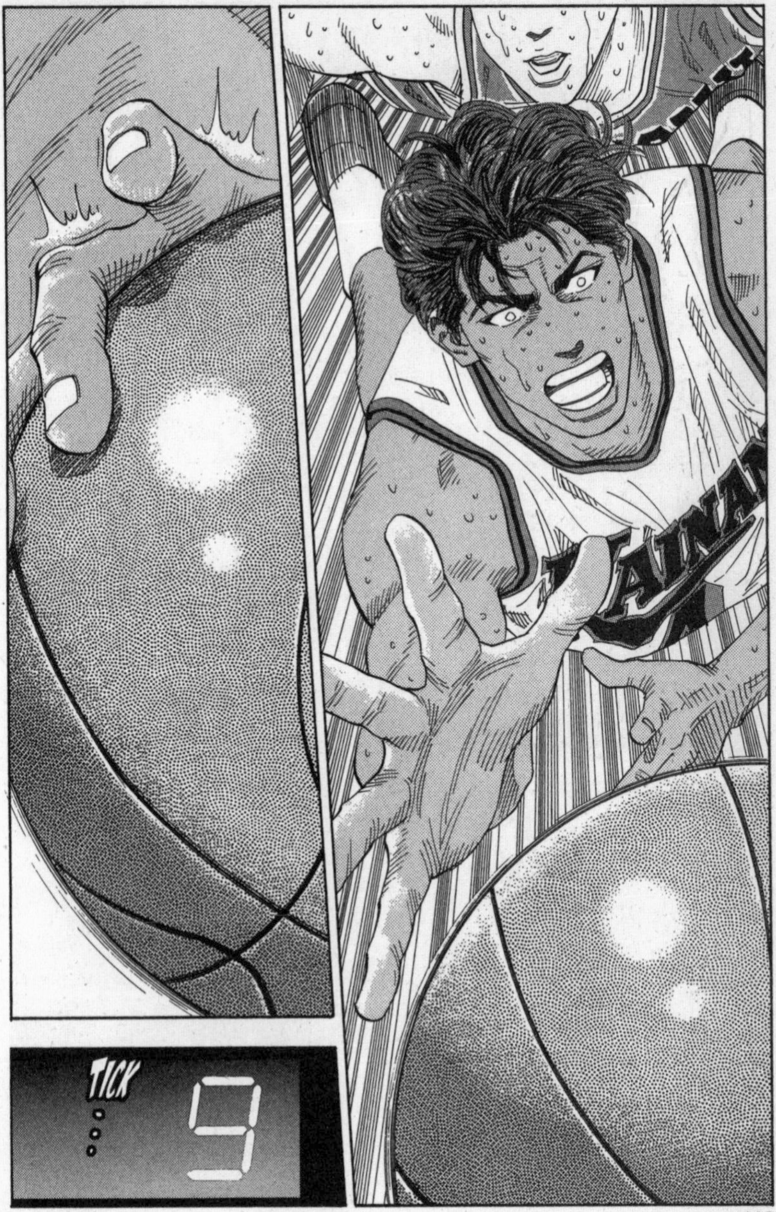
TICK
9

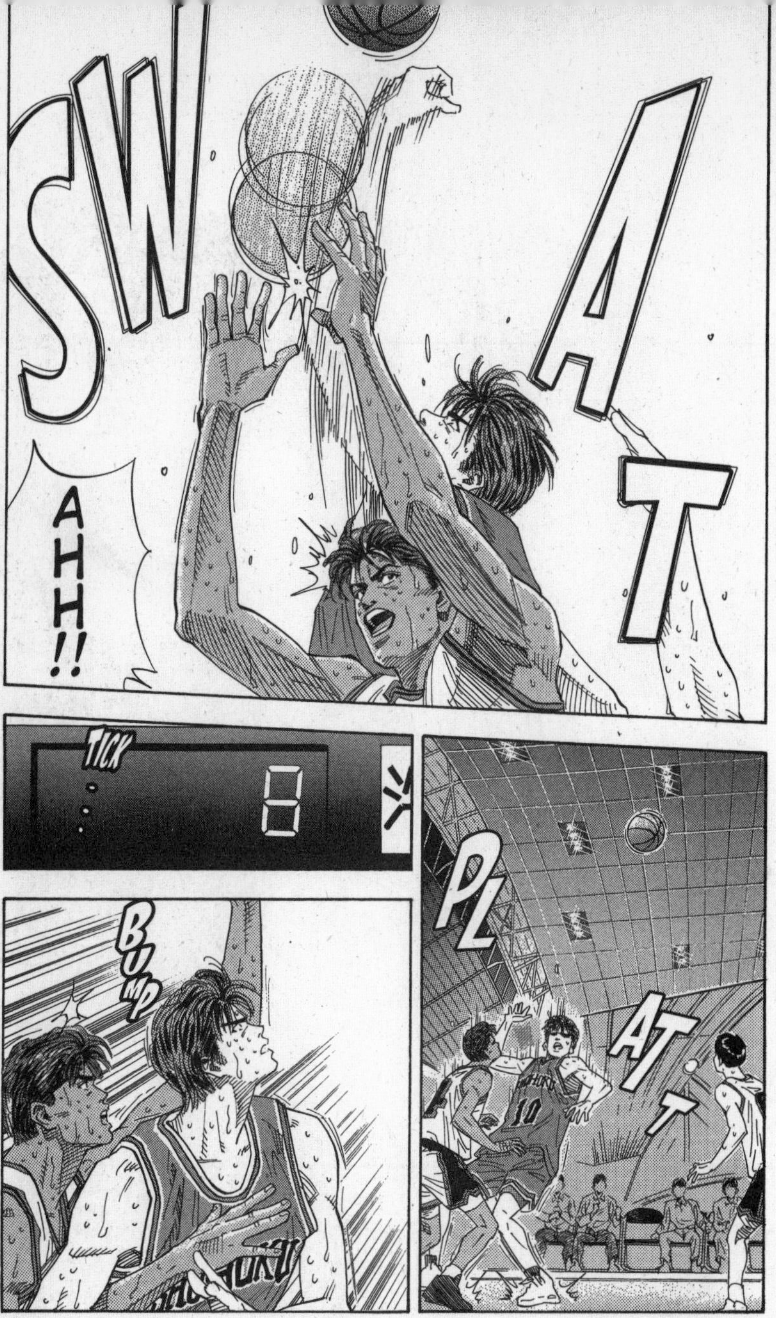
SWAT
AHH!!
PLAT
TICK
BUMP

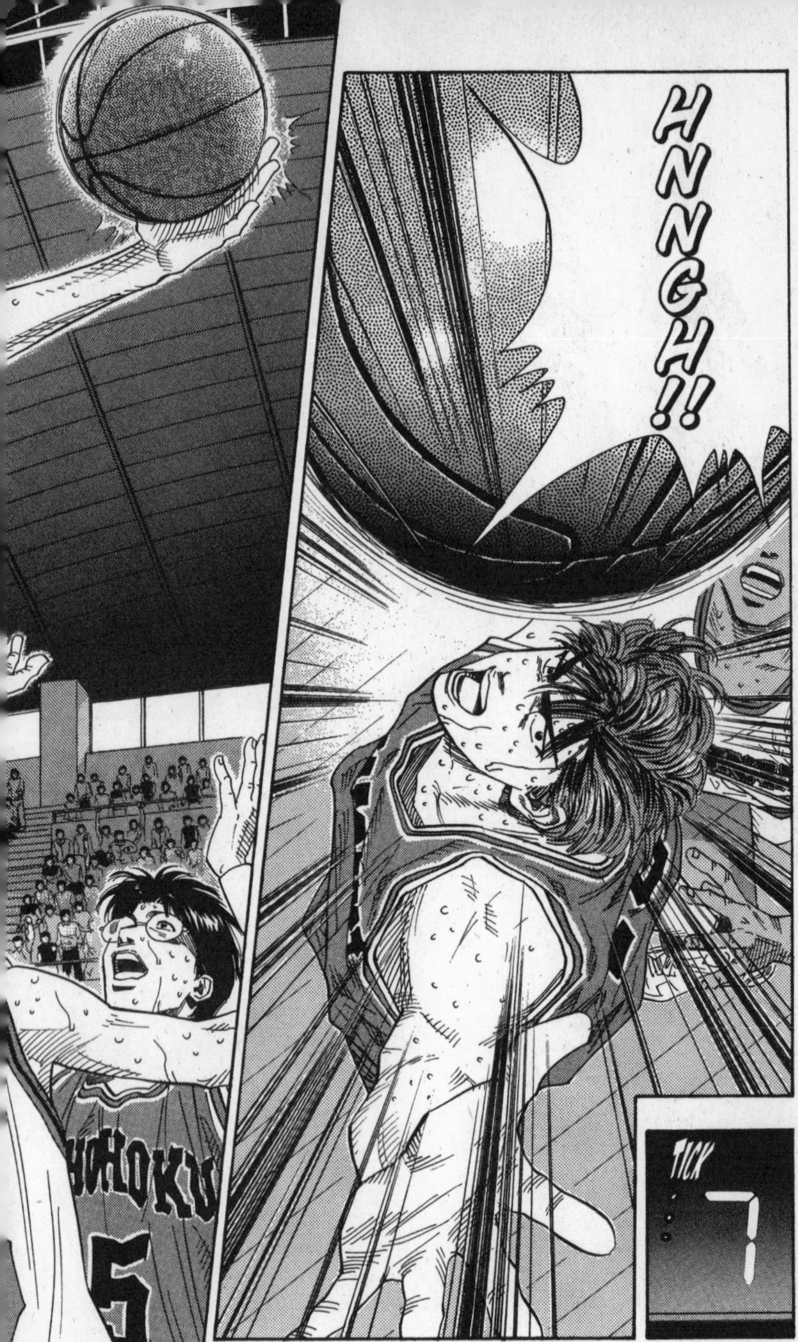
HNNGH!!
SHOHOKU
5
TICK
7

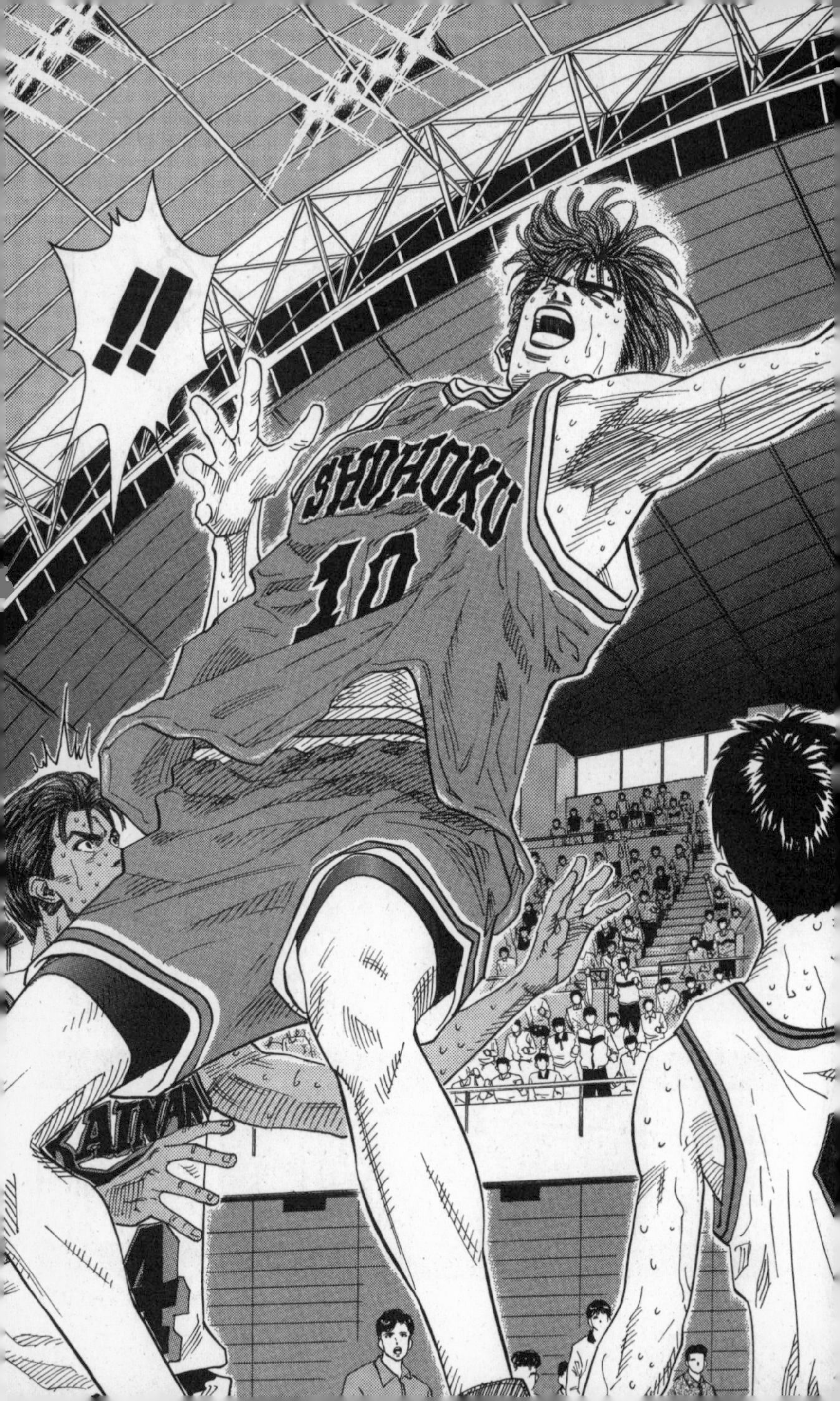
!!
SHOHOKU
10
KAINAN
4

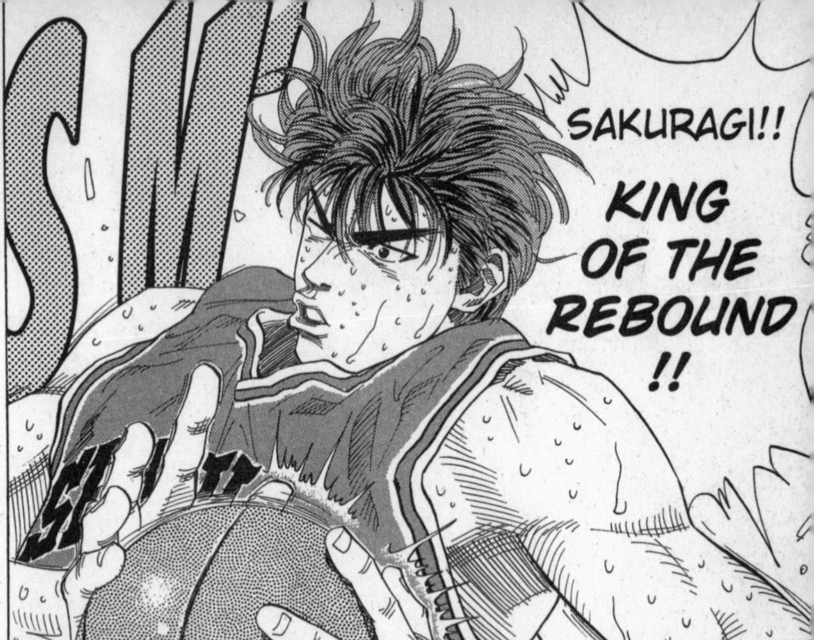
SAKURAGI!!
KING OF THE REBOUND !!

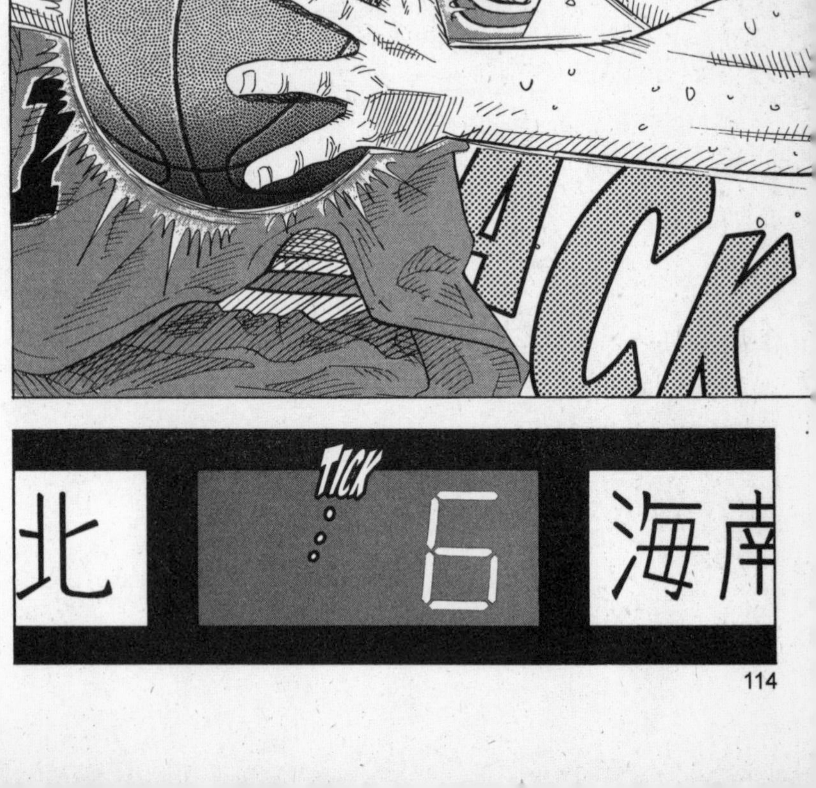
北
TICK
6
海

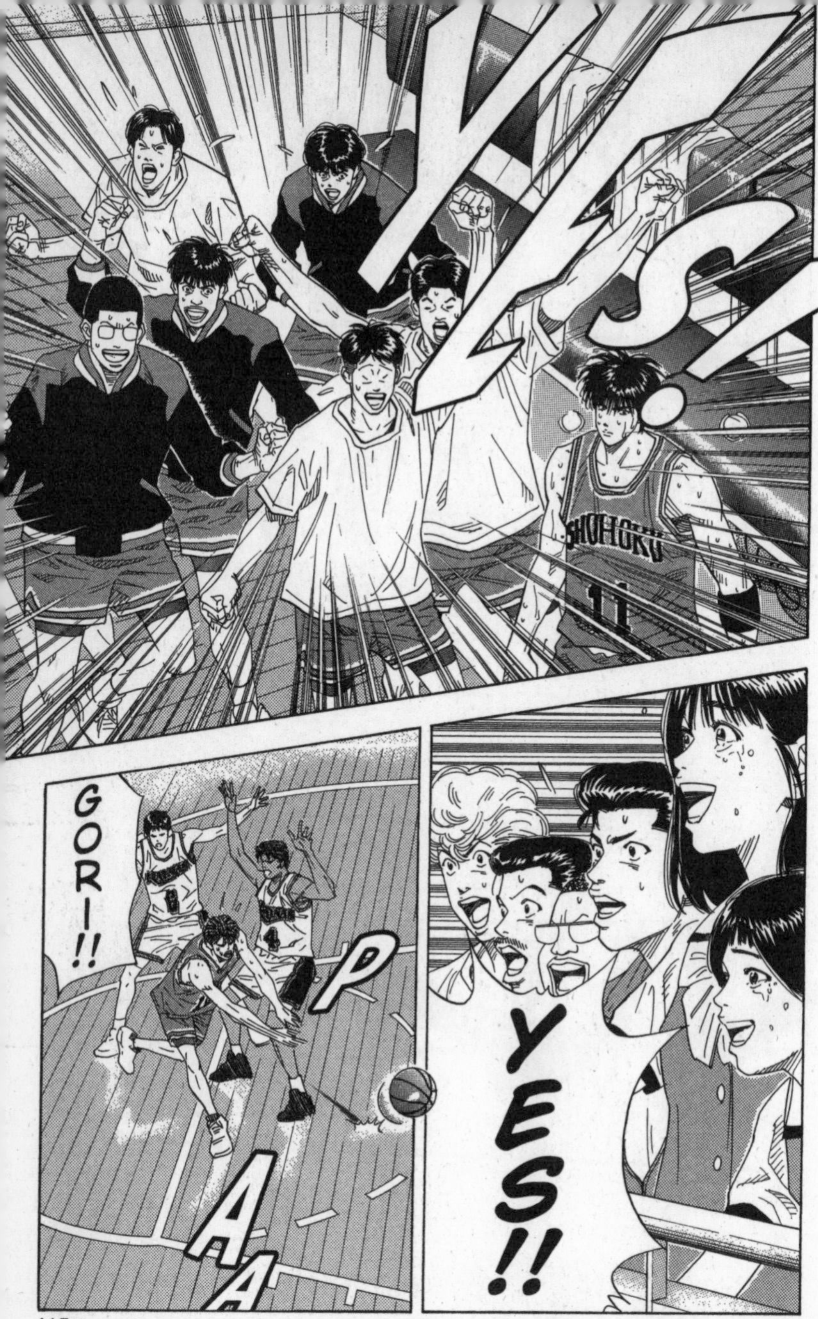
YES!
YES!!
GORI!!
PAA

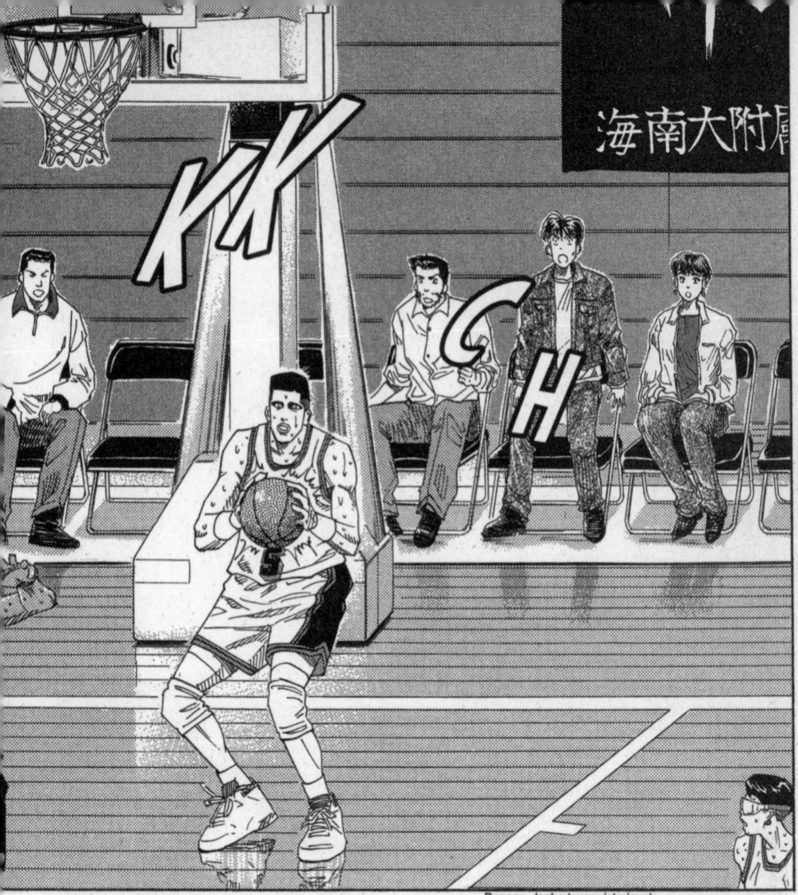
KK
CH
海南大附

Banner: *Josho* (ever victorious)
Kainan Dai Fuzoku High School Basketball Team

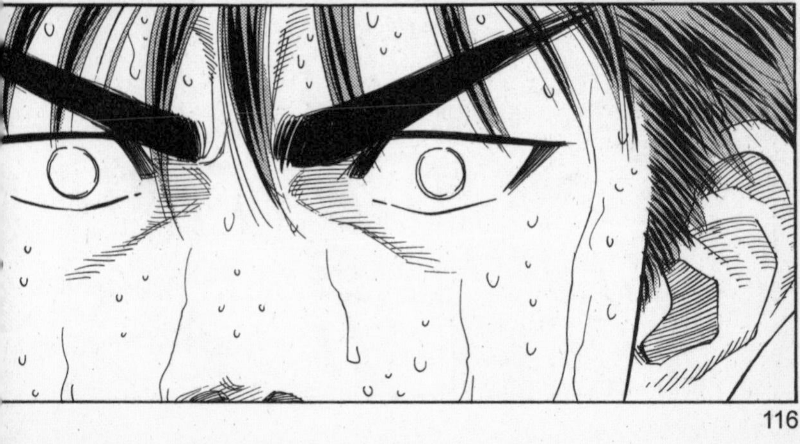

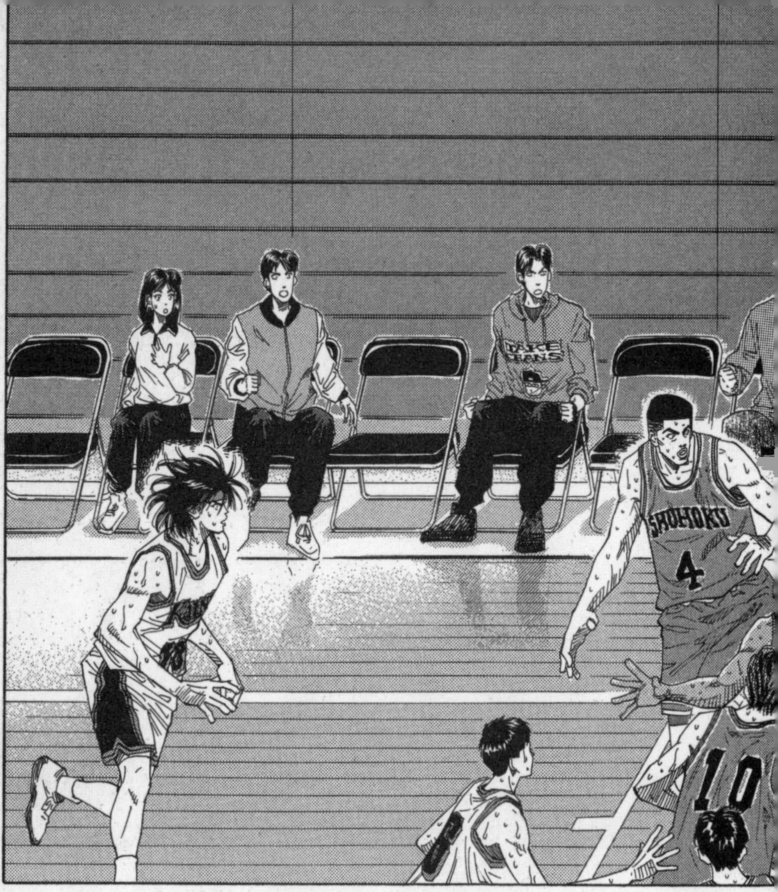
SHOHOKU

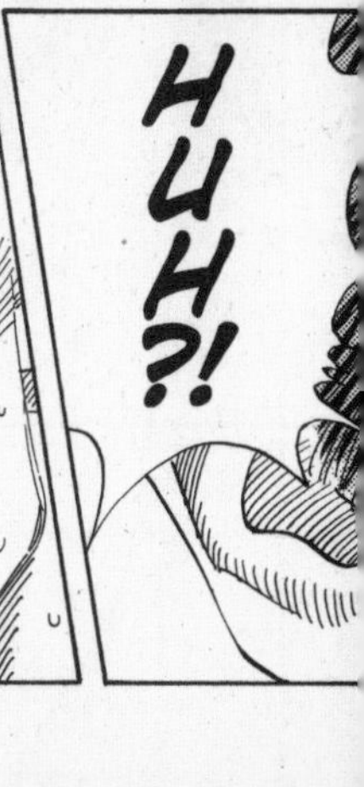
HUH?!

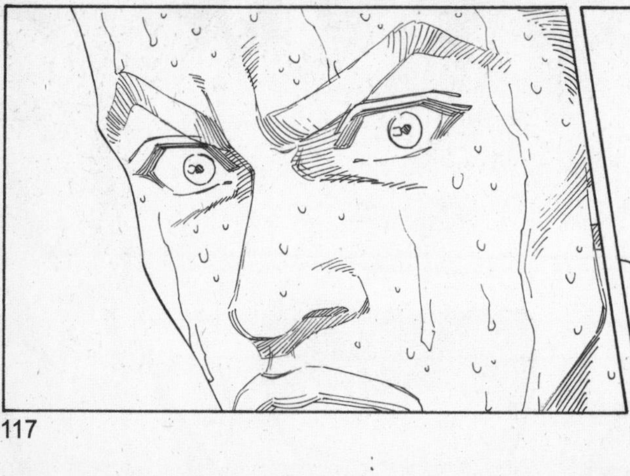

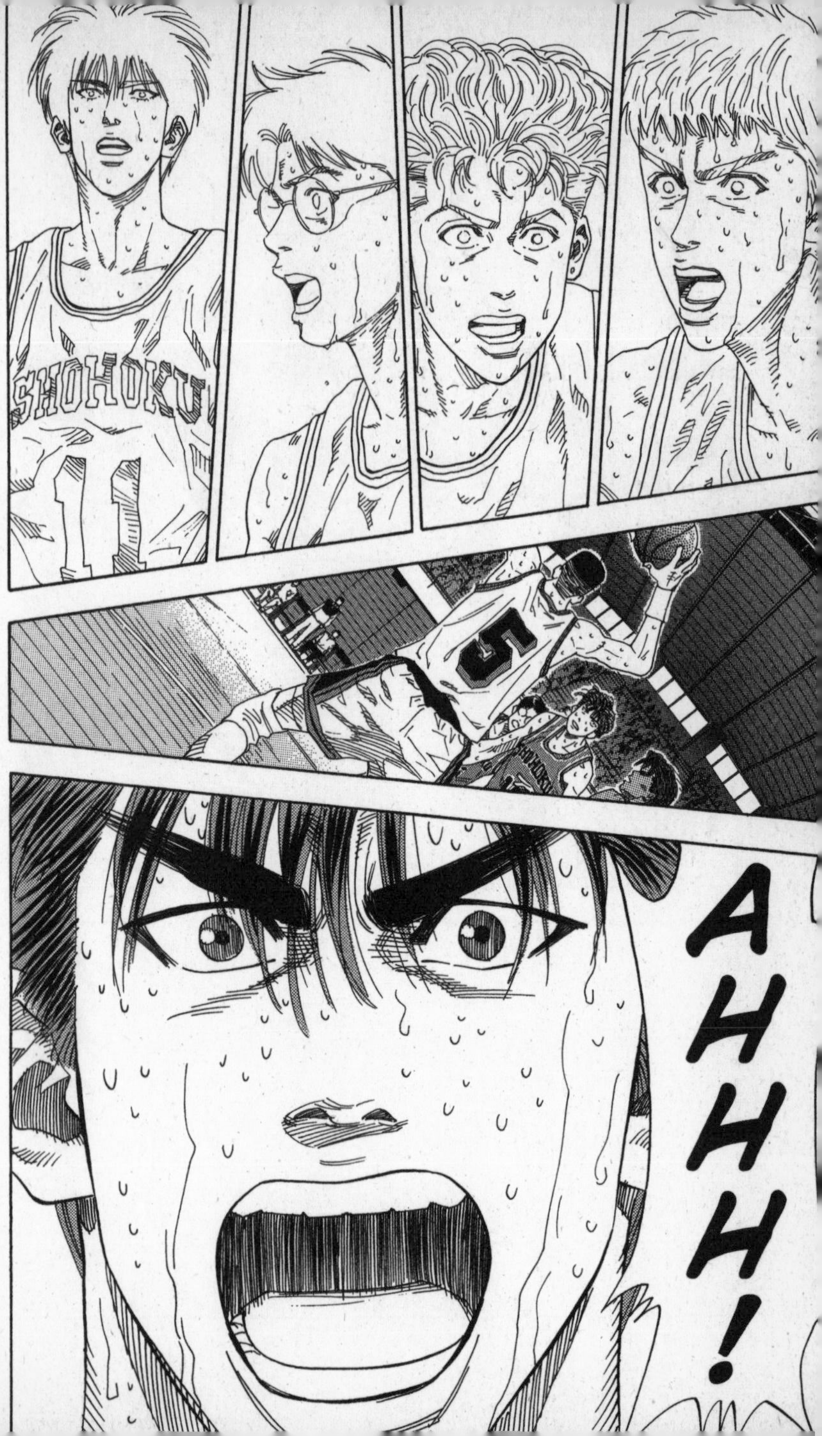
SHOHOKU
11
AHHH!

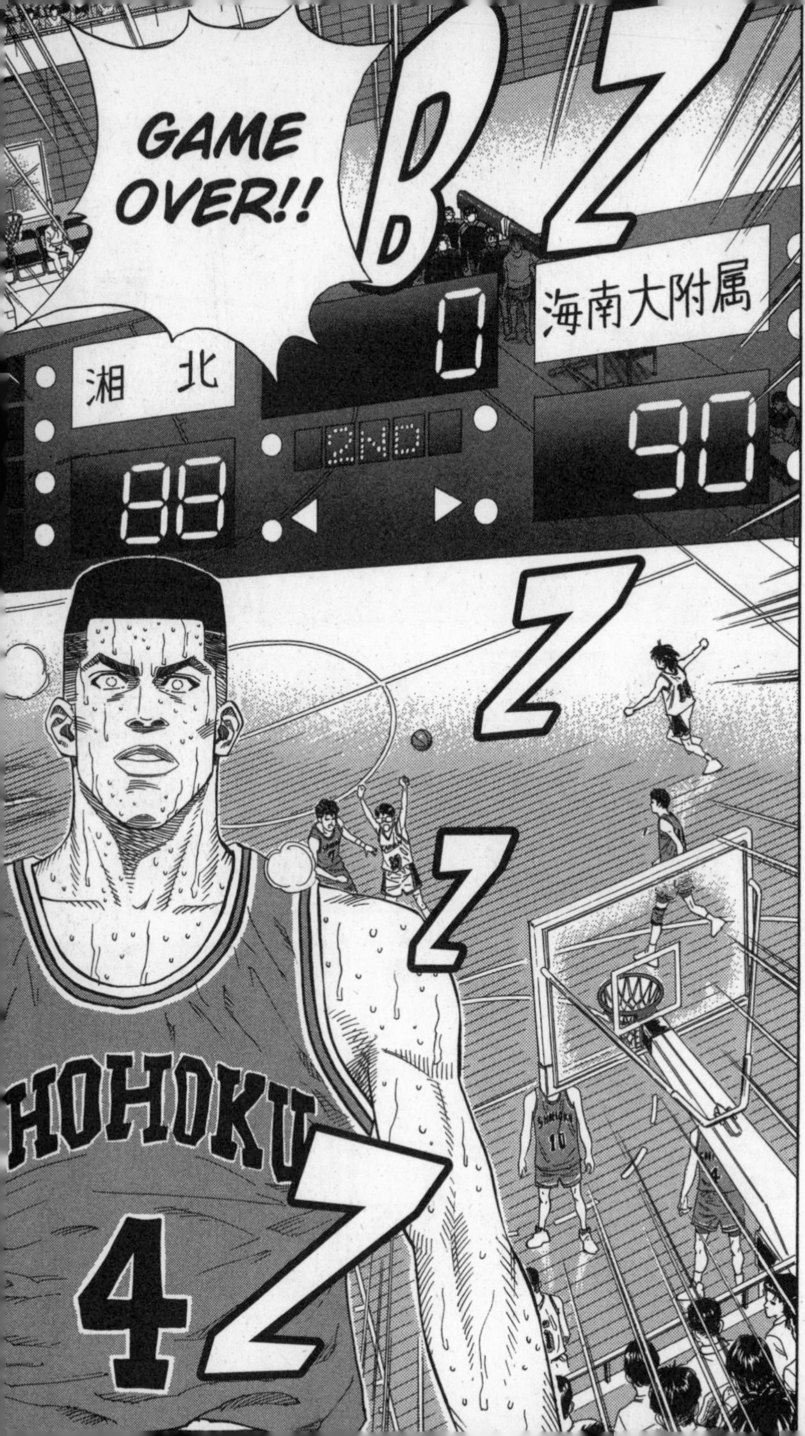

GAME OVER!!
BZZZZ
海南大附属
0
湘北
2ND
88
90
SHOHOKU
4
Scoreboard: Shohoku Kainan Dai Fuzoku

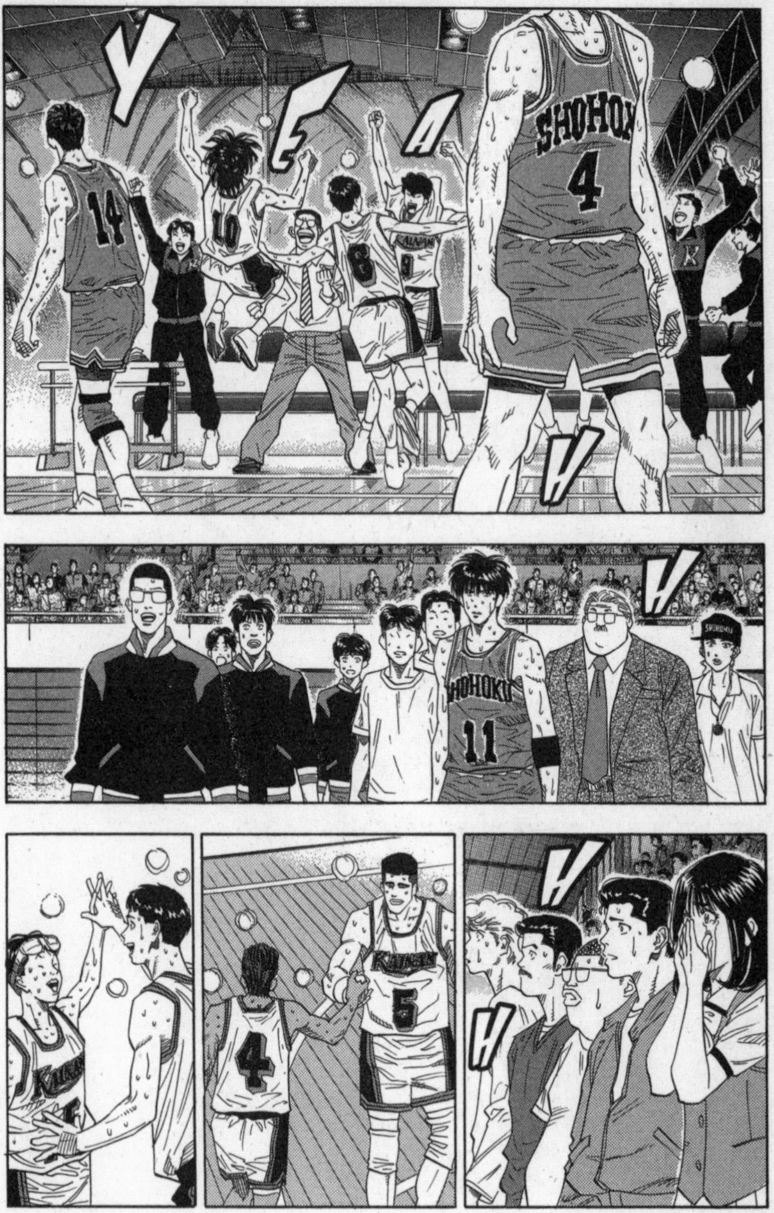
YEAH
H
H
H

READ THIS WAY

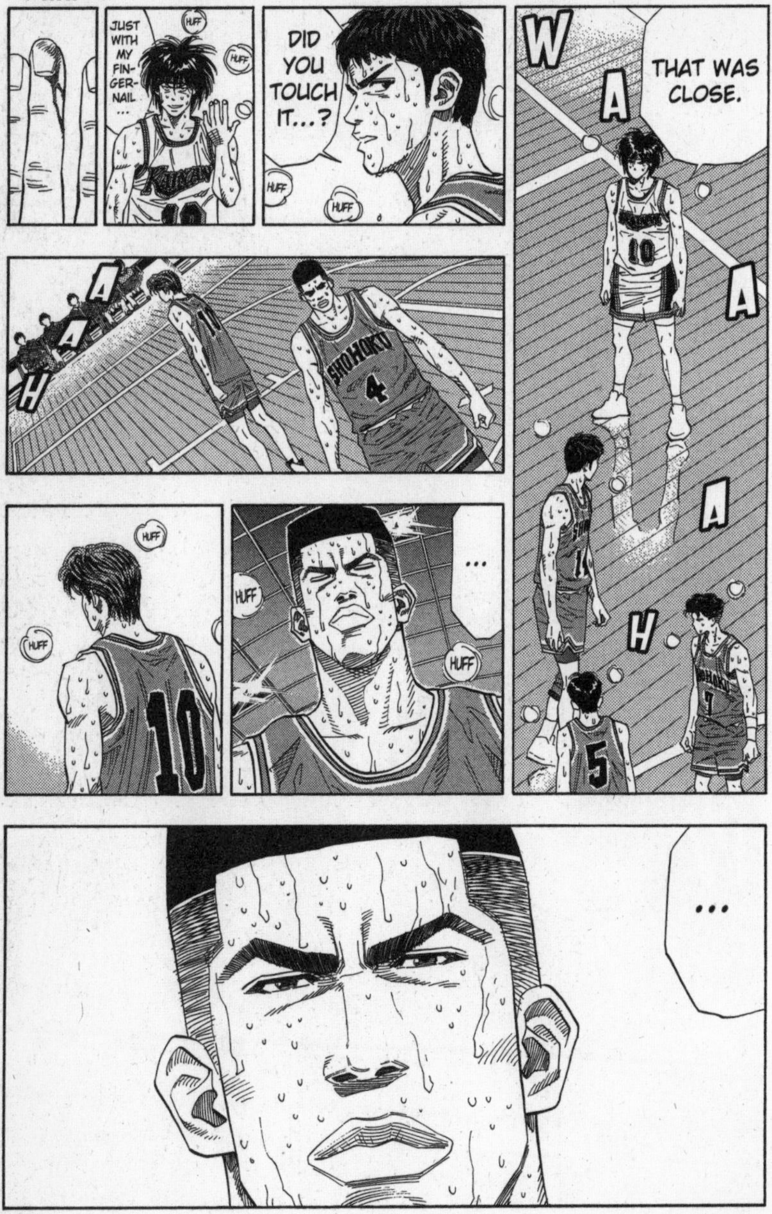
W
A
THAT WAS CLOSE.
A
A
H
DID YOU TOUCH IT...?
HUFF
HUFF
JUST WITH MY FIN-GER-NAIL ...
HUFF
HUFF
A
A
H
...
HUFF
HUFF
HUFF
HUFF
...

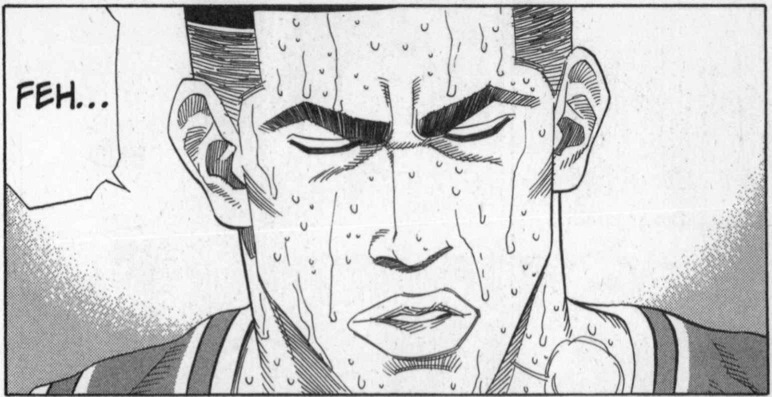
FEH...

Banner: *Josho* (ever victorious)
Kainan Dai Fuzoku High School Basketball Team

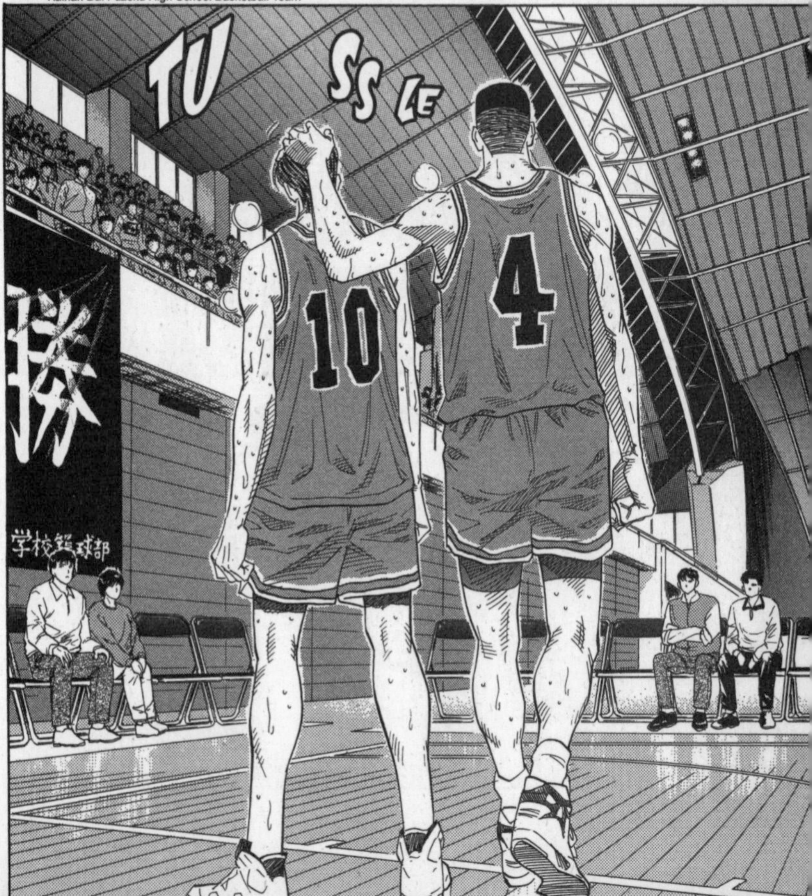
TUSSLE
勝
学校籠球部

READ THIS WAY

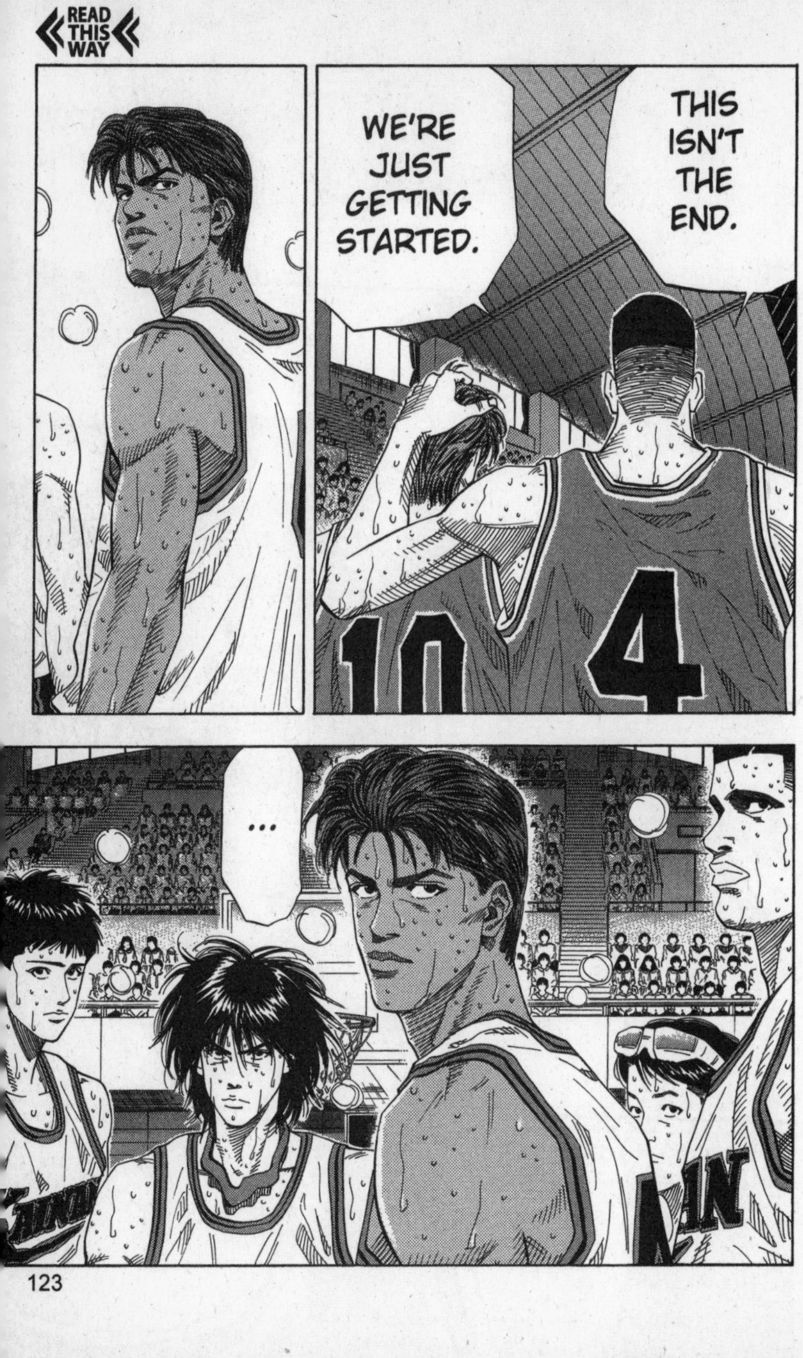
THIS ISN'T THE END.
WE'RE JUST GETTING STARTED.
...

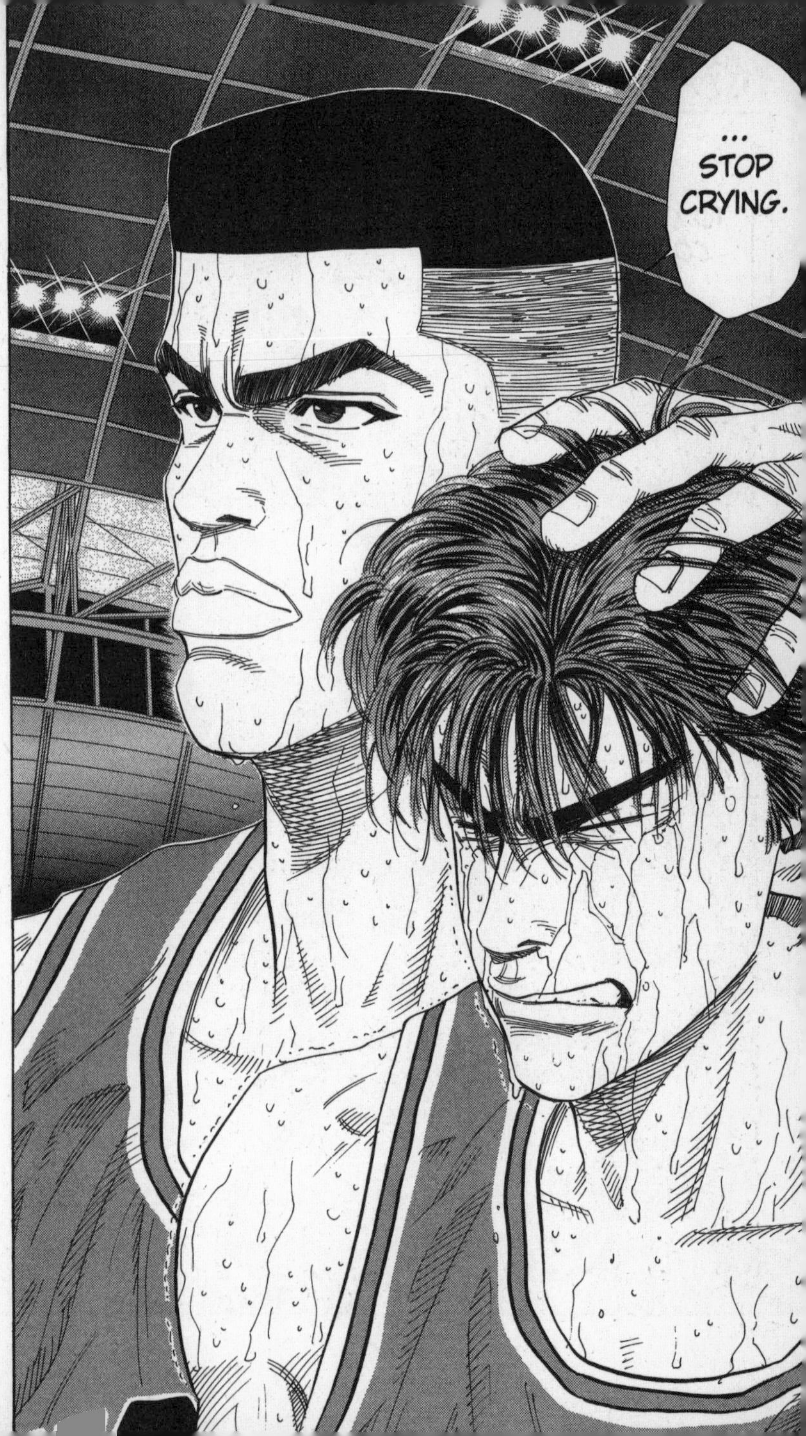
... STOP CRYING.

READ THIS WAY

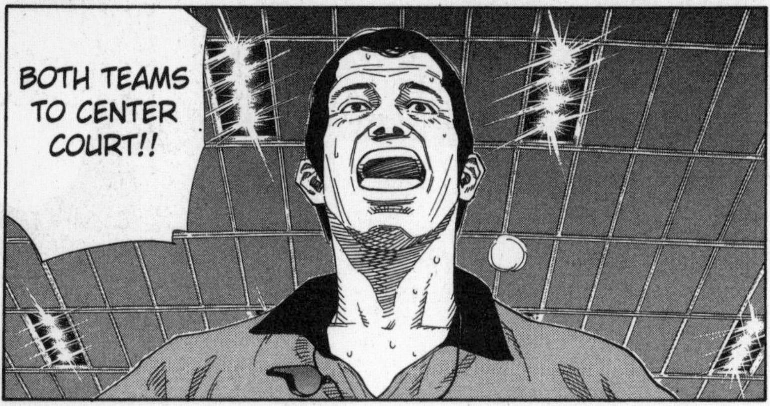
BOTH TEAMS TO CENTER COURT!!

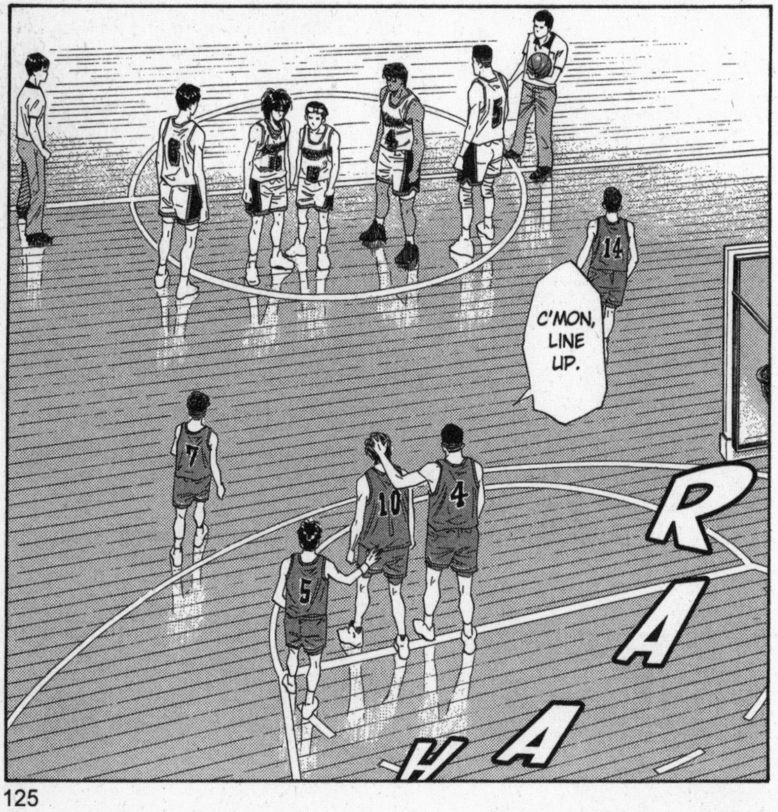
C'MON, LINE UP.
RAAH

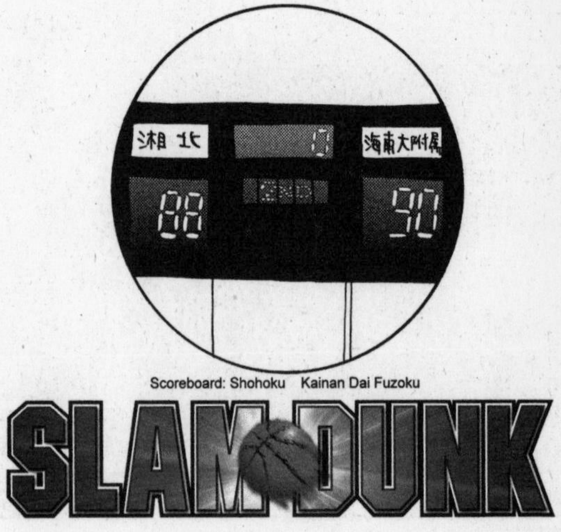
湘北
0
海南大附属
88
2ND
90

Scoreboard: Shohoku Kainan Dai Fuzoku

SLAM DUNK

ON THE BRINK

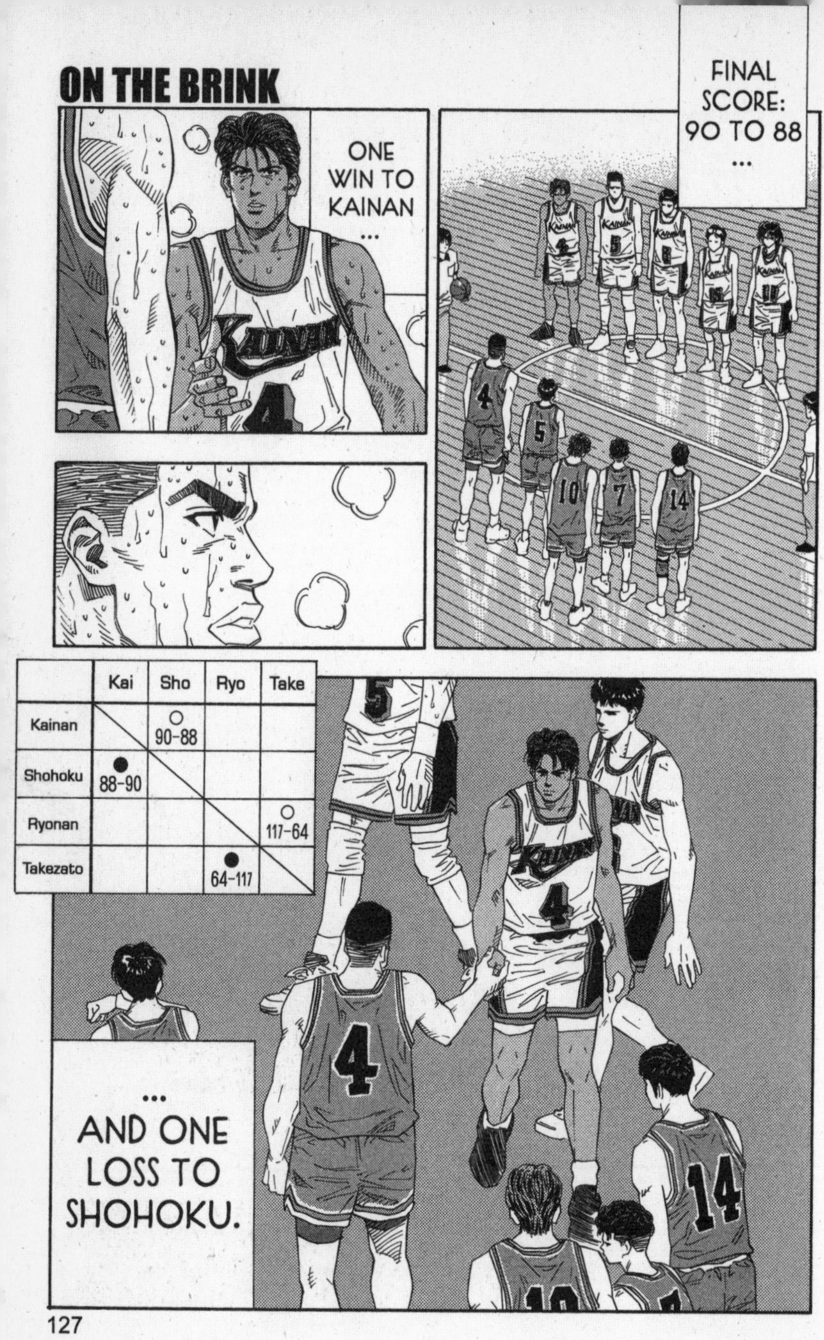
FINAL SCORE: 90 TO 88 ...
ONE WIN TO KAINAN ...
... AND ONE LOSS TO SHOHOKU.

	Kai	Sho	Ryo	Take
Kainan		○ 90-88		
Shohoku	● 88-90			
Ryonan				○ 117-64
Takezato			● 64-117	

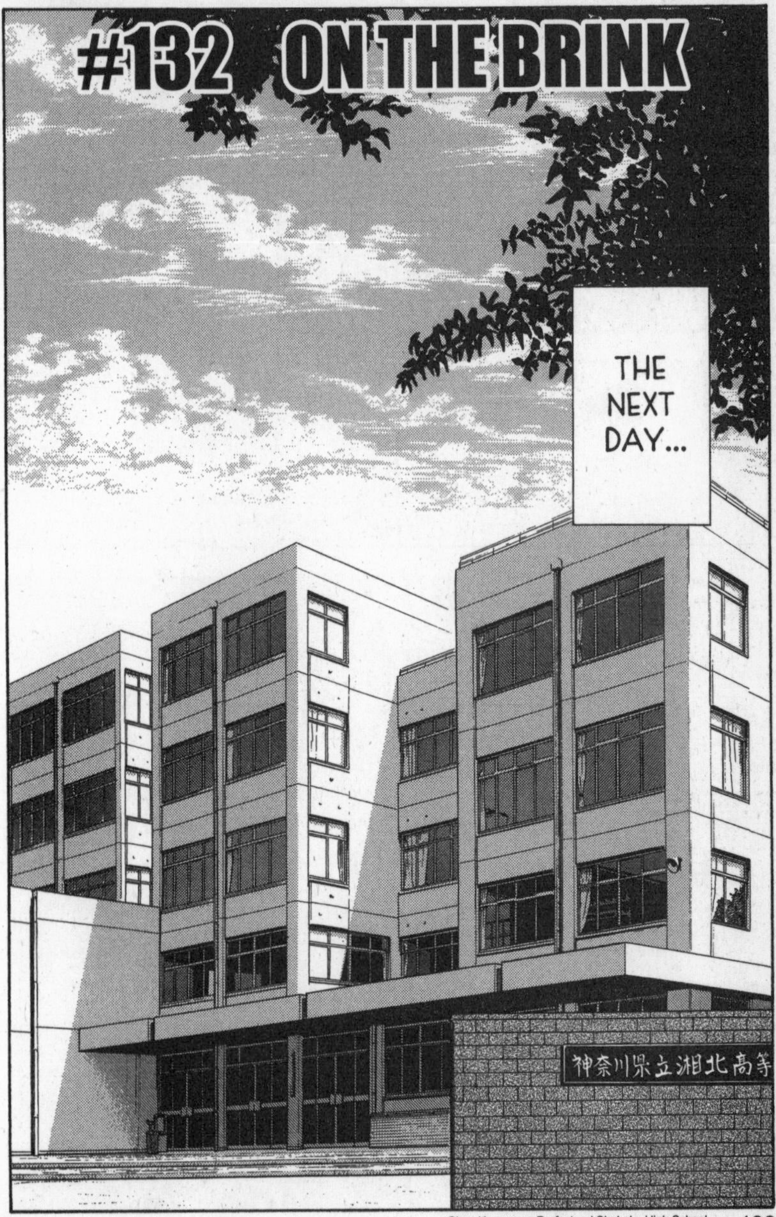
#132 ON THE BRINK
THE NEXT DAY...
神奈川県立湘北高等
Sign: Kanagawa Prefectural Shohoku High School

READ THIS WAY

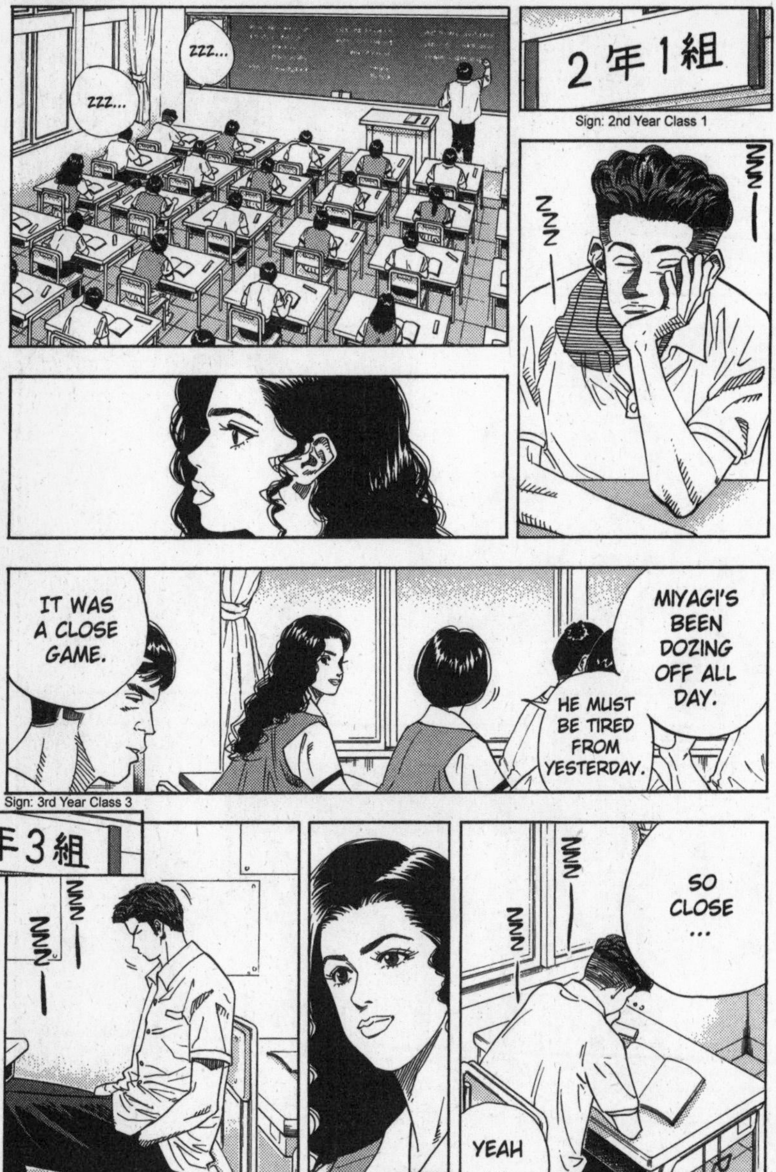

2年1組
Sign: 2nd Year Class 1
ZZZ— ZZZ—
ZZZ...
ZZZ...
MIYAGI'S BEEN DOZING OFF ALL DAY.
HE MUST BE TIRED FROM YESTERDAY.
IT WAS A CLOSE GAME.
ZZZ— ZZZ—
SO CLOSE ...
YEAH ...
Sign: 3rd Year Class 3
3年3組
ZZZ— ZZZ—

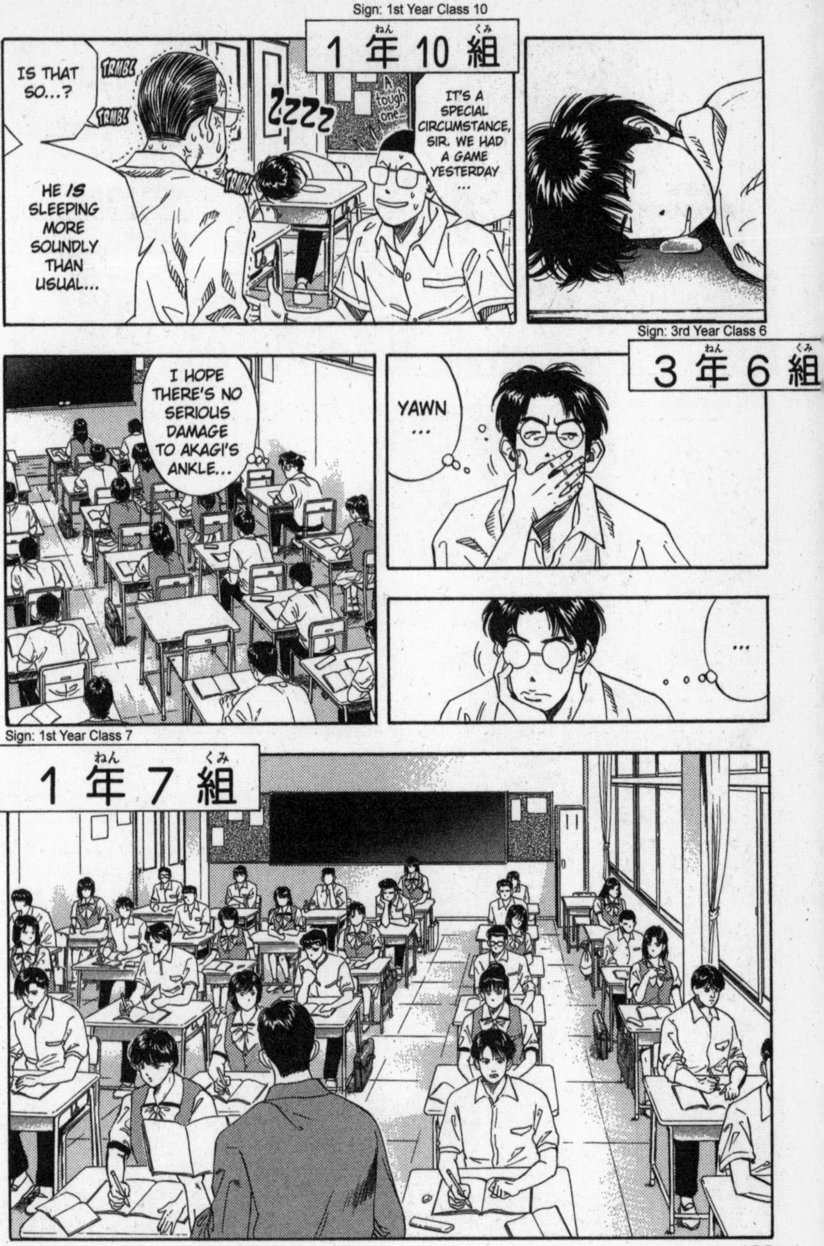
Sign: 1st Year Class 10
1 年 10 組
IT'S A SPECIAL CIRCUMSTANCE, SIR. WE HAD A GAME YESTERDAY ...
A tough one...
ZZZZ
TRMBL
TRMBL
TRMBL
IS THAT SO...?
HE IS SLEEPING MORE SOUNDLY THAN USUAL...
Sign: 3rd Year Class 6
3 年 6 組
YAWN ...
...
I HOPE THERE'S NO SERIOUS DAMAGE TO AKAGI'S ANKLE...
Sign: 1st Year Class 7
1 年 7 組

HM...

HE'S PROBABLY STILL IN BED...

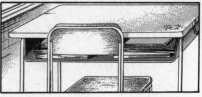

...

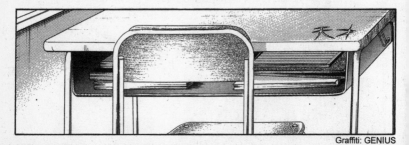

Graffiti: GENIUS

AFTER SCHOOL ...

RIIING RIIING RIIING

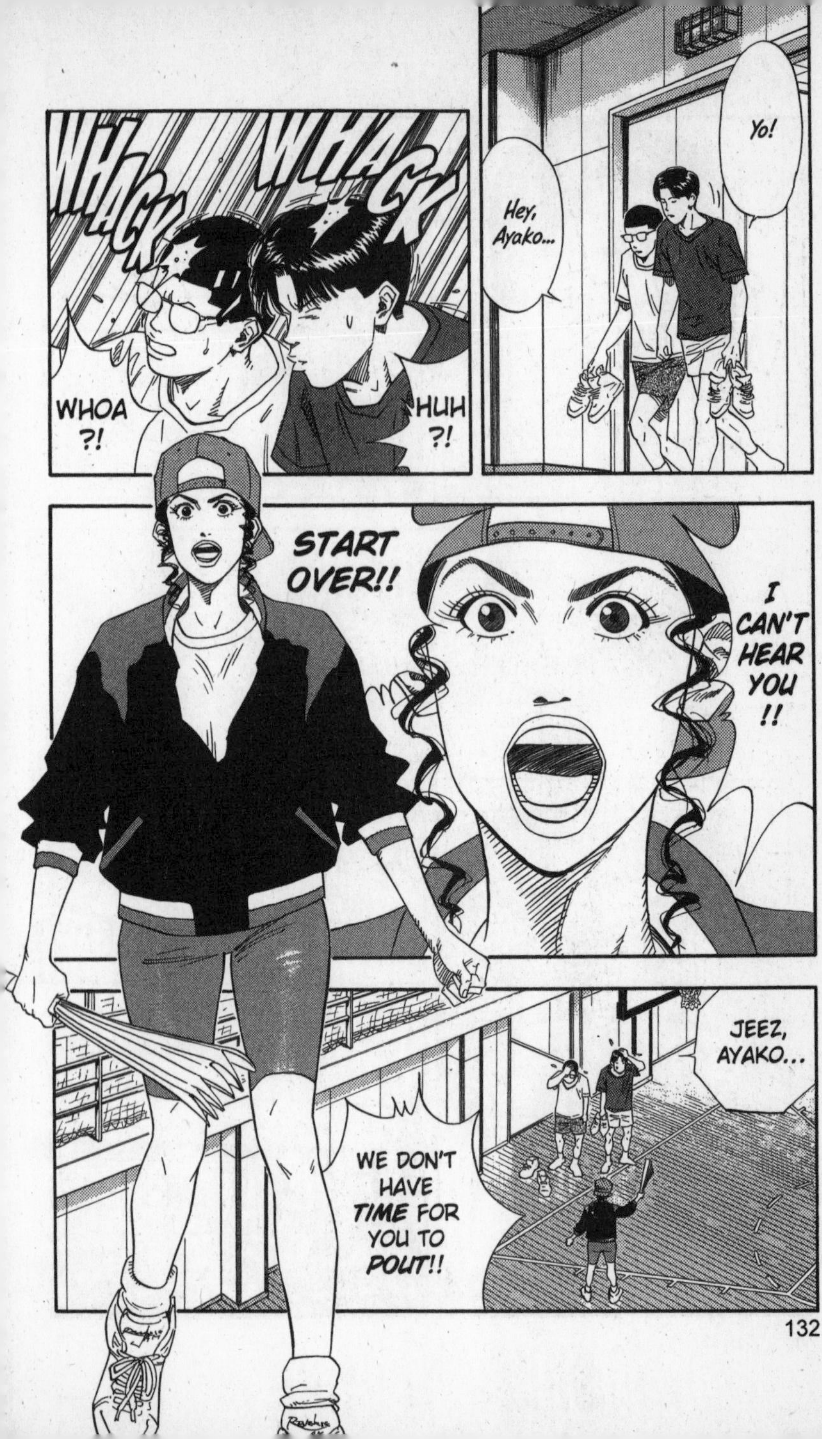
Yo!
Hey, Ayako...
WHACK
WHACK
HUH ?!
WHOA ?!
I CAN'T HEAR YOU !!
START OVER!!
JEEZ, AYAKO...
WE DON'T HAVE TIME FOR YOU TO POUT!!

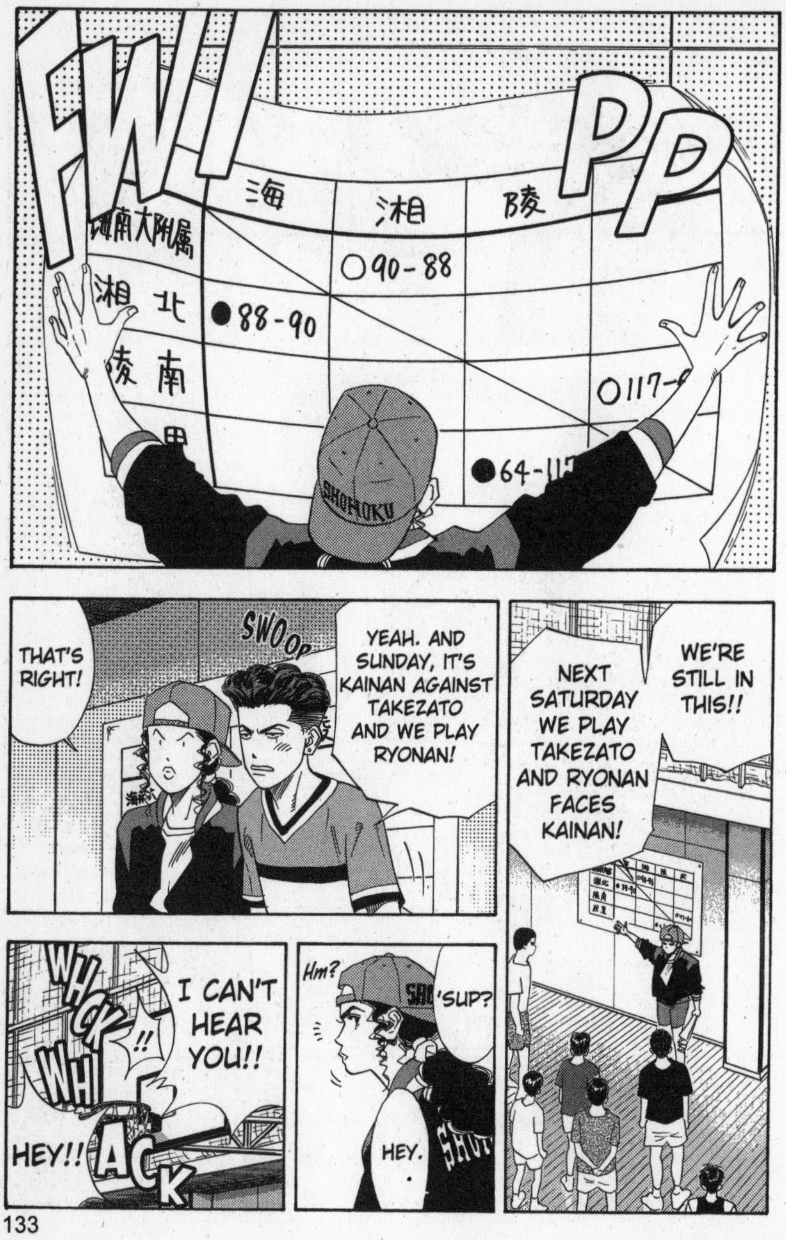
FWIIPP
海
湘
陵
海南大附属
湘北
陵南
○90-88
●88-90
○117-
●64-11
WE'RE STILL IN THIS!!
NEXT SATURDAY WE PLAY TAKEZATO AND RYONAN FACES KAINAN!
YEAH. AND SUNDAY, IT'S KAINAN AGAINST TAKEZATO AND WE PLAY RYONAN!
SWOOP
THAT'S RIGHT!
'SUP?
Hm?
HEY.
I CAN'T HEAR YOU!!
!!
WHCK WHACK
HEY!!

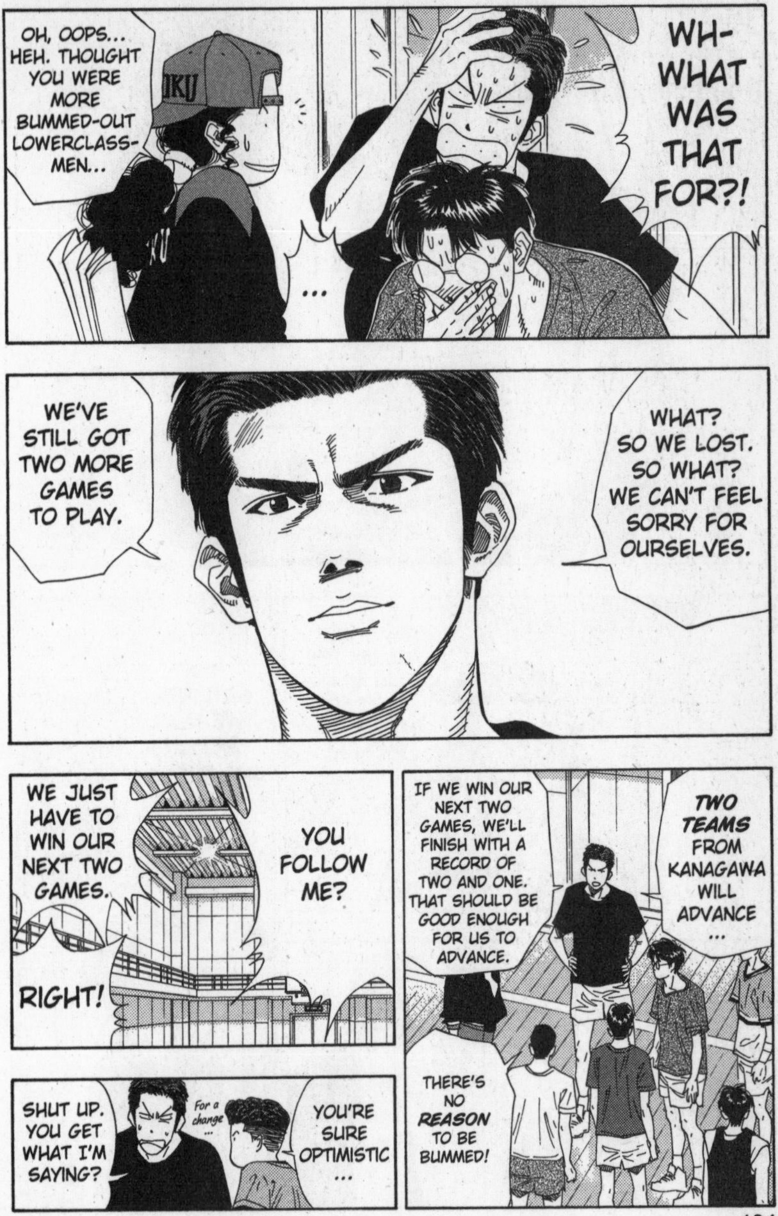
WH- WHAT WAS THAT FOR?!
OH, OOPS... HEH. THOUGHT YOU WERE MORE BUMMED-OUT LOWERCLASS- MEN...
...
WHAT? SO WE LOST. SO WHAT? WE CAN'T FEEL SORRY FOR OURSELVES.
WE'VE STILL GOT TWO MORE GAMES TO PLAY.
IF WE WIN OUR NEXT TWO GAMES, WE'LL FINISH WITH A RECORD OF TWO AND ONE. THAT SHOULD BE GOOD ENOUGH FOR US TO ADVANCE.
TWO TEAMS FROM KANAGAWA WILL ADVANCE ...
THERE'S NO REASON TO BE BUMMED!
WE JUST HAVE TO WIN OUR NEXT TWO GAMES.
YOU FOLLOW ME?
RIGHT!
YOU'RE SURE OPTIMISTIC ...
For a change ...
SHUT UP. YOU GET WHAT I'M SAYING?

READ THIS WAY

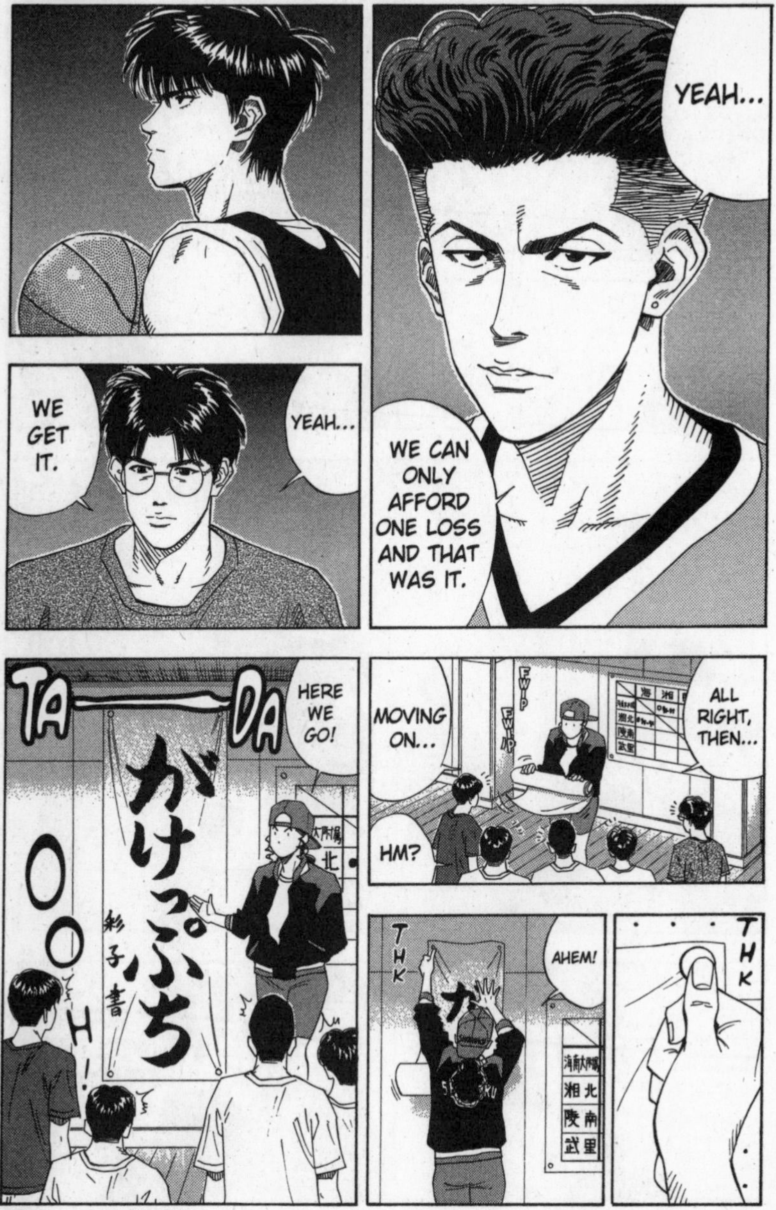
YEAH...
WE CAN ONLY AFFORD ONE LOSS AND THAT WAS IT.
YEAH...
WE GET IT.
ALL RIGHT, THEN...
FWIP
FWIP
MOVING ON...
HM?
. . . .
THK
AHEM!
THK
海南大附属
湘北
陵南
武里
TA—DA
HERE WE GO!
がけっぷち
彩子書
OOOH!

Paper: On the Brink
By Ayako

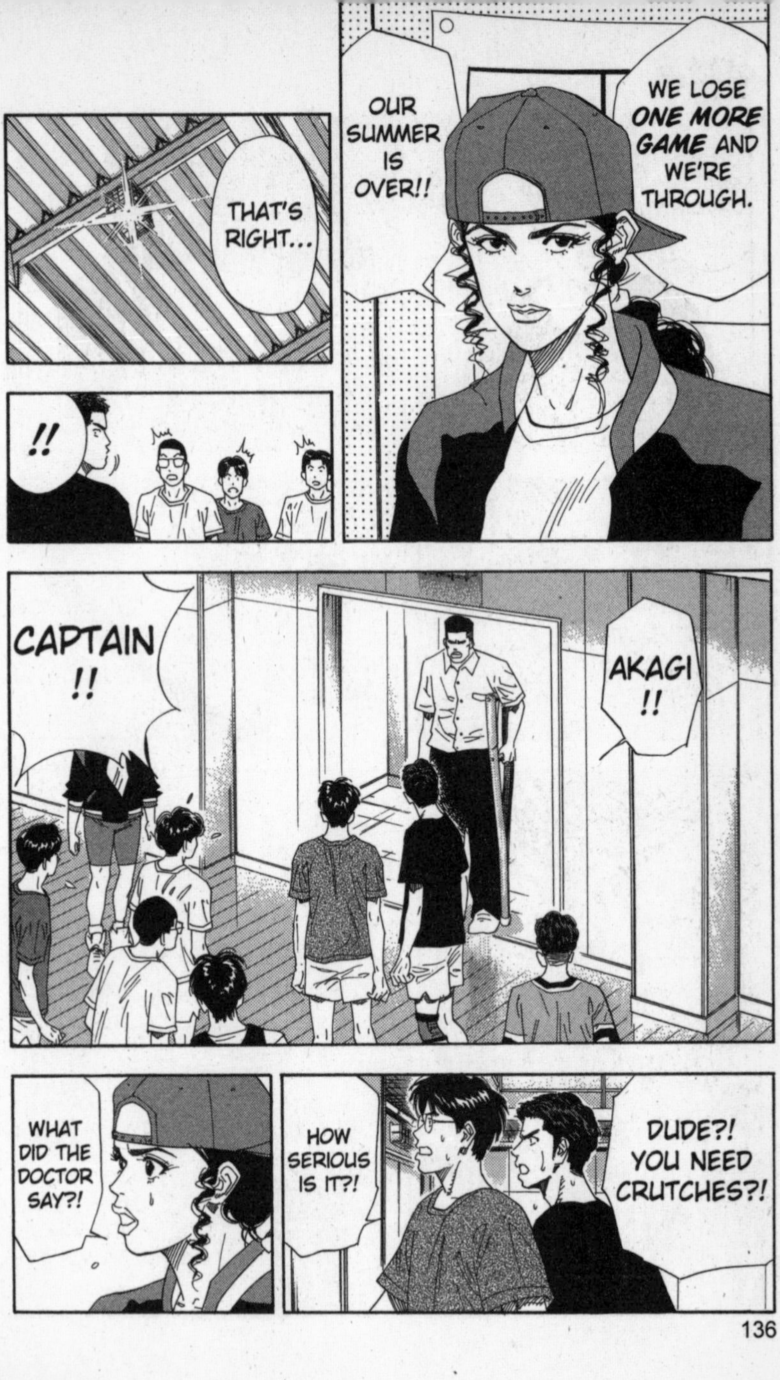
WE LOSE ONE MORE GAME AND WE'RE THROUGH.
OUR SUMMER IS OVER!!
THAT'S RIGHT...
!!
AKAGI !!
CAPTAIN !!
DUDE?! YOU NEED CRUTCHES?!
HOW SERIOUS IS IT?!
WHAT DID THE DOCTOR SAY?!

READ THIS WAY

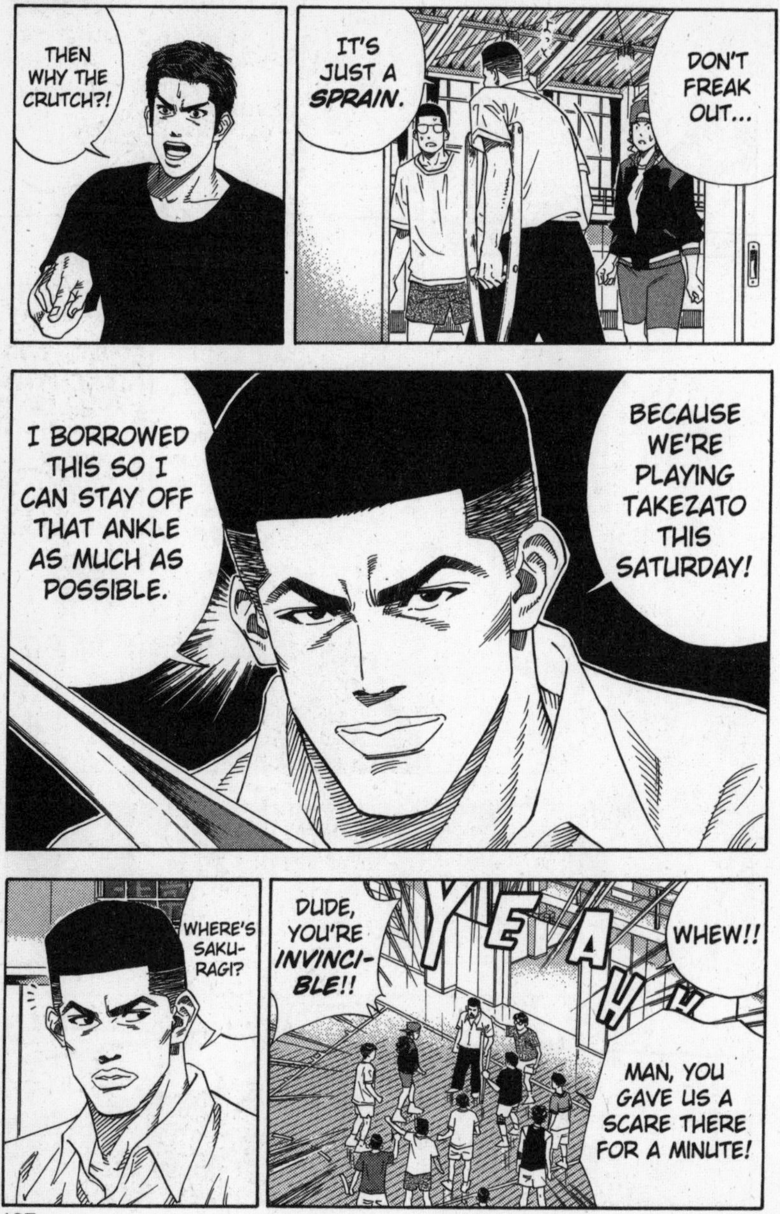
DON'T FREAK OUT...
IT'S JUST A *SPRAIN*.
THEN WHY THE CRUTCH?!
BECAUSE WE'RE PLAYING TAKEZATO THIS SATURDAY!
I BORROWED THIS SO I CAN STAY OFF THAT ANKLE AS MUCH AS POSSIBLE.
WHEW!!
YEAAH
DUDE, YOU'RE *INVINCIBLE*!!
MAN, YOU GAVE US A SCARE THERE FOR A MINUTE!
WHERE'S SAKURAGI?

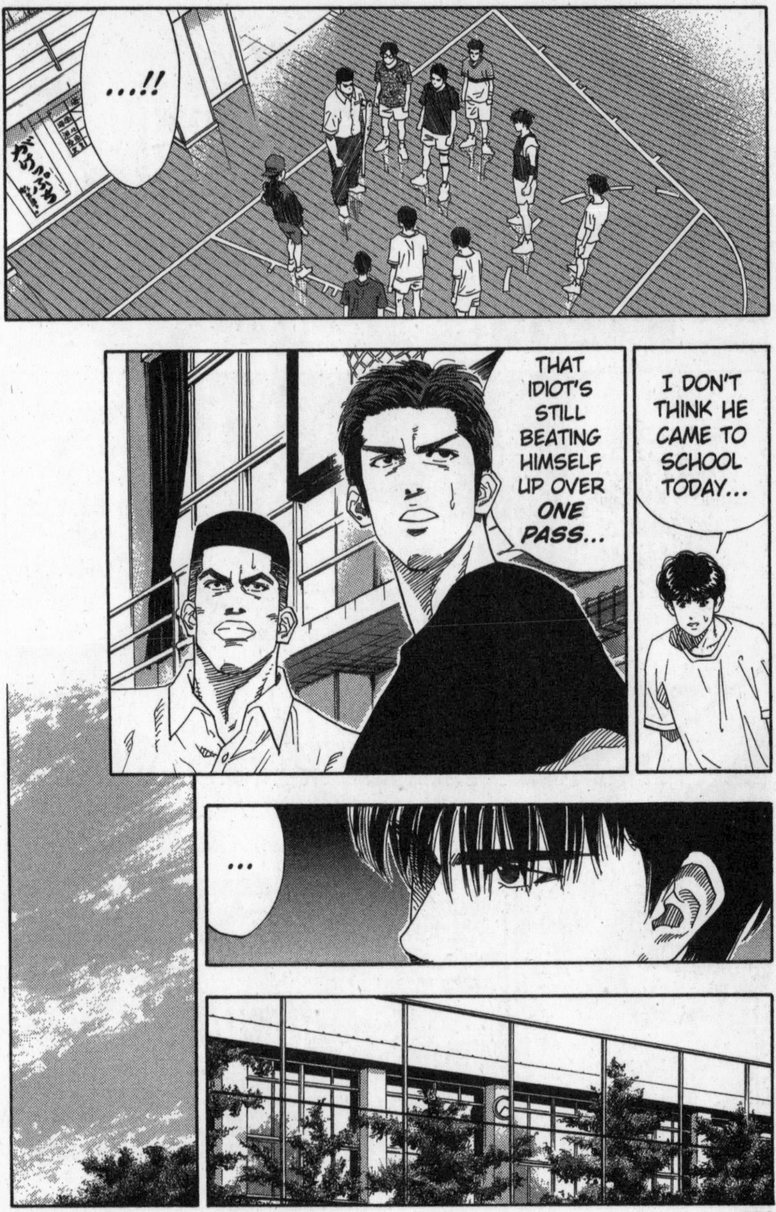
...!!
I DON'T THINK HE CAME TO SCHOOL TODAY...
THAT IDIOT'S STILL BEATING HIMSELF UP OVER *ONE PASS*...
...

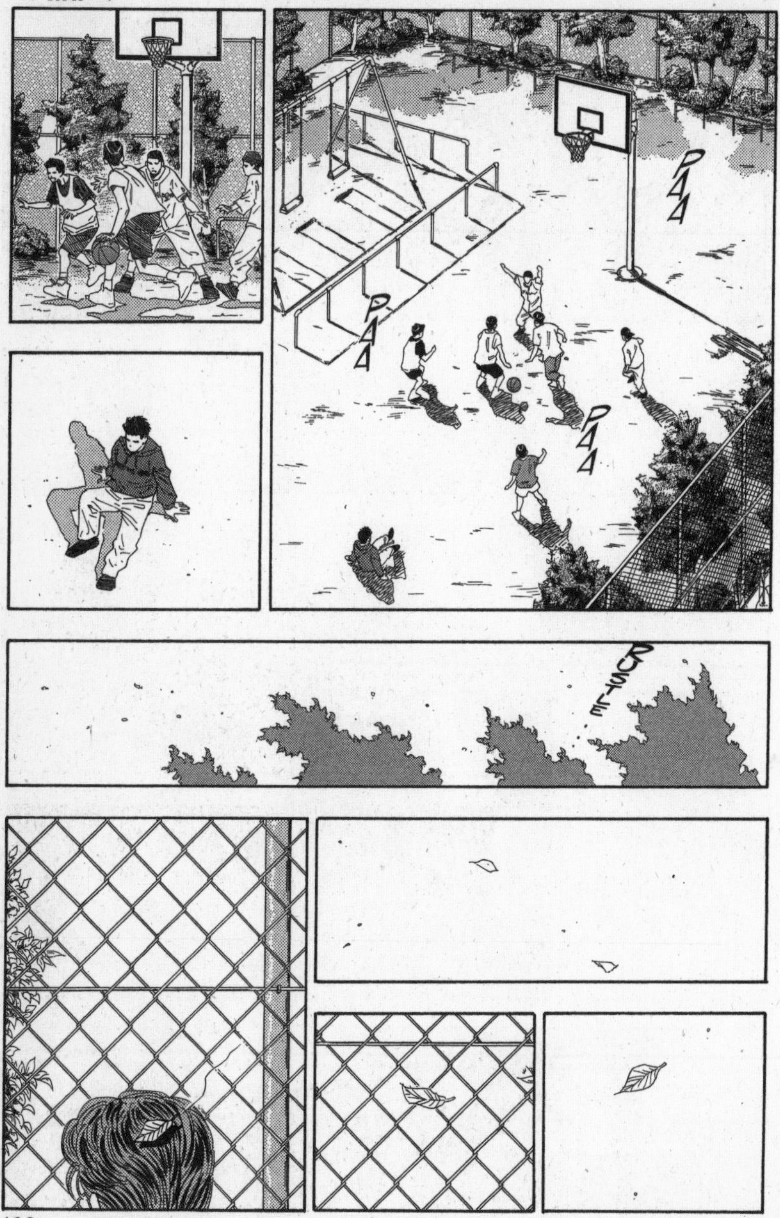
PAA
PAA
PAA
RUSTLE

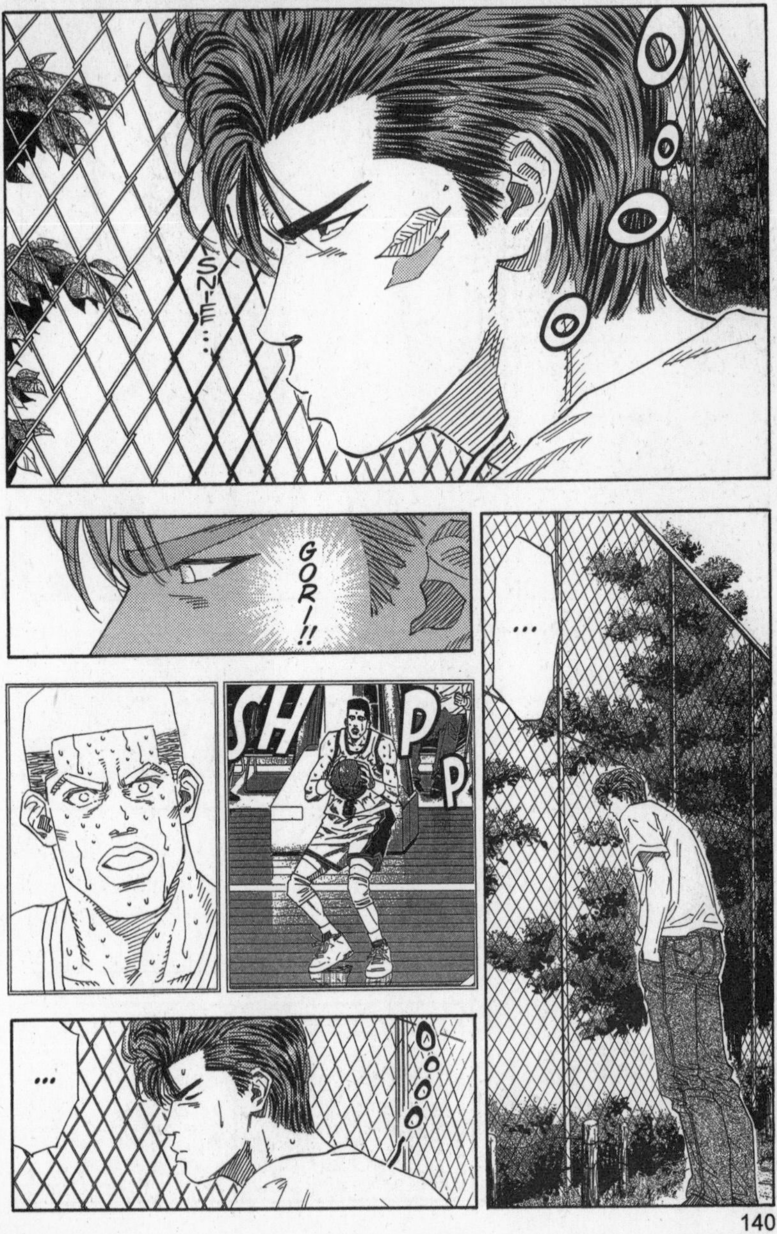
SNIFF...
...
GORI!!
SHPP
...
...OOO!

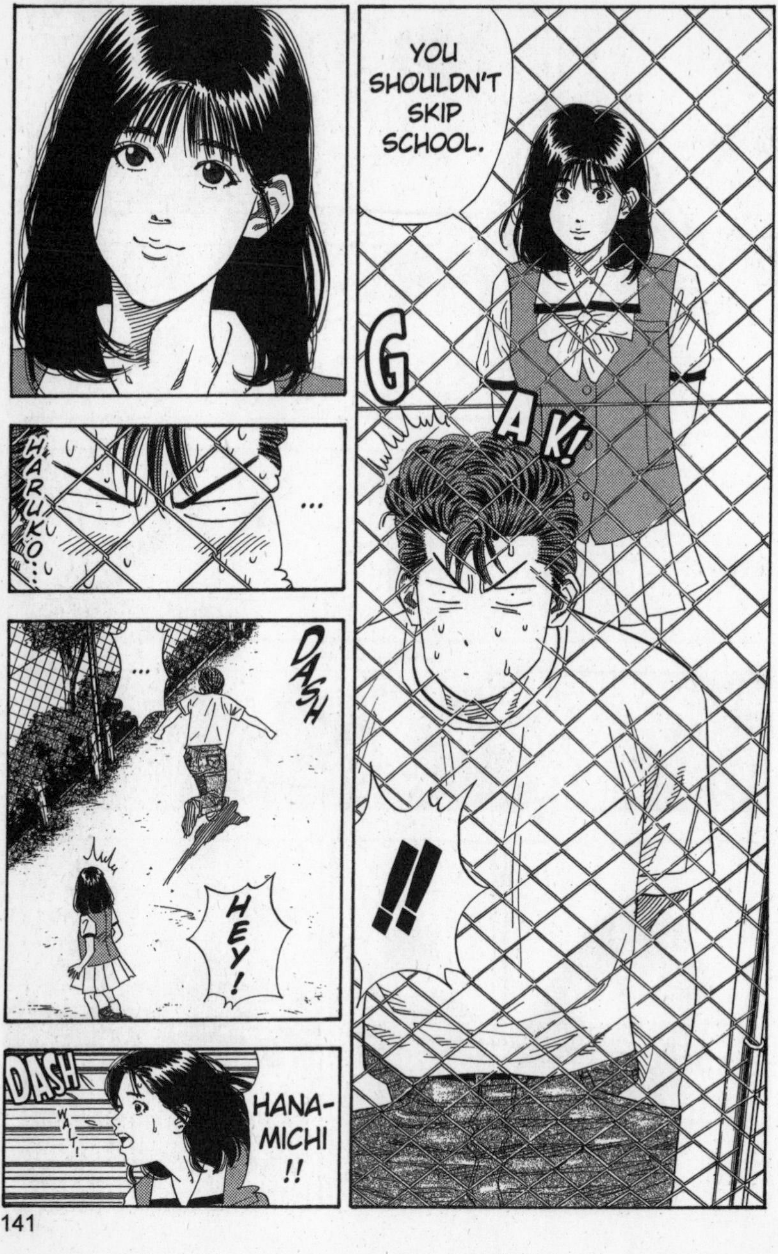
YOU SHOULDN'T SKIP SCHOOL.
GAK!
!!
HARUKO...
...
DASH
...
HEY!
HANA-MICHI !!
WAIT!
DASH

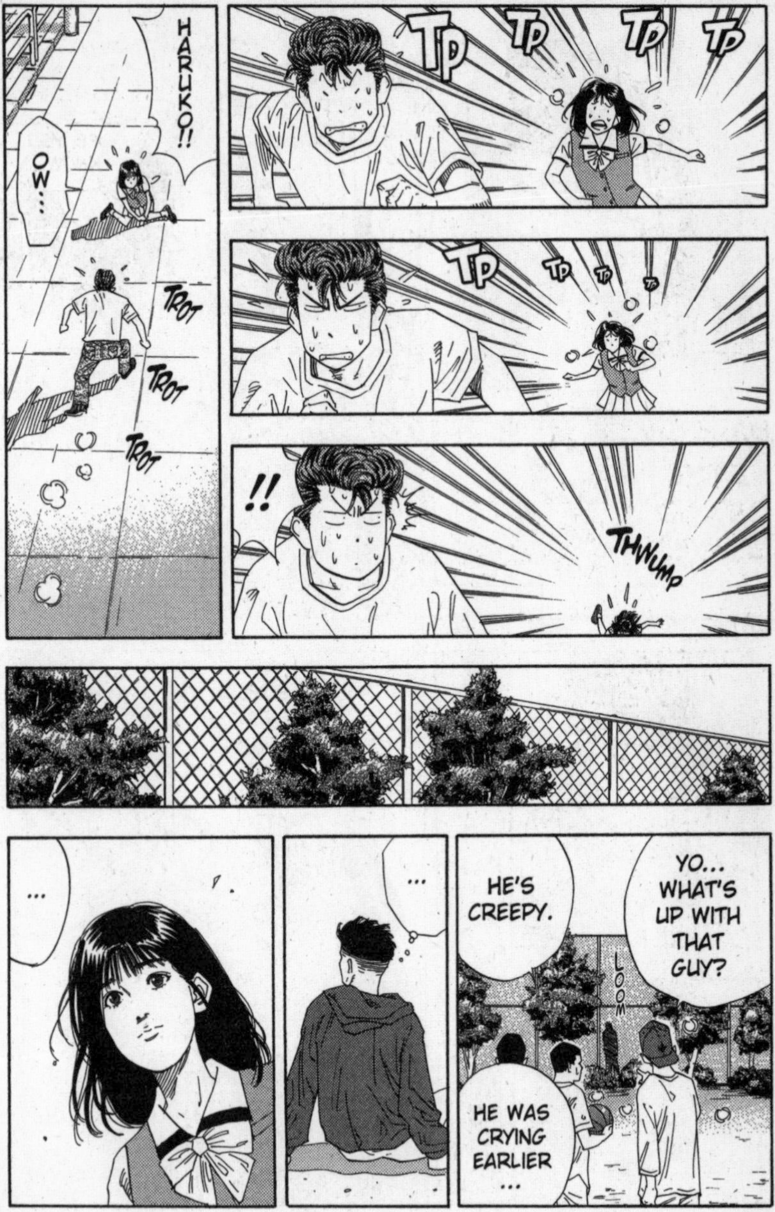

Tp Tp Tp Tp
Tp Tp Tp Tp
!!
THWUMP
HARUKO!!
OW...
TROT
TROT
TROT
YO... WHAT'S UP WITH THAT GUY?
HE'S CREEPY.
LOOM
HE WAS CRYING EARLIER ...
...
...

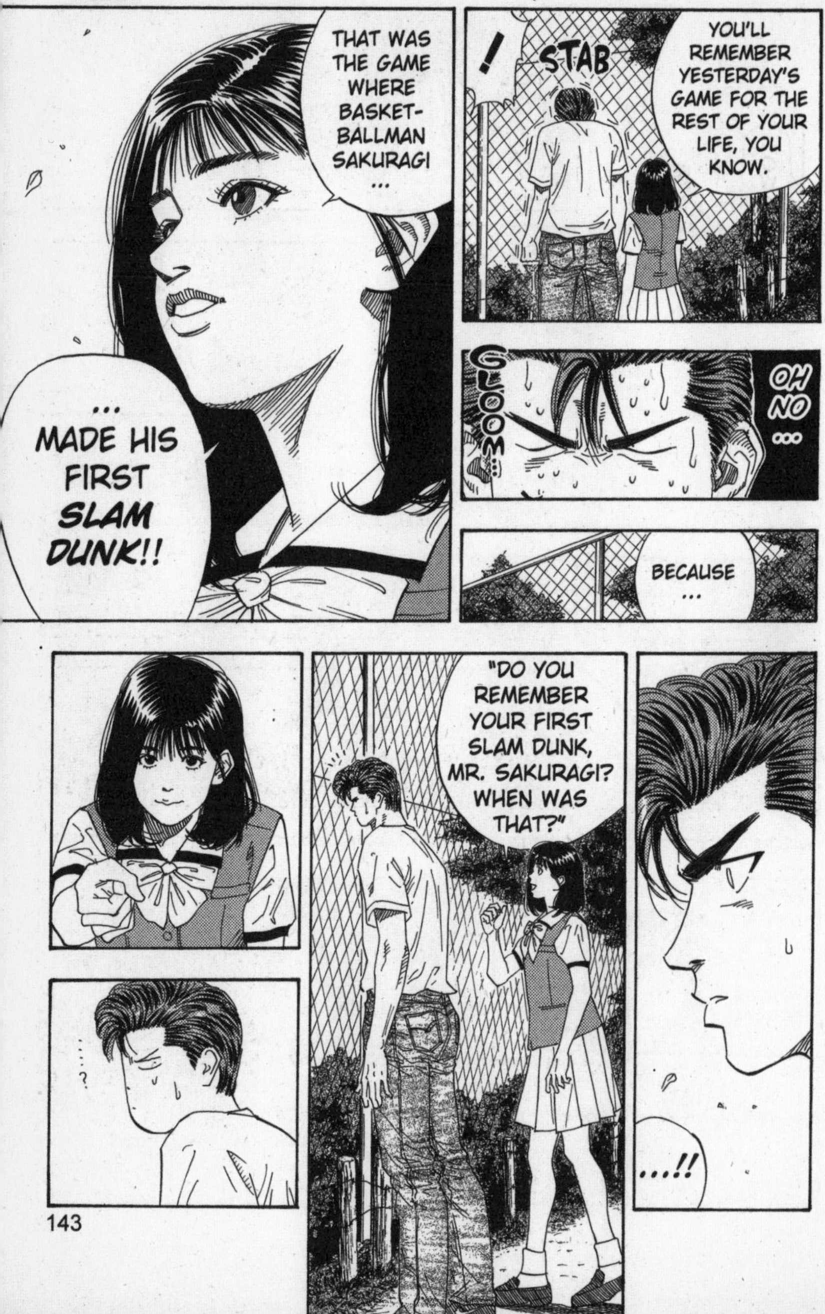
YOU'LL REMEMBER YESTERDAY'S GAME FOR THE REST OF YOUR LIFE, YOU KNOW.
!
STAB
GLOOM...
OH NO...
BECAUSE...
THAT WAS THE GAME WHERE BASKET-BALLMAN SAKURAGI...
...MADE HIS FIRST SLAM DUNK!!
...!!
"DO YOU REMEMBER YOUR FIRST SLAM DUNK, MR. SAKURAGI? WHEN WAS THAT?"
...?

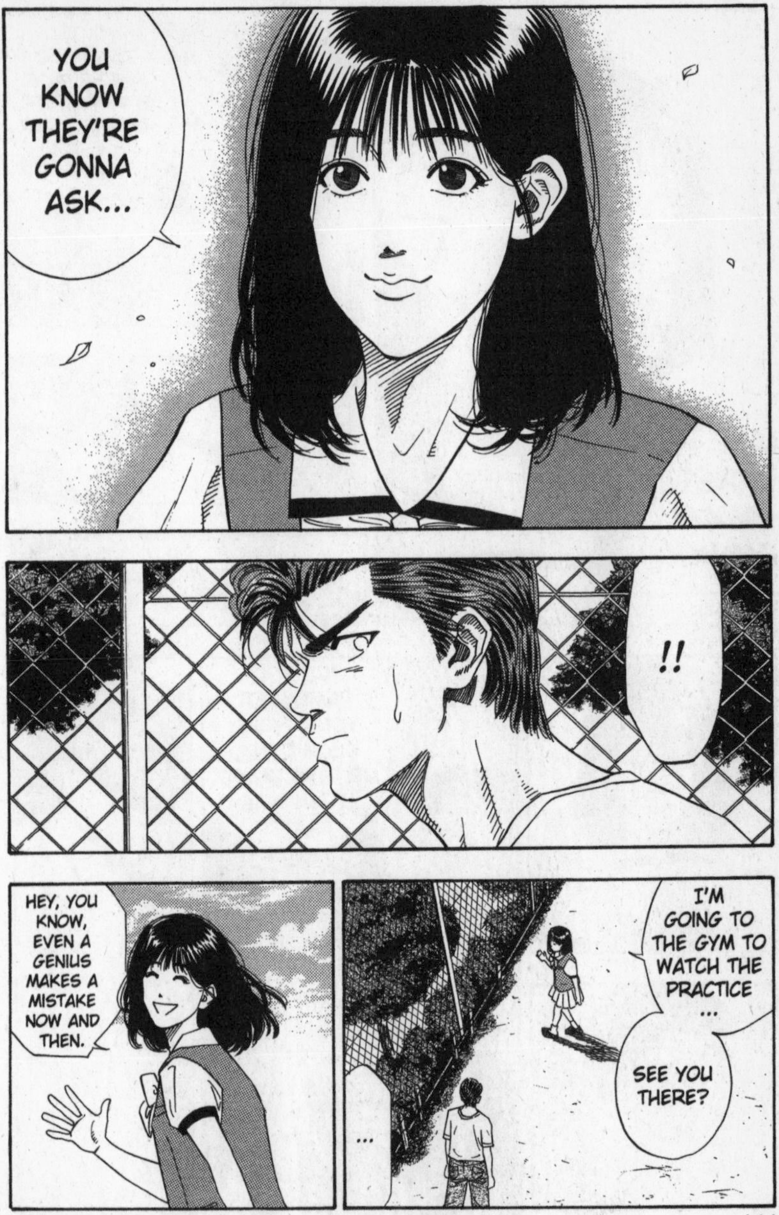
YOU KNOW THEY'RE GONNA ASK...
!!
I'M GOING TO THE GYM TO WATCH THE PRACTICE ...
SEE YOU THERE?
...
HEY, YOU KNOW, EVEN A GENIUS MAKES A MISTAKE NOW AND THEN.

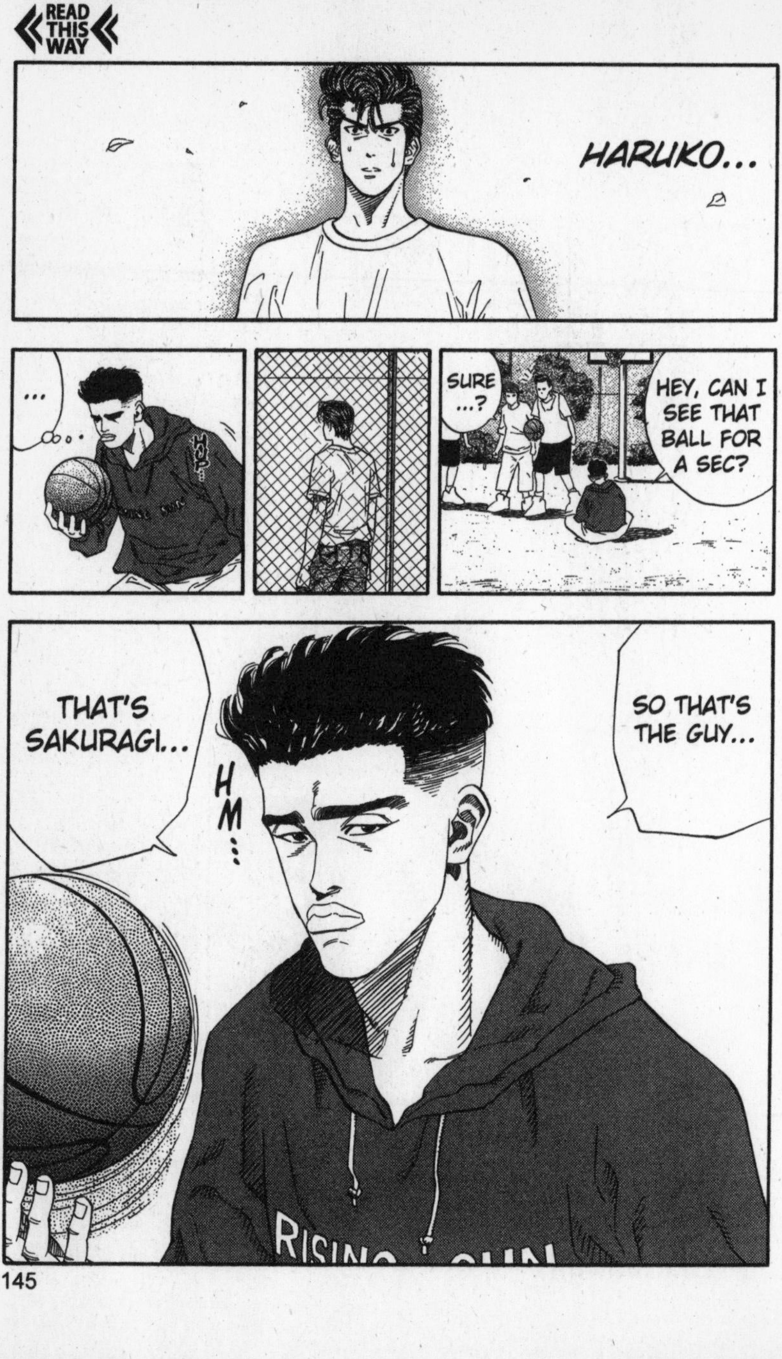
READ THIS WAY
HARUKO...
HEY, CAN I SEE THAT BALL FOR A SEC?
SURE ...?
...
HUP...
SO THAT'S THE GUY...
HM...
THAT'S SAKURAGI...
RISING SUN

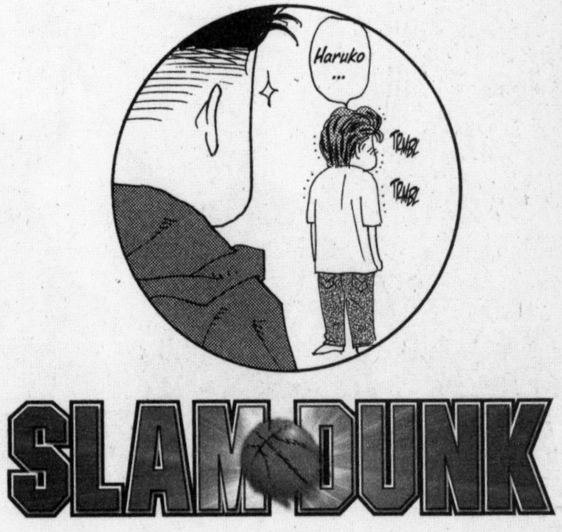
Haruko ...
TRMBL
TRMBL

SLAM DUNK

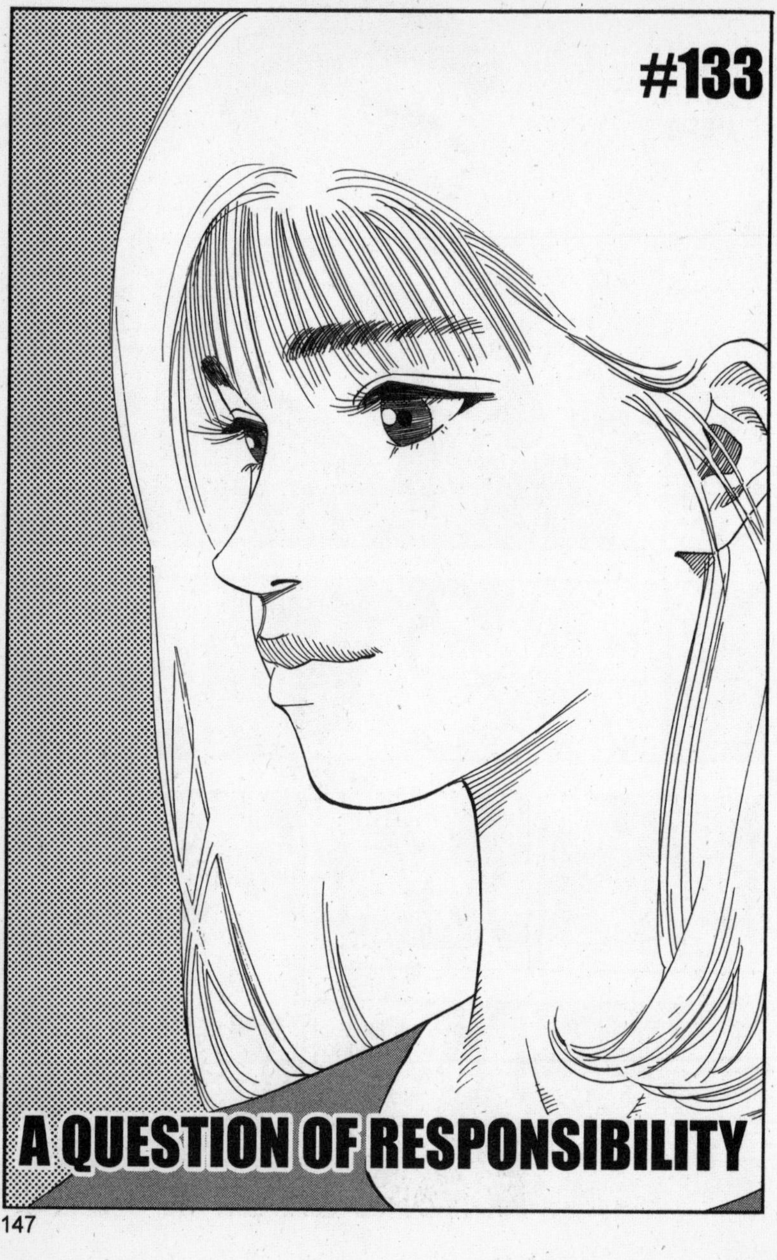
#133
A QUESTION OF RESPONSIBILITY

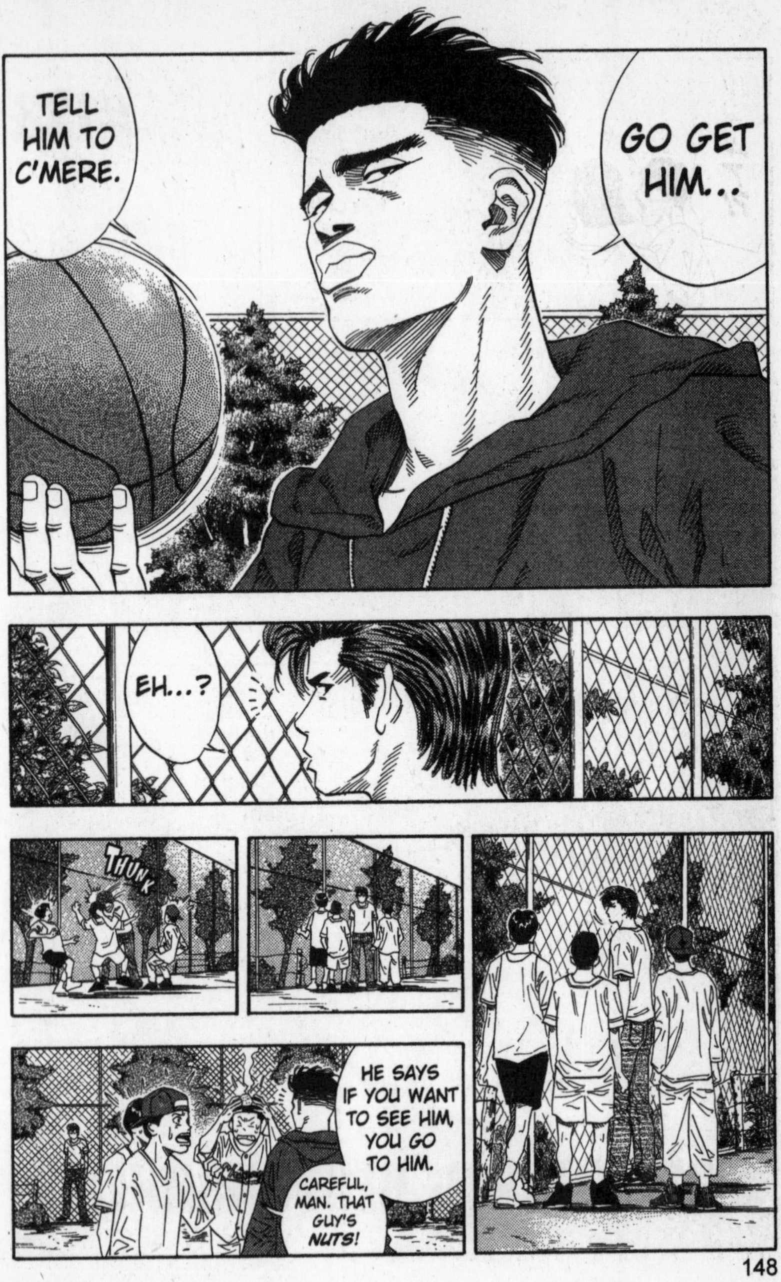
GO GET HIM...
TELL HIM TO C'MERE.
EH...?
THUNK
HE SAYS IF YOU WANT TO SEE HIM, YOU GO TO HIM.
CAREFUL, MAN. THAT GUY'S NUTS!

READ THIS WAY

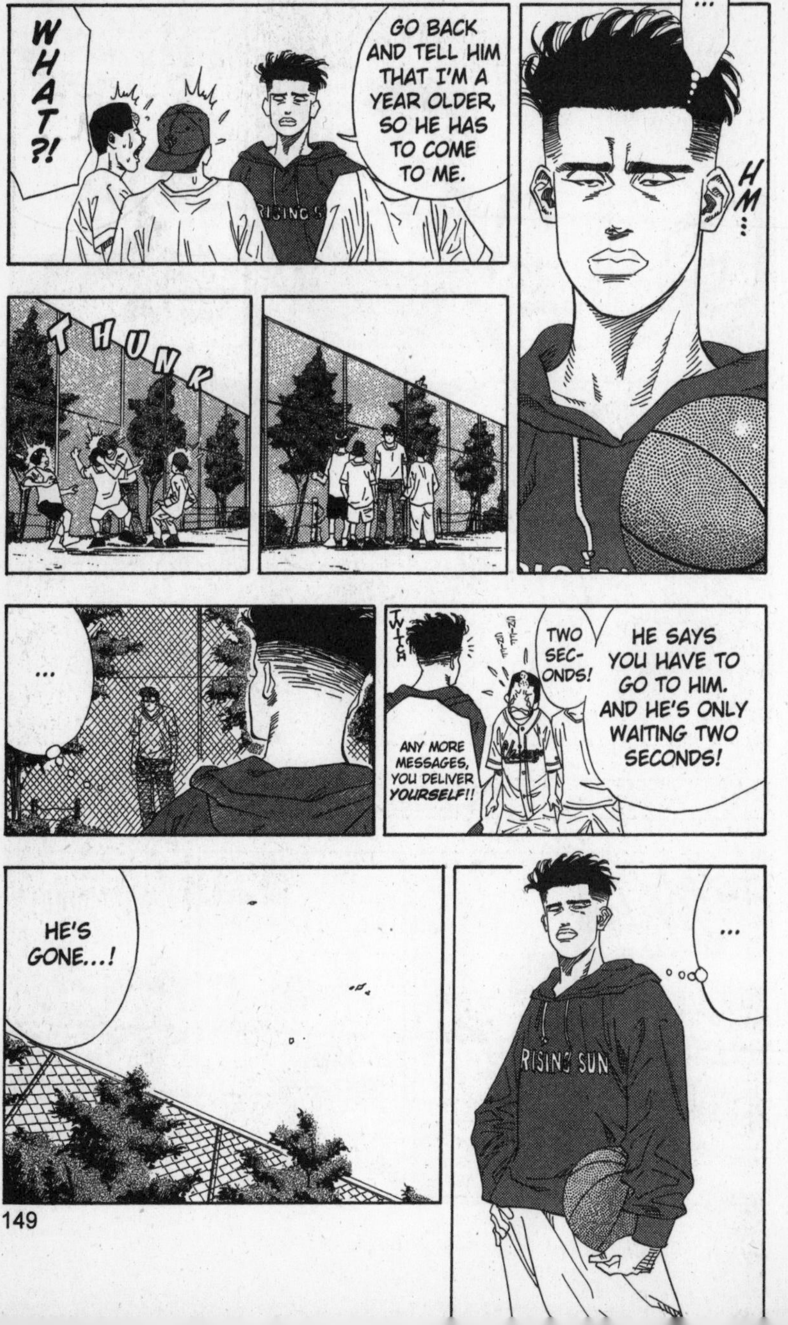
...
HM...
GO BACK AND TELL HIM THAT I'M A YEAR OLDER, SO HE HAS TO COME TO ME.
WHAT?!
THUNK
HE SAYS YOU HAVE TO GO TO HIM. AND HE'S ONLY WAITING TWO SECONDS!
TWO SEC-ONDS!
SNIFF SNIFF
TWITCH
ANY MORE MESSAGES, YOU DELIVER YOURSELF!!
...
...
RISING SUN
HE'S GONE...!

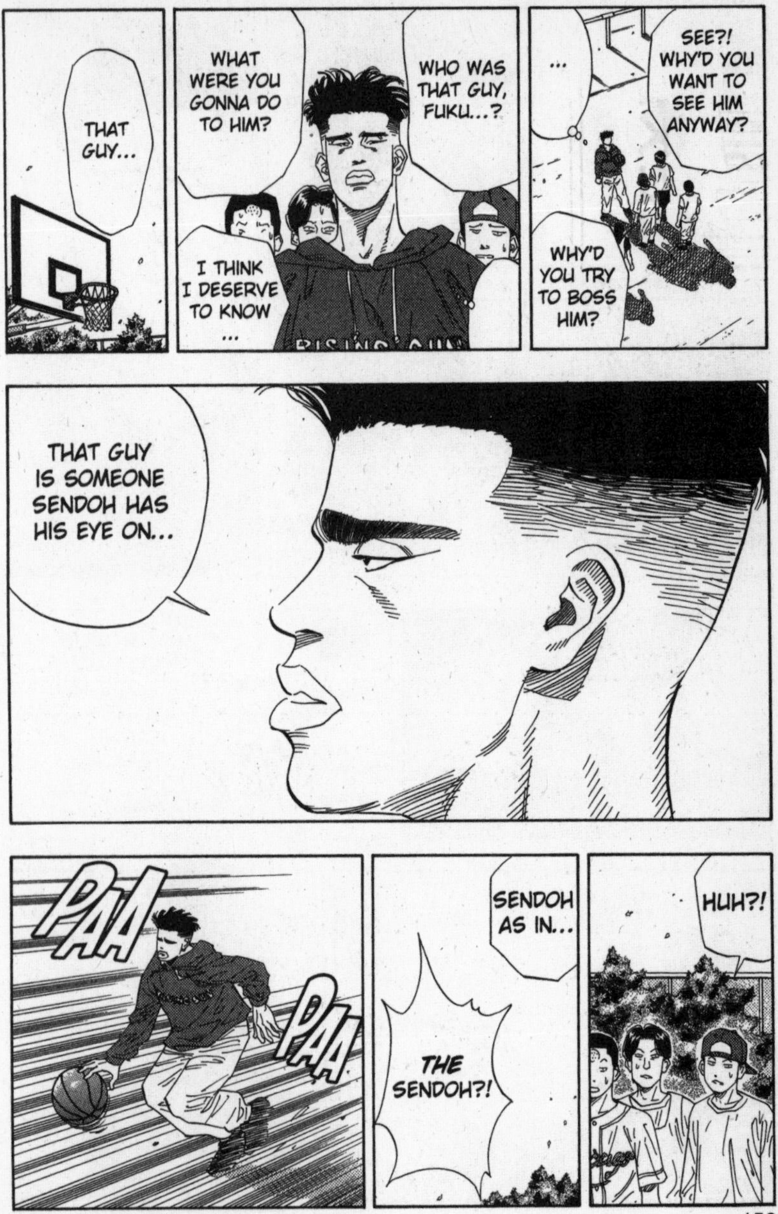
SEE?! WHY'D YOU WANT TO SEE HIM ANYWAY?
...
WHY'D YOU TRY TO BOSS HIM?
WHO WAS THAT GUY, FUKU...?
WHAT WERE YOU GONNA DO TO HIM?
I THINK I DESERVE TO KNOW ...
THAT GUY...
THAT GUY IS SOMEONE SENDOH HAS HIS EYE ON...
HUH?!
SENDOH AS IN...
THE SENDOH?!
PAA
PAA

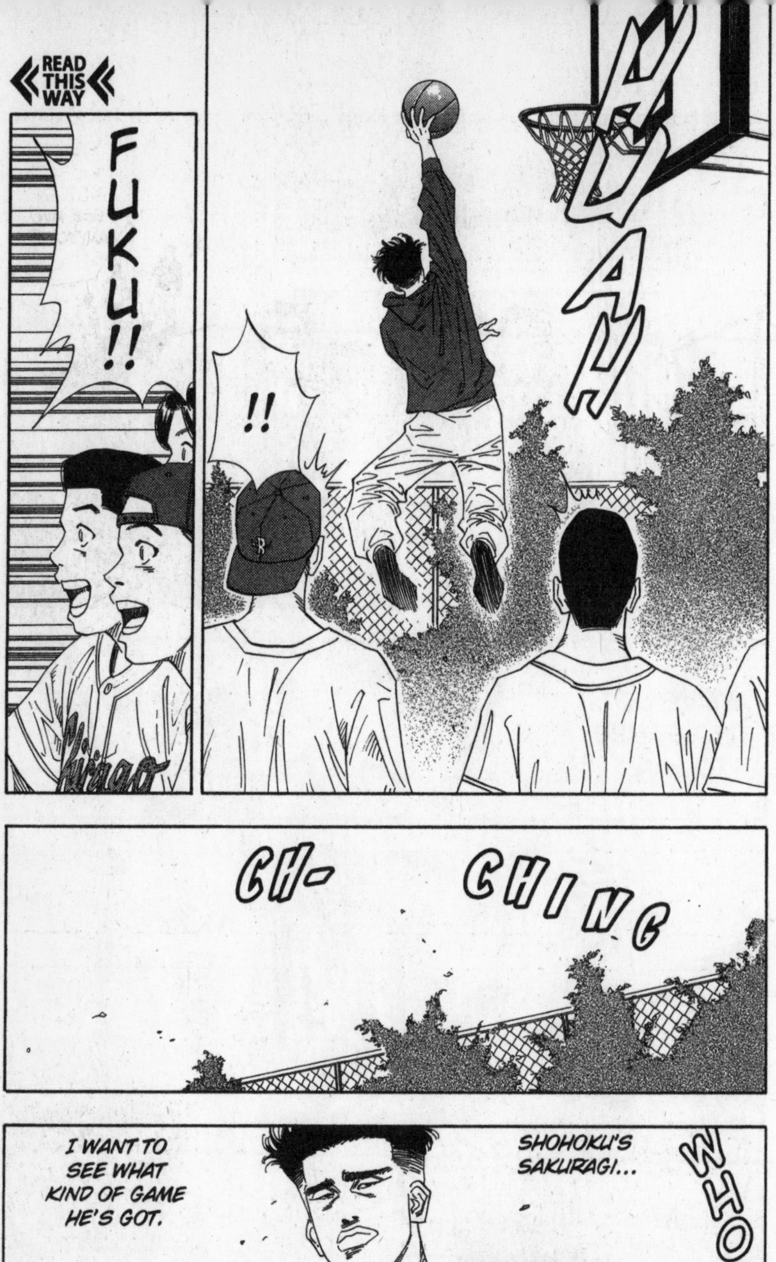
READ THIS WAY
WHAM
!!
FUKU!!
CH- CHING
WHOA
SHOHOKU'S SAKURAGI...
I WANT TO SEE WHAT KIND OF GAME HE'S GOT.

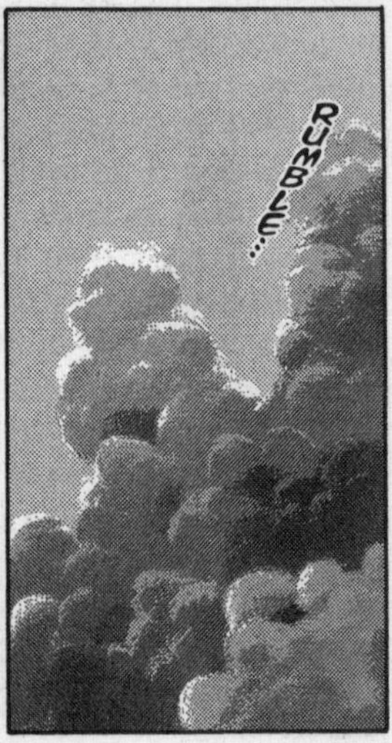
RUMBLE...

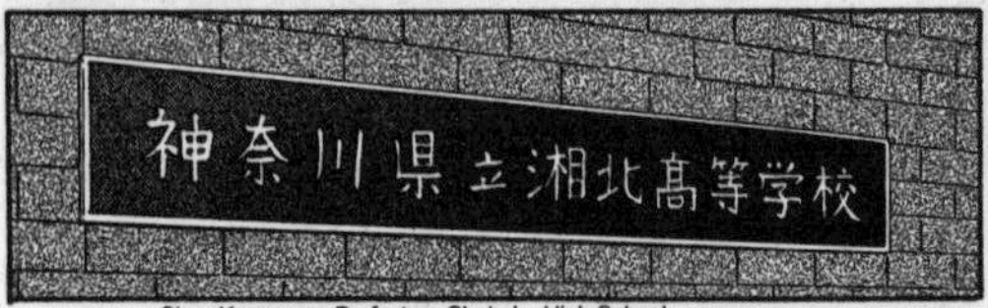
神奈川県立湘北高等学校

Sign: Kanagawa Prefecture Shohoku High School

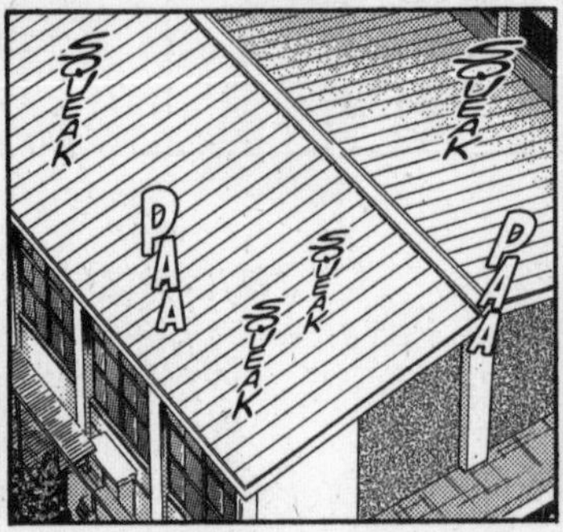
SQUEAK
PAA
SQUEAK
SQUEAK
PAA
SQUEAK

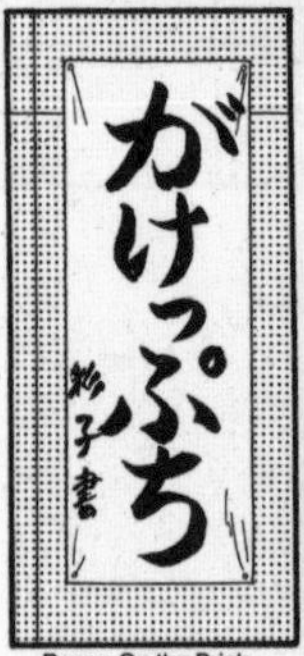
がけっぷち
彩子書

Paper: On the Brink
By Ayako

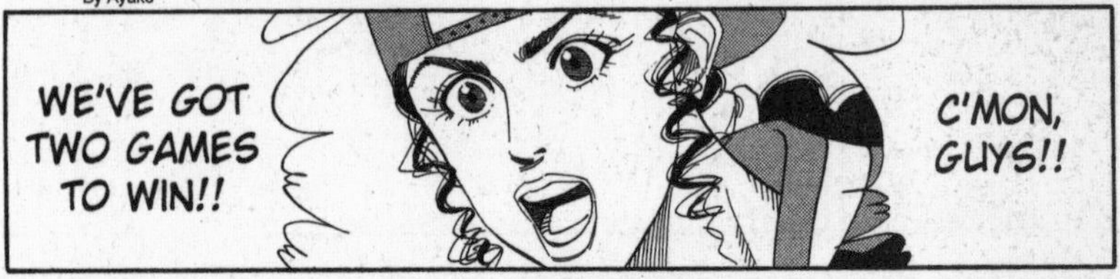
C'MON, GUYS!!
WE'VE GOT TWO GAMES TO WIN!!

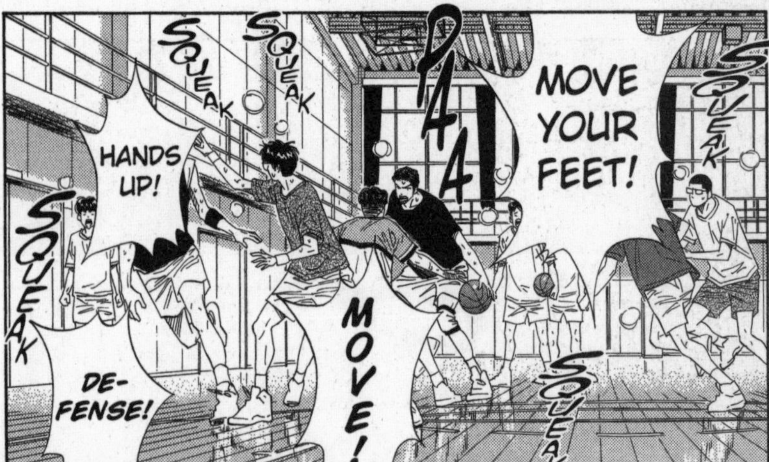
SQUEAK
MOVE YOUR FEET!
SQUEAK
PAA
SQUEAK
SQUEAK
HANDS UP!
MOVE!
SQUEAK
DEFENSE!

READ THIS WAY

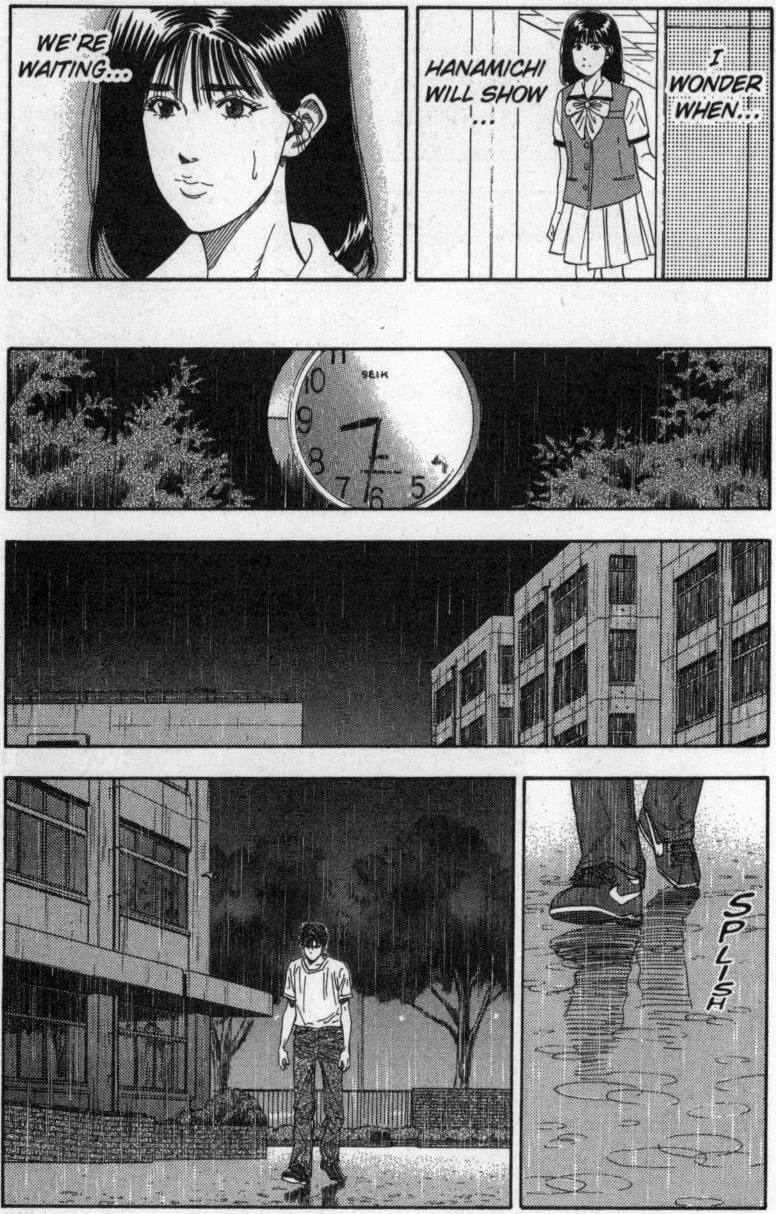
I WONDER WHEN...
HANAMICHI WILL SHOW ...
WE'RE WAITING...
SEIK
SPLISH

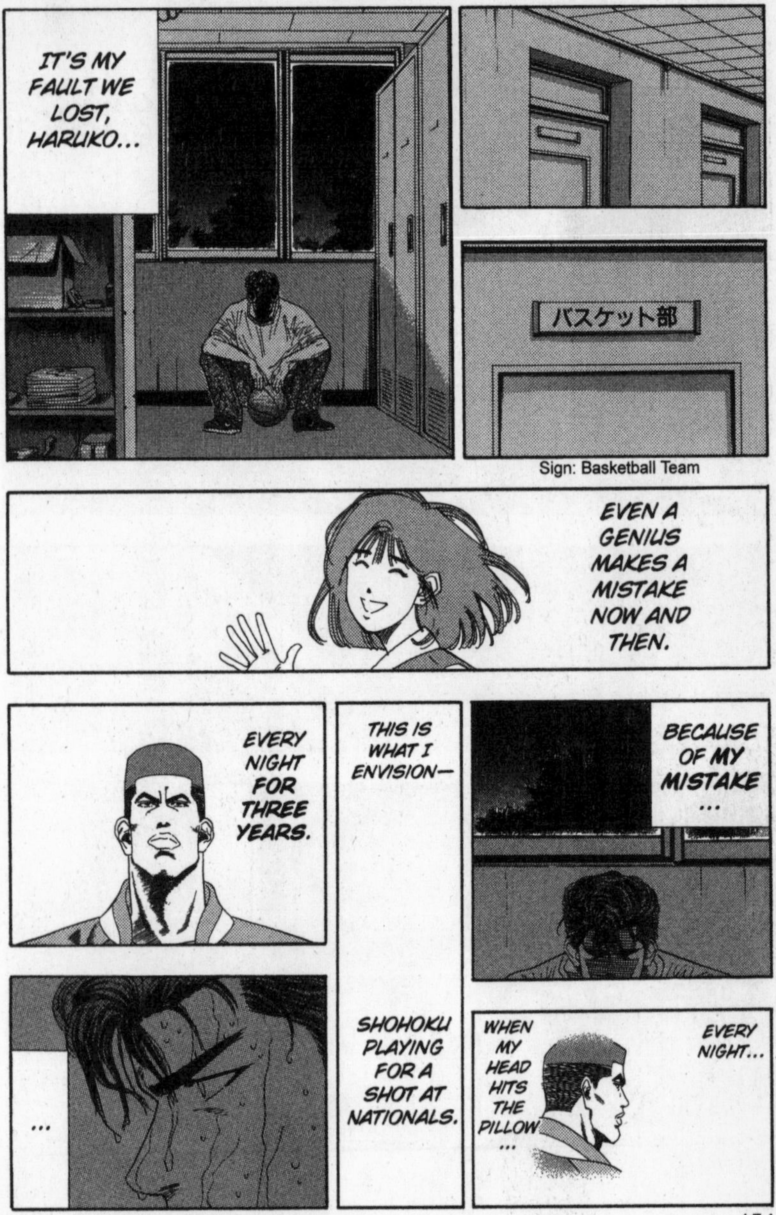
バスケット部
IT'S MY FAULT WE LOST, HARUKO...
EVEN A GENIUS MAKES A MISTAKE NOW AND THEN.
BECAUSE OF MY MISTAKE...
EVERY NIGHT...
WHEN MY HEAD HITS THE PILLOW...
THIS IS WHAT I ENVISION—
SHOHOKU PLAYING FOR A SHOT AT NATIONALS.
EVERY NIGHT FOR THREE YEARS.
...
Sign: Basketball Team

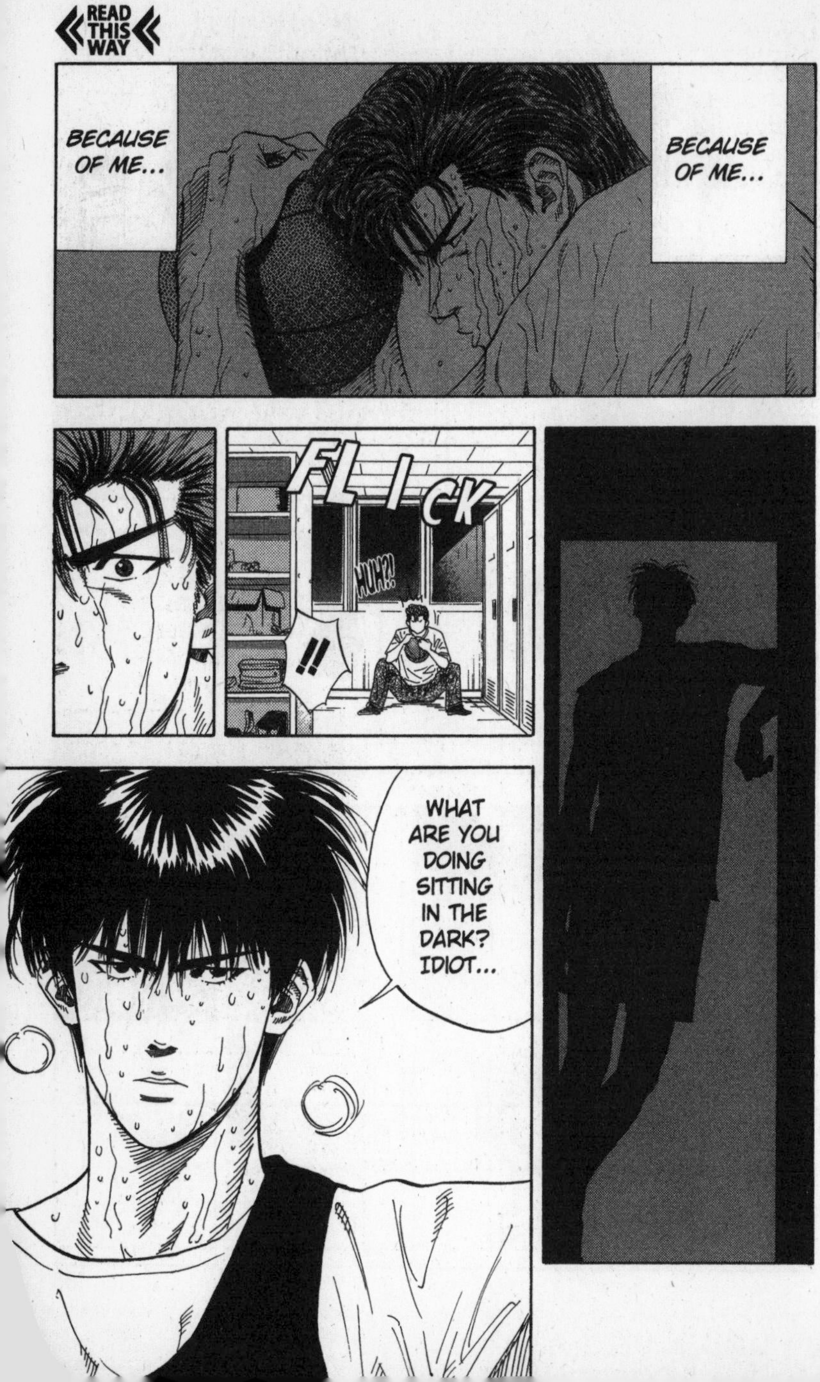
READ THIS WAY
BECAUSE OF ME...
BECAUSE OF ME...
FLICK
HUH?!
!!
WHAT ARE YOU DOING SITTING IN THE DARK? IDIOT...

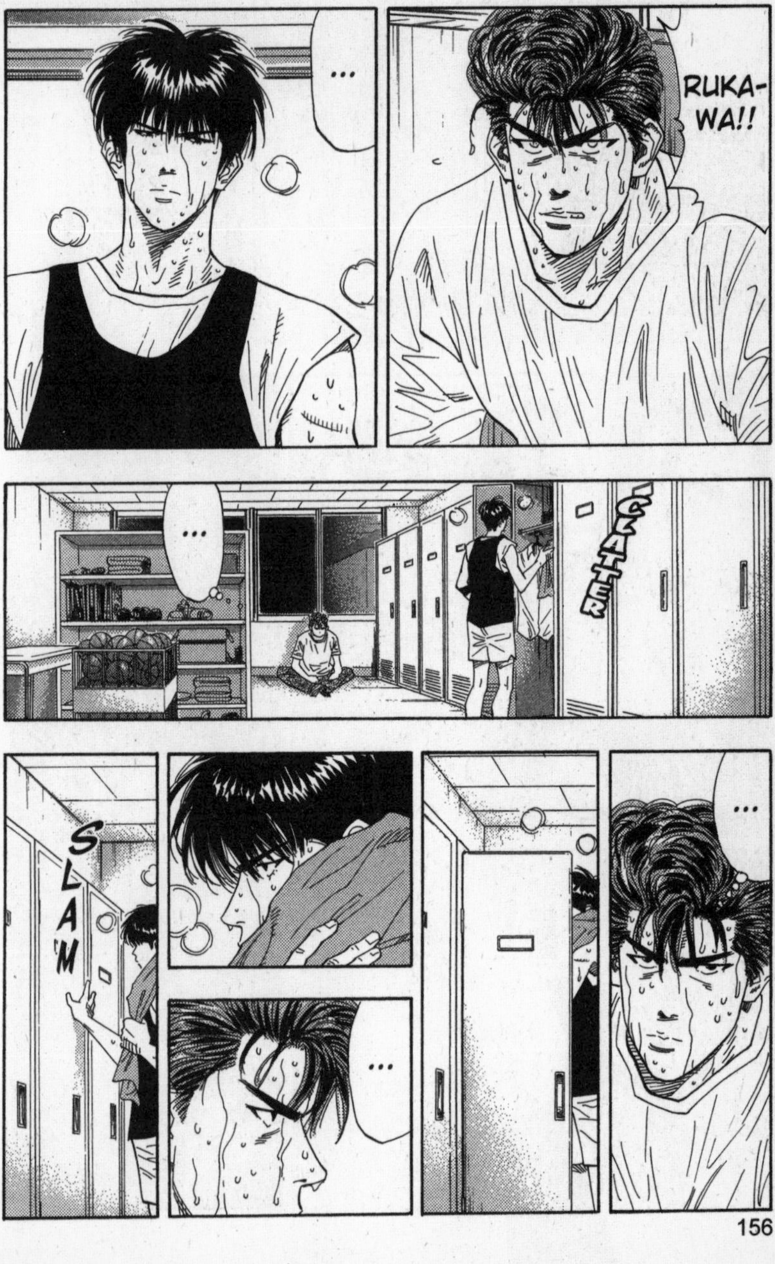
RUKA-
WA!!
...
CLATTER
...
...
...
SLAM

READ THIS WAY

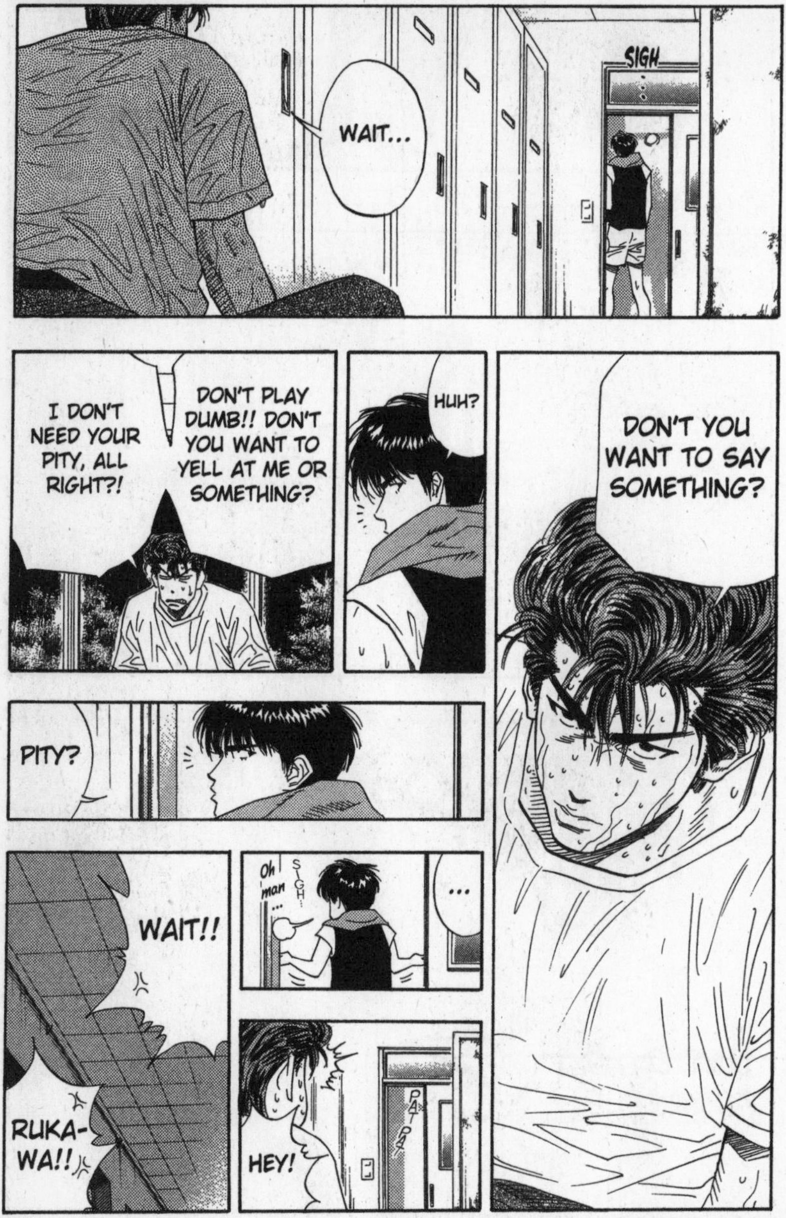
SIGH
WAIT...
DON'T YOU WANT TO SAY SOMETHING?
HUH?
DON'T PLAY DUMB!! DON'T YOU WANT TO YELL AT ME OR SOMETHING?
I DON'T NEED YOUR PITY, ALL RIGHT?!
PITY?
...
SIGH...
Oh man...
HEY!
PAT PAT
WAIT!!
RUKA-WA!!

HMPH. IDIOT...

ER ...?

YOU THINK WE LOST BECAUSE OF *YOU*?

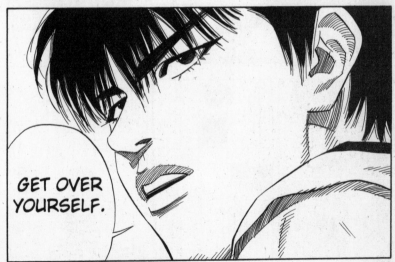

GET OVER YOURSELF.

READ THIS WAY

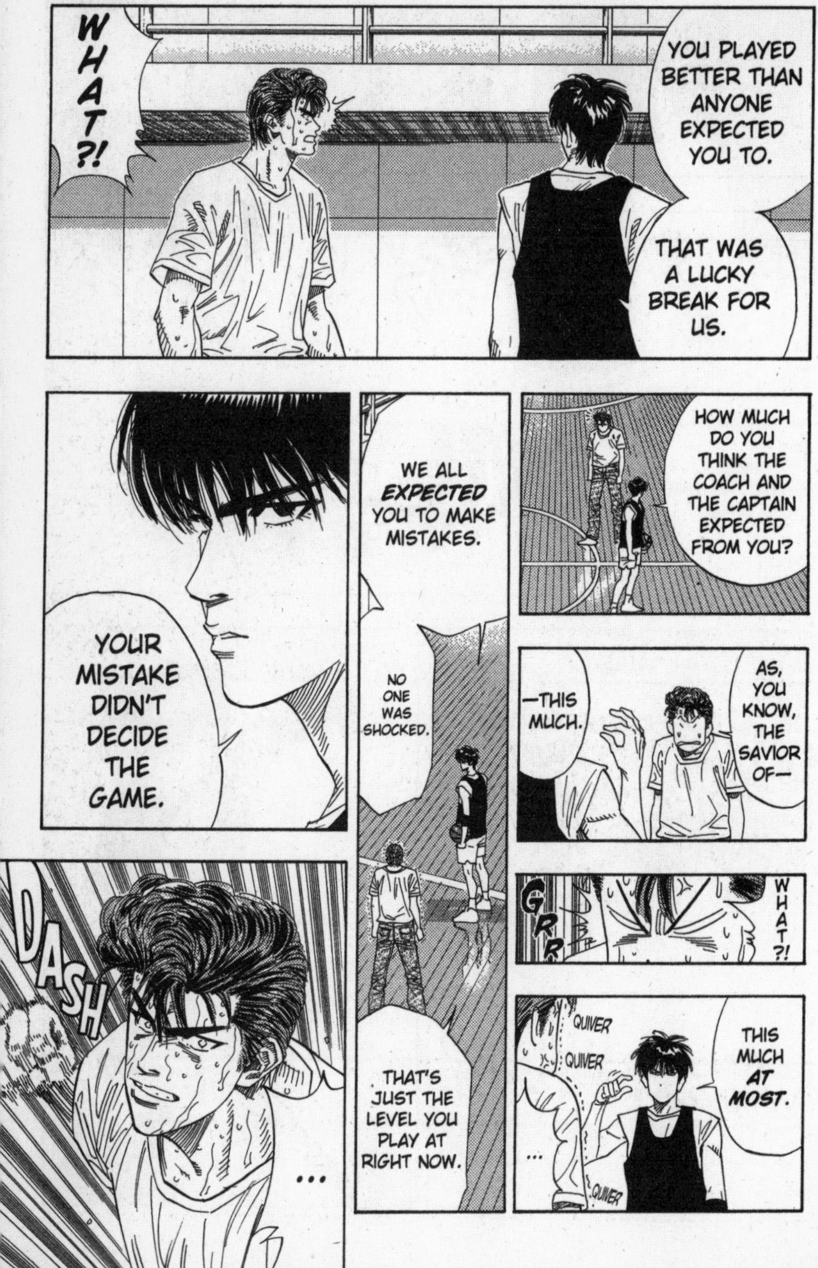
YOU PLAYED BETTER THAN ANYONE EXPECTED YOU TO.
THAT WAS A LUCKY BREAK FOR US.
WHAT?!
HOW MUCH DO YOU THINK THE COACH AND THE CAPTAIN EXPECTED FROM YOU?
AS, YOU KNOW, THE SAVIOR OF—
—THIS MUCH.
WHAT?!
GRR
THIS MUCH AT MOST.
QUIVER
QUIVER
...
QUIVER
WE ALL EXPECTED YOU TO MAKE MISTAKES.
NO ONE WAS SHOCKED.
THAT'S JUST THE LEVEL YOU PLAY AT RIGHT NOW.
YOUR MISTAKE DIDN'T DECIDE THE GAME.
DASH
...

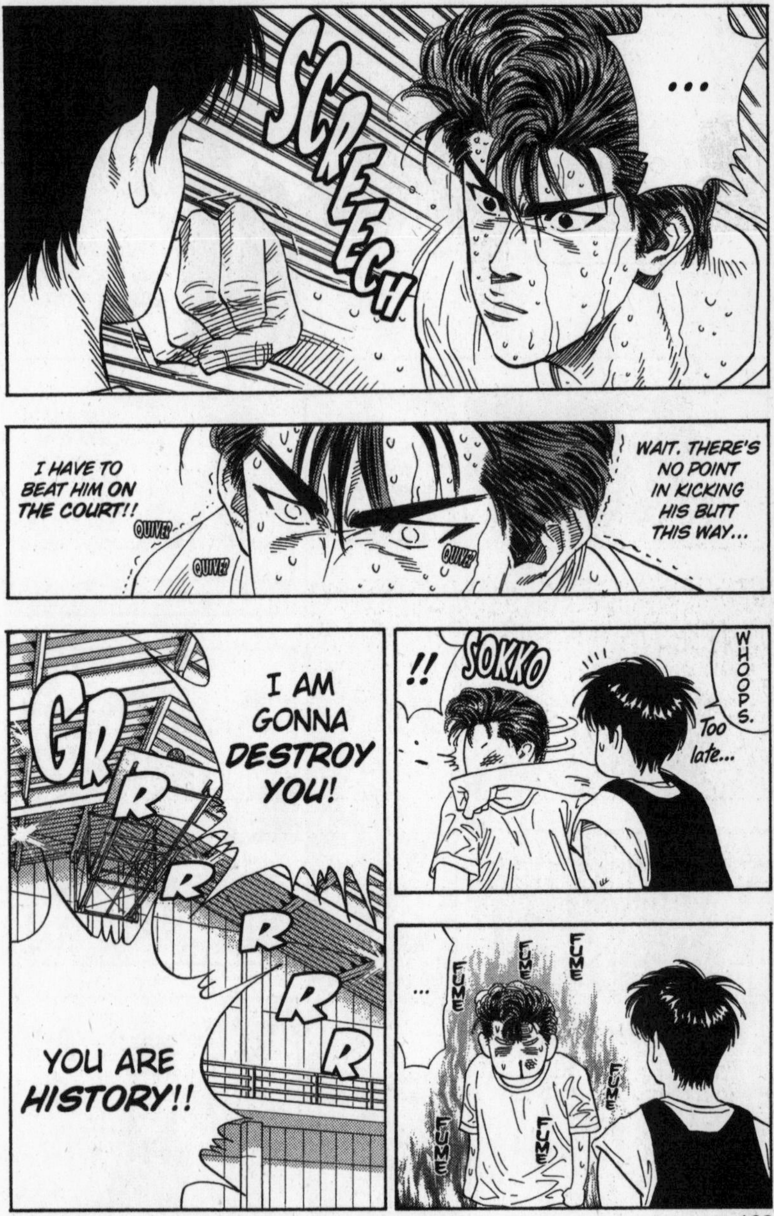
...
SCREECH
WAIT. THERE'S NO POINT IN KICKING HIS BUTT THIS WAY...
QUIVER
QUIVER
QUIVER
I HAVE TO BEAT HIM ON THE COURT!!
WHOOPS.
Too late...
SOKKO
!!
FUME
FUME
FUME
...
FUME
FUME
FUME
FUME
I AM GONNA DESTROY YOU!
GRRRRRR
YOU ARE HISTORY!!

READ THIS WAY

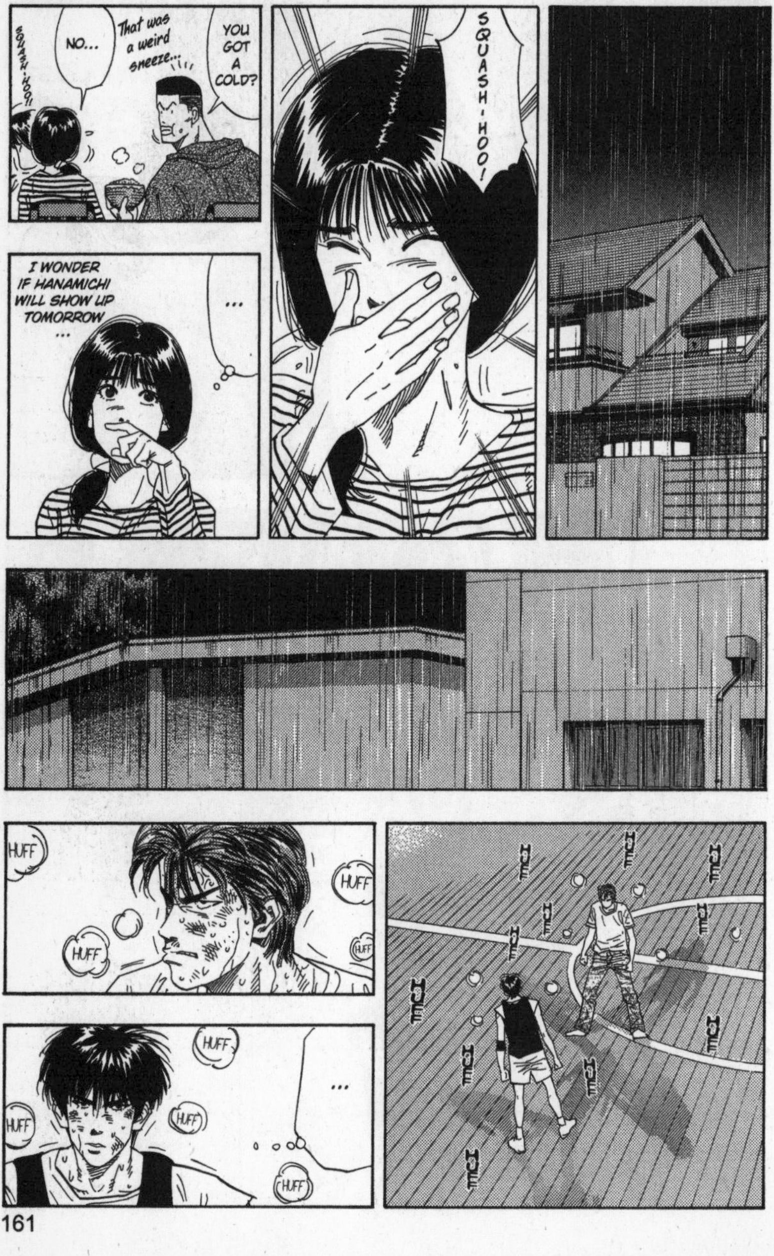
SQUASH-HOO!
YOU GOT A COLD?
That was a weird sneeze...
NO...
SQUASH-HOO!!
...
I WONDER IF HANAMICHI WILL SHOW UP TOMORROW ...
HUFF
HUFF
HUFF
HUFF
HUFF
HUFF
...
HUFF
HUFF
HUFF
HUFF

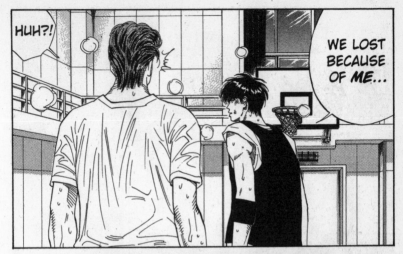

WE LOST BECAUSE OF ME...
HUH?!
IF I'D HAD THE STAMINA TO STAY IN THE GAME...
WE WOULD'VE WON.
YOU... YOU...
YOU'RE THE ONE WHO NEEDS TO GET OVER YOUR-SELF!!
WHAM

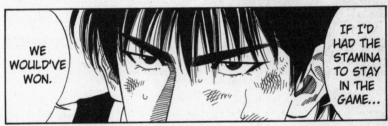

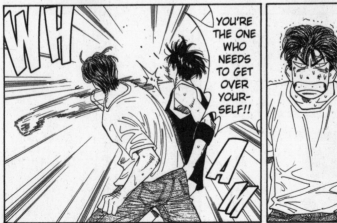

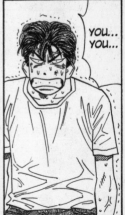

READ THIS WAY

IT WAS MY FAULT!
HAA
A
GAH!!
IT WAS MY FAULT!!
POW
WHAM
NO, IT WAS MINE!
IT WAS ME!
WHACK
CRASH
IT WAS ME!
THUD
IT WAS ME!
BAM
IT WAS ME!
THE NEXT DAY...
SAKURAGI SKIPPED AGAIN.
THINK HE'S STILL BLAMING HIMSELF?
PROBABLY.
'SUP?
YO...

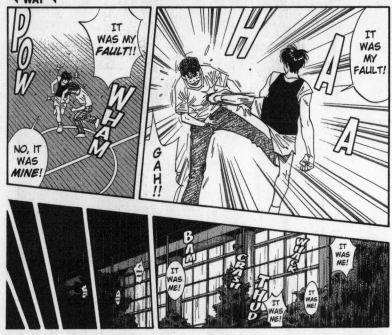

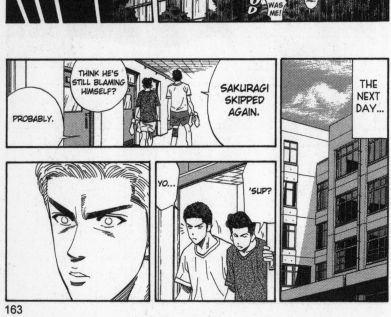

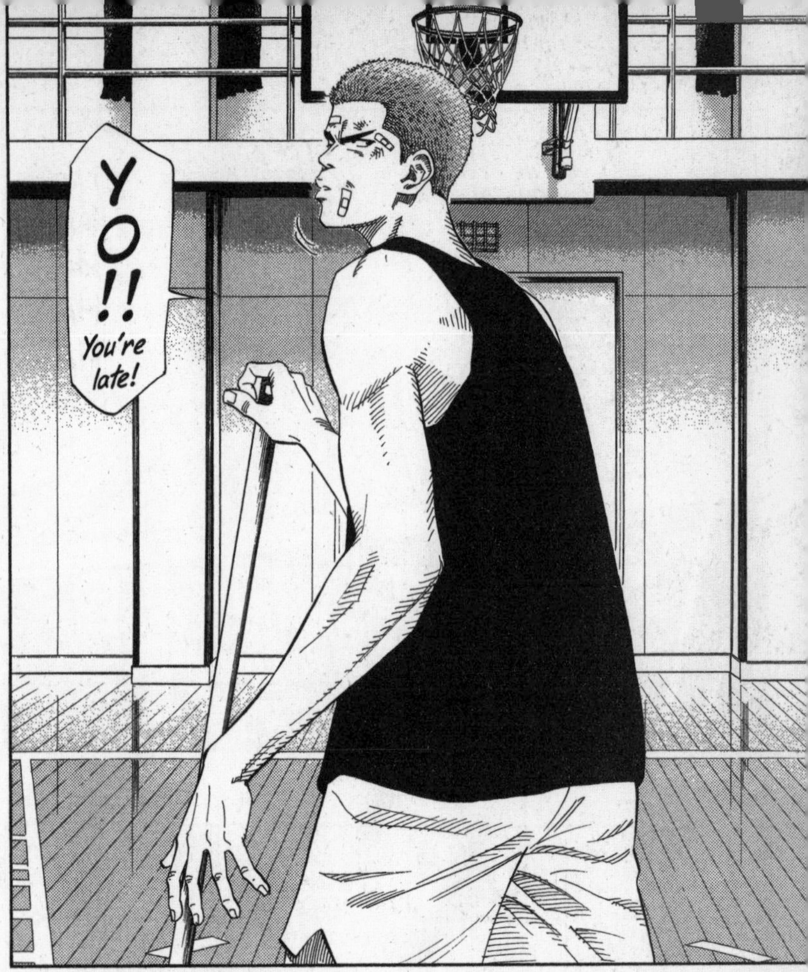
YO!! You're late!
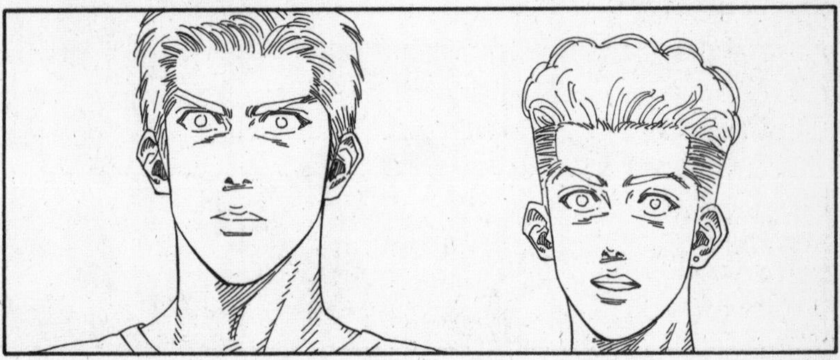

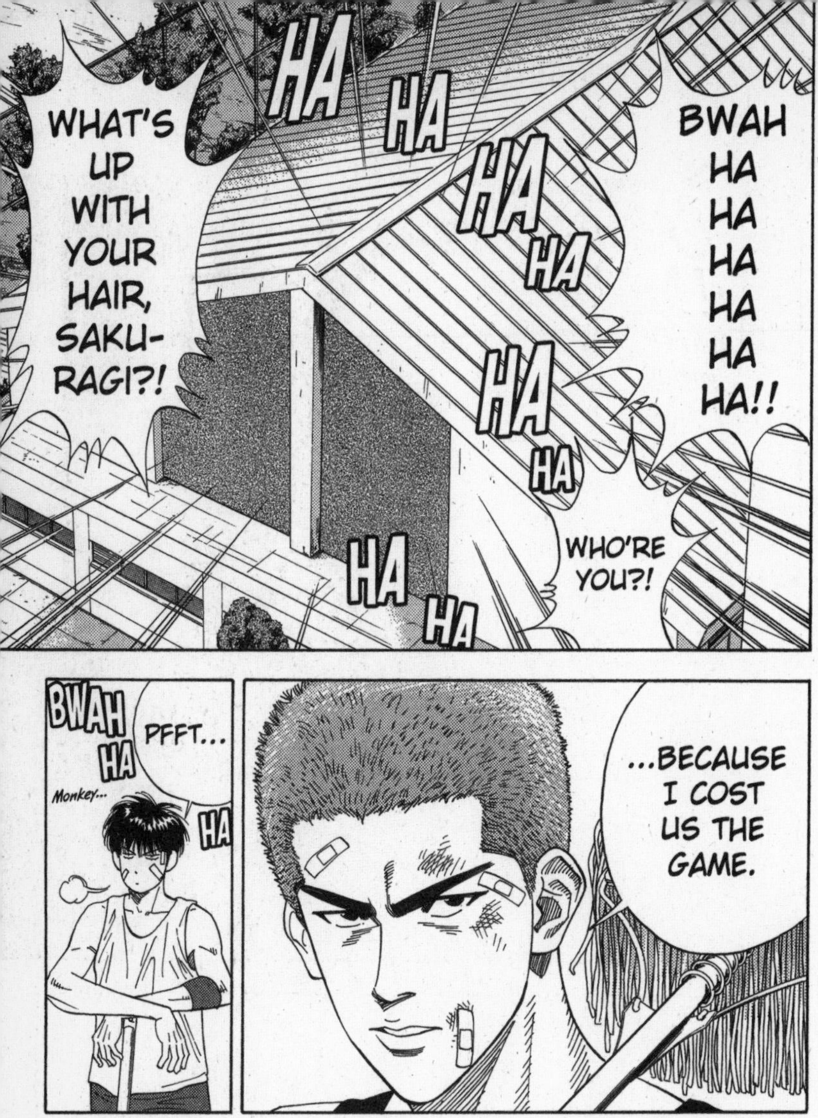
BWAH HA HA HA HA HA HA!!
HA HA HA HA HA HA HA HA
WHAT'S UP WITH YOUR HAIR, SAKU-RAGI?!
WHO'RE YOU?!
...BECAUSE I COST US THE GAME.
PFFT...
BWAH HA HA
Monkey...
My tummy hurts...
IT'S CUTE, HANAMICHI. ♥
REALLY?
THREE MORE DAYS UNTIL THE NEXT GAME!

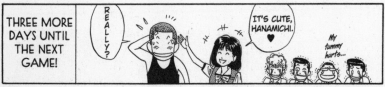

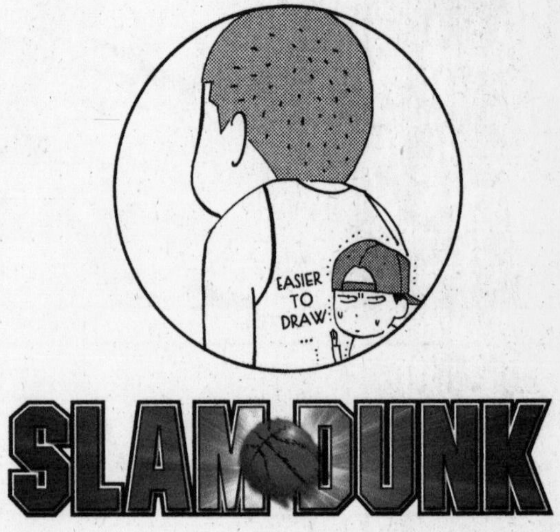
EASIER TO DRAW...

SLAM DUNK

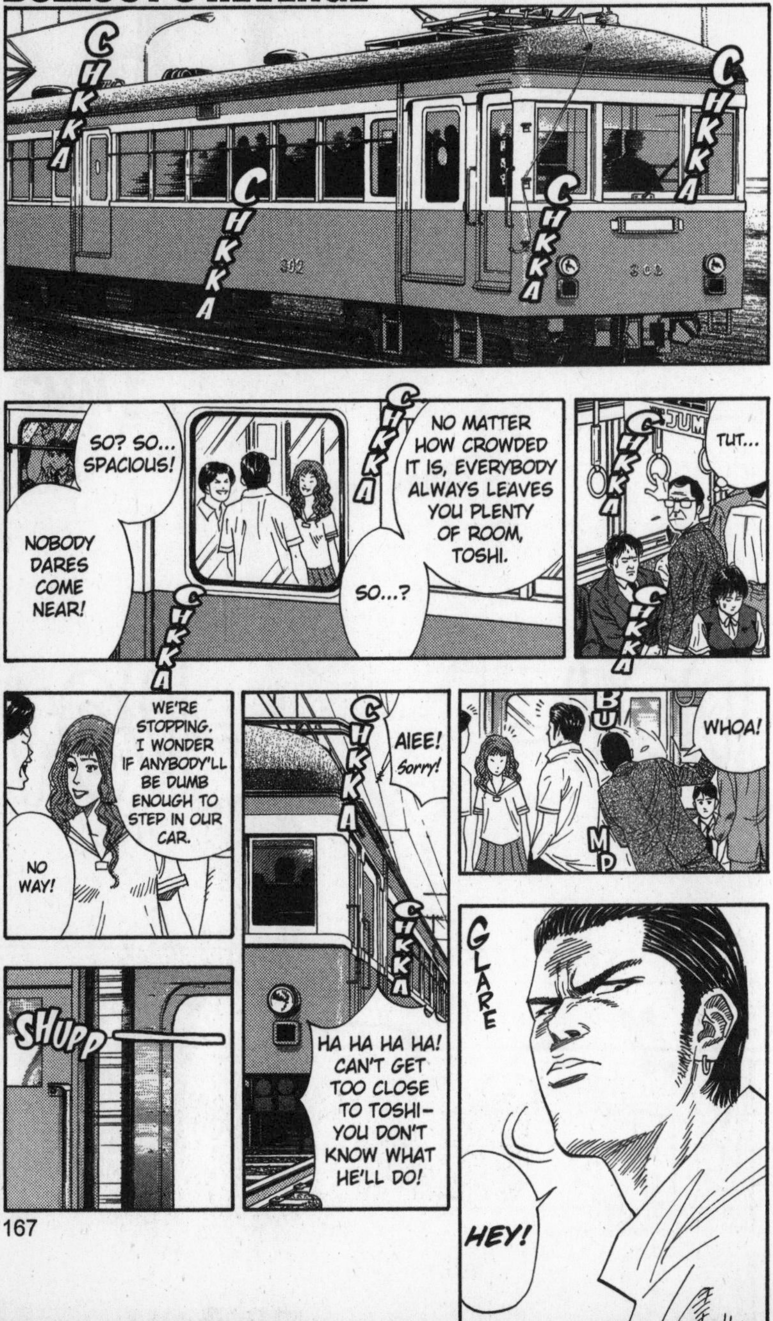
CHKKA
CHKKA
CHKKA
CHKKA
SO? SO... SPACIOUS!
NOBODY DARES COME NEAR!
CHKKA
CHKKA
NO MATTER HOW CROWDED IT IS, EVERYBODY ALWAYS LEAVES YOU PLENTY OF ROOM, TOSHI.
SO...?
CHKKA
TUT...
CHKKA
WE'RE STOPPING. I WONDER IF ANYBODY'LL BE DUMB ENOUGH TO STEP IN OUR CAR.
NO WAY!
SHUPP
CHKKA
AIEE! Sorry!
CHKKA
HA HA HA HA! CAN'T GET TOO CLOSE TO TOSHI- YOU DON'T KNOW WHAT HE'LL DO!
BUMP
WHOA!
GLARE
HEY!

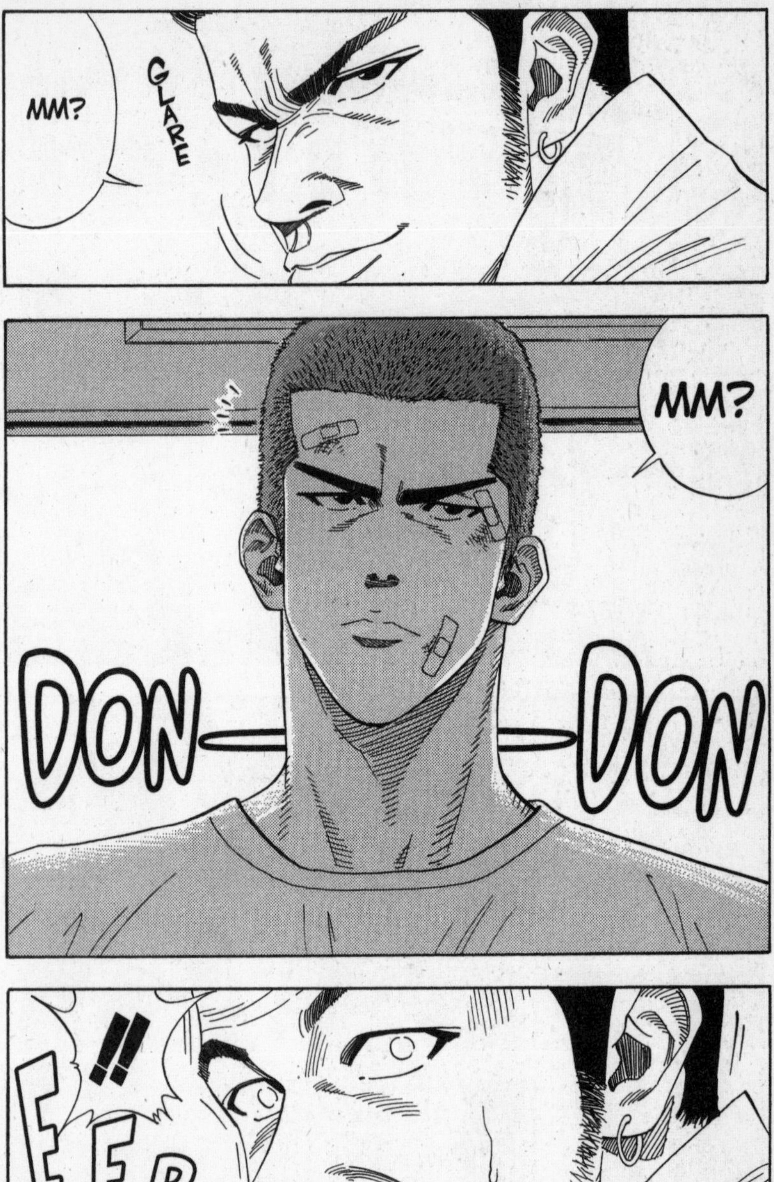
GLARE
MM?
MM?
DON
DON
!!
EEP

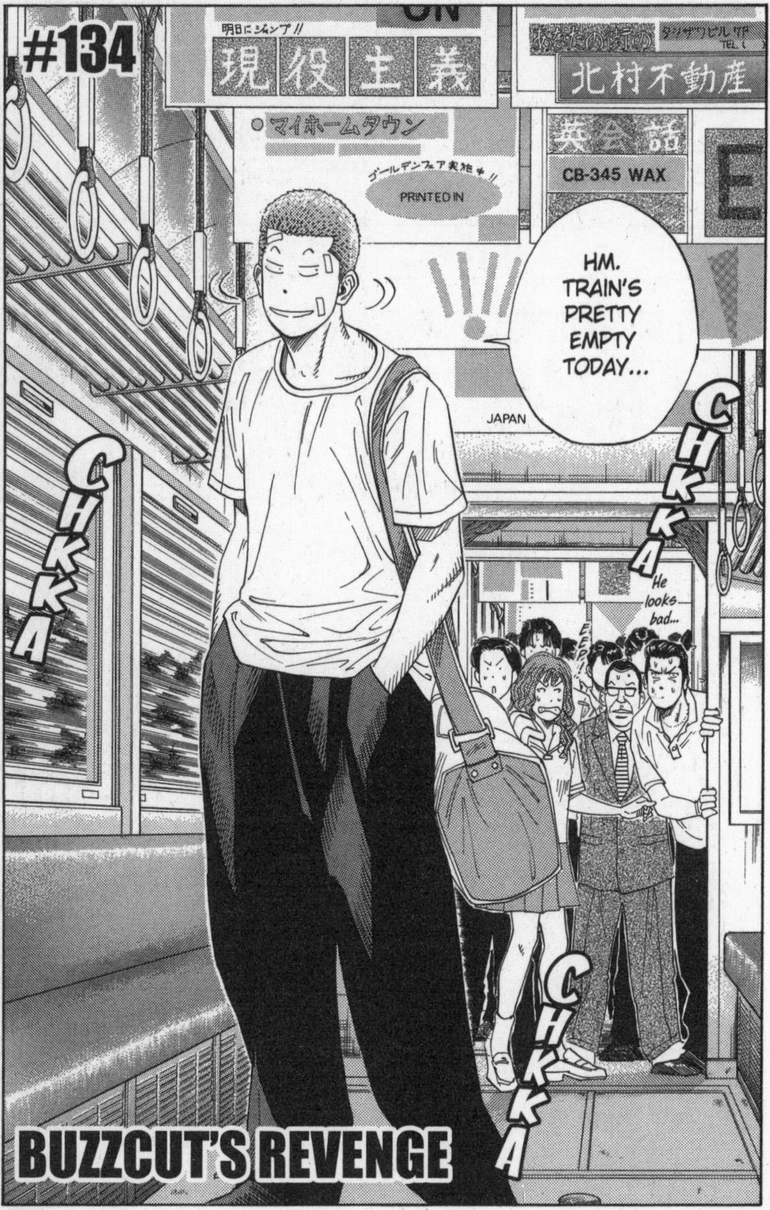
#134
明日にジャンプ!!
現役主義
マイホームタウン
ゴールデンフェア実施中!!
PRINTED IN
JAPAN
あなたの街の
北村不動産
英会話
CB-345 WAX
HM. TRAIN'S PRETTY EMPTY TODAY...
CHKKA
CHKKA
He looks bad...
EEP!!
CHKKA
BUZZCUT'S REVENGE

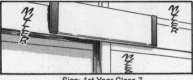

MUTTER
MUTTER
MUTTER
MUTTER
MUTTER
Sign: 1st Year Class 7
MUTTER
MUTTER
MUTTER
MUTTER
MUTTER
MUTTER
HE'S EVEN SCARIER NOW...
YEAH ...
MUTTER
MUTTER
BRIGHT RED SHAVED HEAD...
NOW THAT'S FREAKY ...
MUTTER
MUTTER
STOP STARING AT ME!!
RARR
AHHHH!!

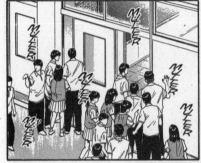

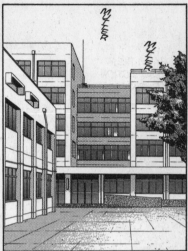

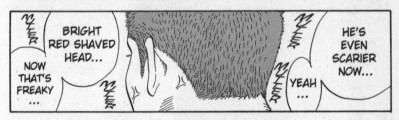

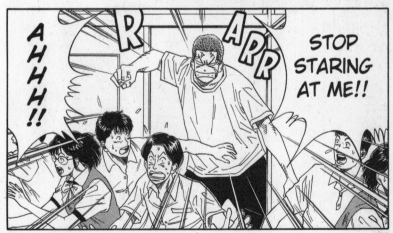

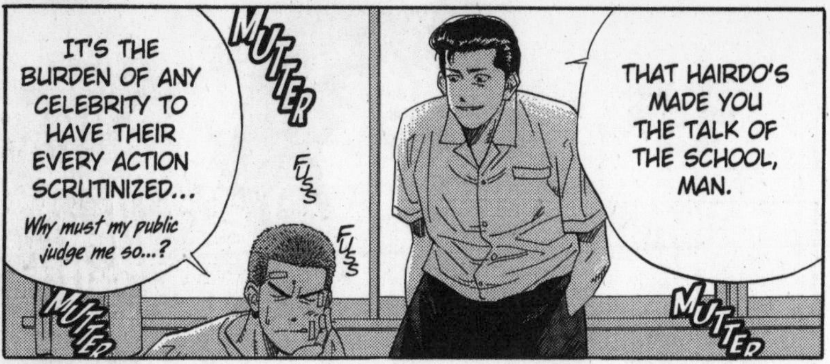
THAT HAIRDO'S MADE YOU THE TALK OF THE SCHOOL, MAN.
MUTTER
FUSS
FUSS
MUTTER
IT'S THE BURDEN OF ANY CELEBRITY TO HAVE THEIR EVERY ACTION SCRUTINIZED...
Why must my public judge me so...?
MUTTER

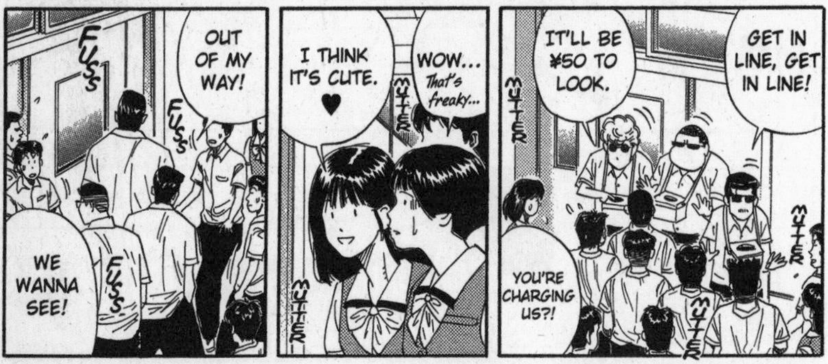
GET IN LINE, GET IN LINE!
IT'LL BE ¥50 TO LOOK.
MUTTER
MUTTER
YOU'RE CHARGING US?!
MUTTER
WOW... *That's freaky...*
MUTTER
I THINK IT'S CUTE. ♥
MUTTER
OUT OF MY WAY!
FUSS
FUSS
FUSS
WE WANNA SEE!

Sign: 1st Year Class 7

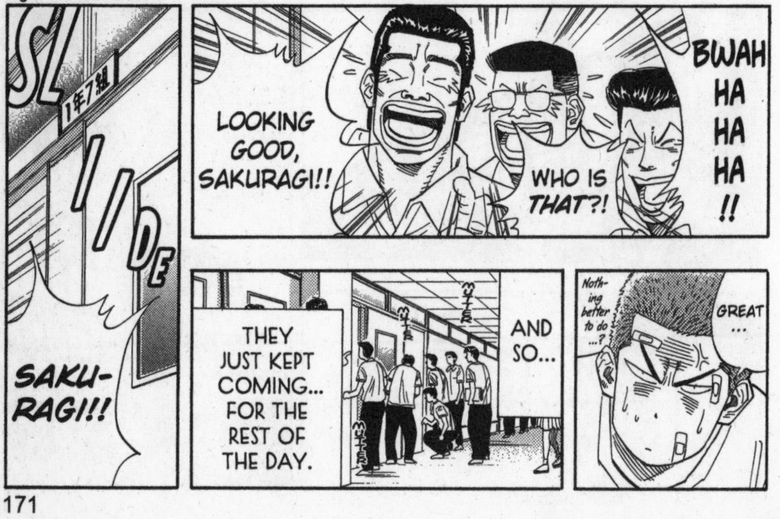
BWAH HA HA HA !!
WHO IS *THAT*?!
LOOKING GOOD, SAKURAGI!!
GREAT ...
Nothing better to do ...?
AND SO...
MUTTER
MUTTER
MUTTER
THEY JUST KEPT COMING... FOR THE REST OF THE DAY.
1年7組
SLIIDE
SAKURAGI!!

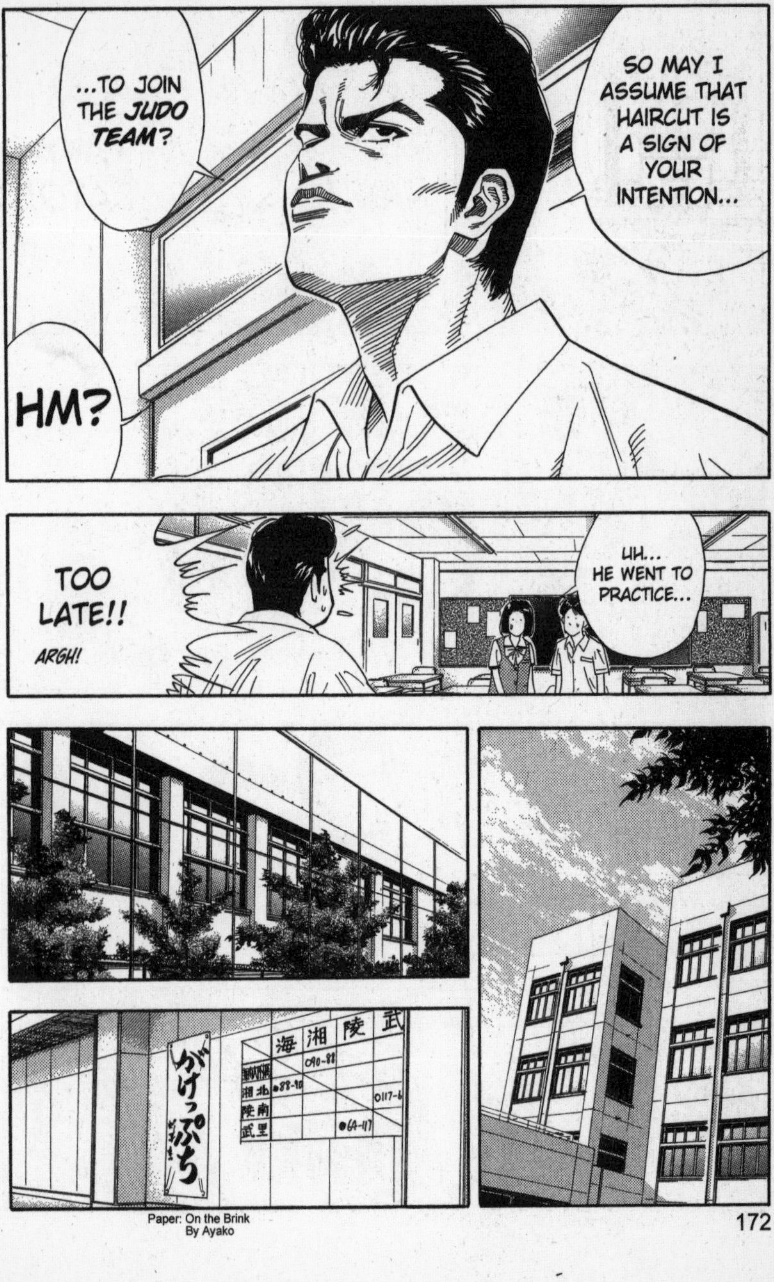
SO MAY I ASSUME THAT HAIRCUT IS A SIGN OF YOUR INTENTION...
...TO JOIN THE JUDO TEAM?
HM?
UH... HE WENT TO PRACTICE...
TOO LATE!!
ARGH!
海 湘 陵 武
湘北
陵南
武里
がけっぷち

Paper: On the Brink
By Ayako

READ THIS WAY

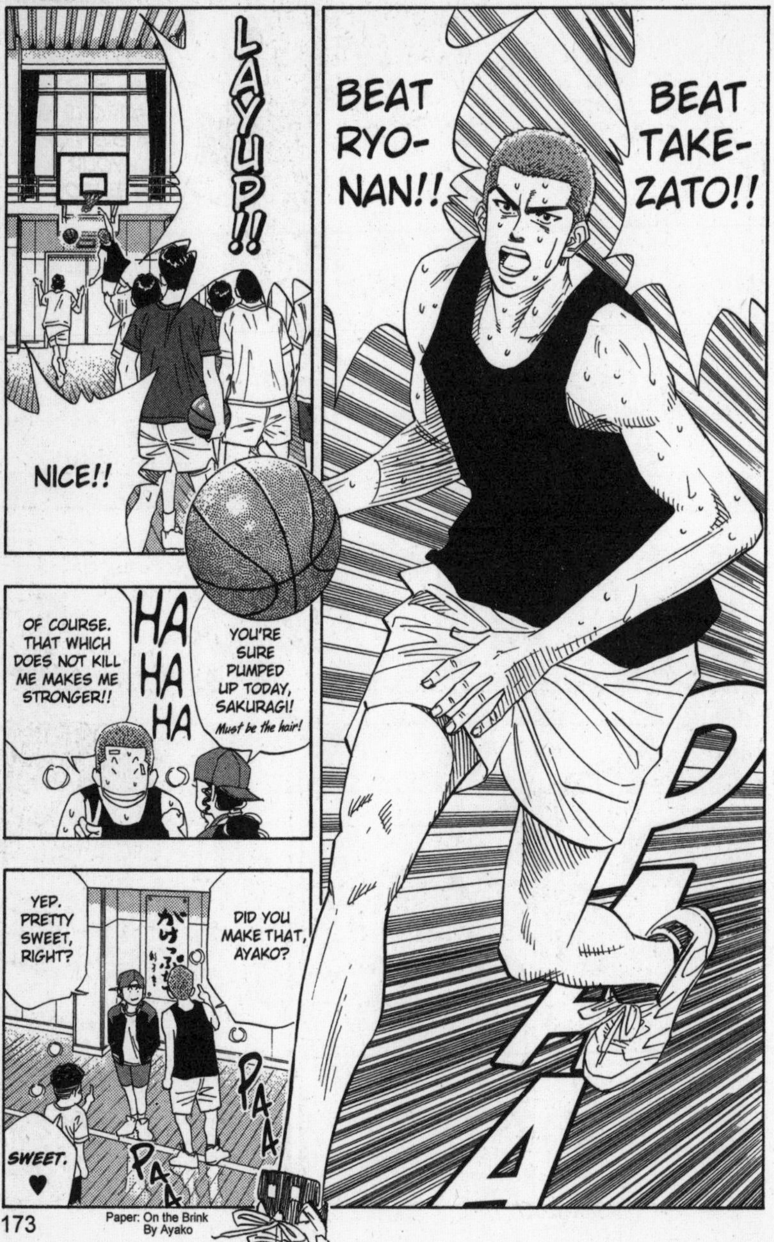
BEAT TAKE-ZATO!!
BEAT RYO-NAN!!
LAYUP!!
NICE!!
YOU'RE SURE PUMPED UP TODAY, SAKURAGI!
Must be the hair!
HA HA HA
OF COURSE. THAT WHICH DOES NOT KILL ME MAKES ME STRONGER!!
DID YOU MAKE THAT, AYAKO?
YEP. PRETTY SWEET, RIGHT?
PAA
PAA
SWEET. ♥

Paper: On the Brink
By Ayako

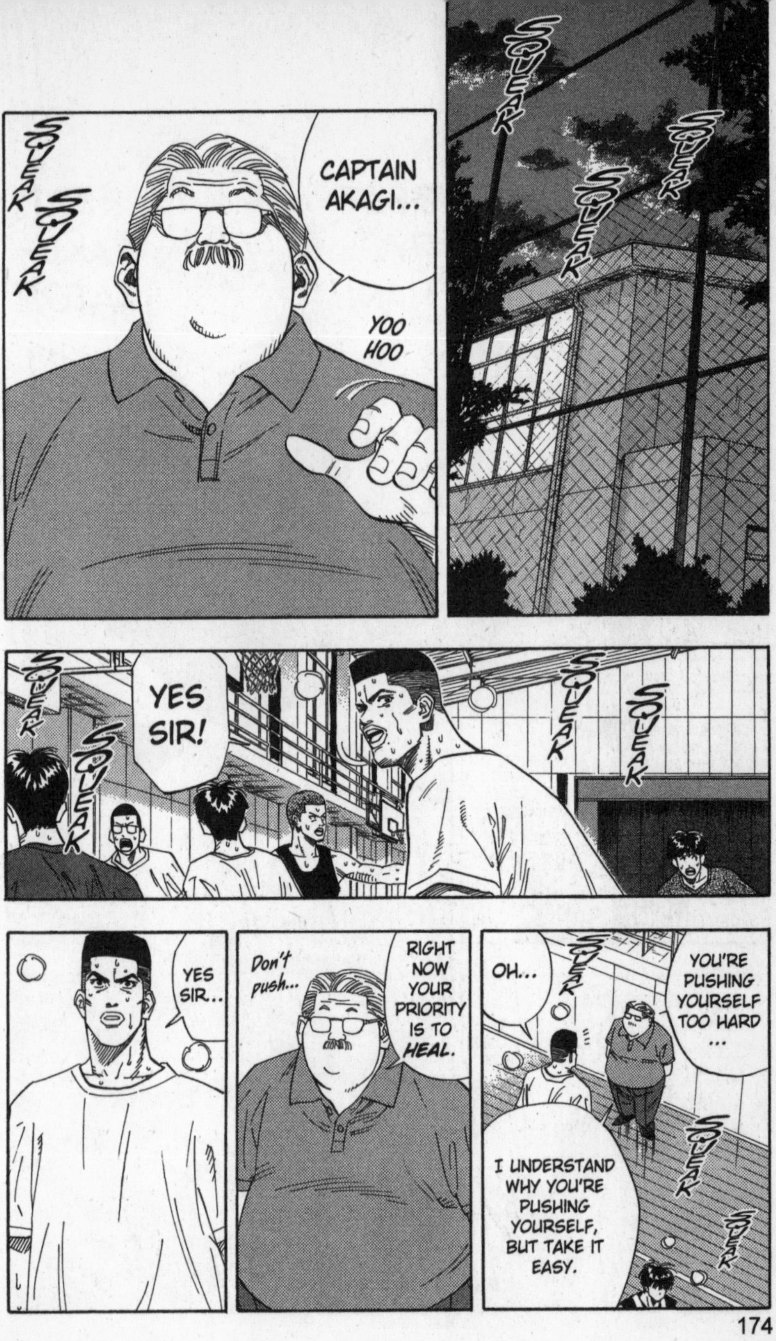
SQUEAK
SQUEAK
SQUEAK
CAPTAIN AKAGI...
YOO HOO
SQUEAK
SQUEAK
SQUEAK
SQUEAK
YES SIR!
SQUEAK
SQUEAK
YOU'RE PUSHING YOURSELF TOO HARD ...
SQUEAK
OH...
I UNDERSTAND WHY YOU'RE PUSHING YOURSELF, BUT TAKE IT EASY.
SQUEAK
SQUEAK
RIGHT NOW YOUR PRIORITY IS TO HEAL.
Don't push...
YES SIR...

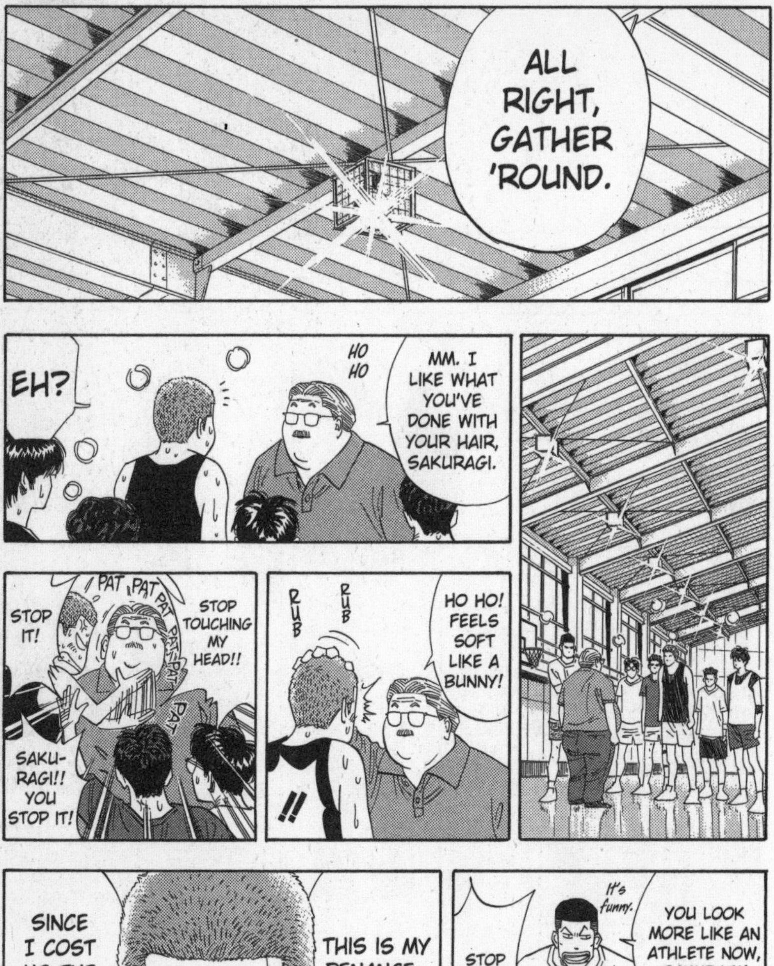
ALL RIGHT, GATHER 'ROUND.
HO HO
MM. I LIKE WHAT YOU'VE DONE WITH YOUR HAIR, SAKURAGI.
EH?
RUB RUB
HO HO! FEELS SOFT LIKE A BUNNY!
!!
PAT PAT PAT PAT PAT PAT
STOP TOUCHING MY HEAD!!
STOP IT!
SAKURAGI!! YOU STOP IT!
It's funny.
YOU LOOK MORE LIKE AN ATHLETE NOW, SAKURAGI! HEH HEH HEH!
STOP LAUGHING!!
Your hair is weirder than mine!!
SINCE I COST US THE GAME...
THIS IS MY PENANCE...

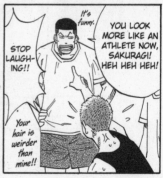

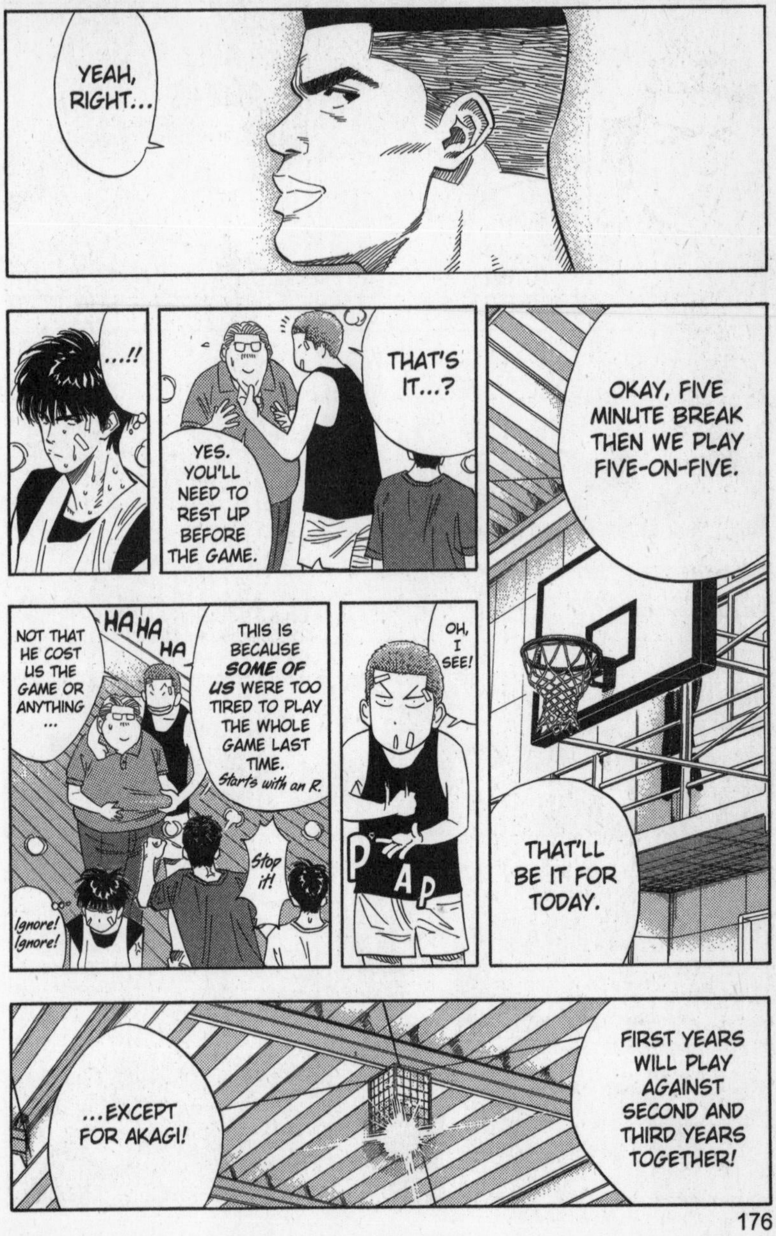
YEAH, RIGHT...
OKAY, FIVE MINUTE BREAK THEN WE PLAY FIVE-ON-FIVE.
THAT'LL BE IT FOR TODAY.
THAT'S IT...?
YES. YOU'LL NEED TO REST UP BEFORE THE GAME.
...!!
OH, I SEE!
PAP
HA HA HA
THIS IS BECAUSE ***SOME OF US*** WERE TOO TIRED TO PLAY THE WHOLE GAME LAST TIME.
Starts with an R.
NOT THAT HE COST US THE GAME OR ANYTHING ...
Stop it!
Ignore! Ignore!
FIRST YEARS WILL PLAY AGAINST SECOND AND THIRD YEARS TOGETHER!
...EXCEPT FOR AKAGI!

READ THIS WAY

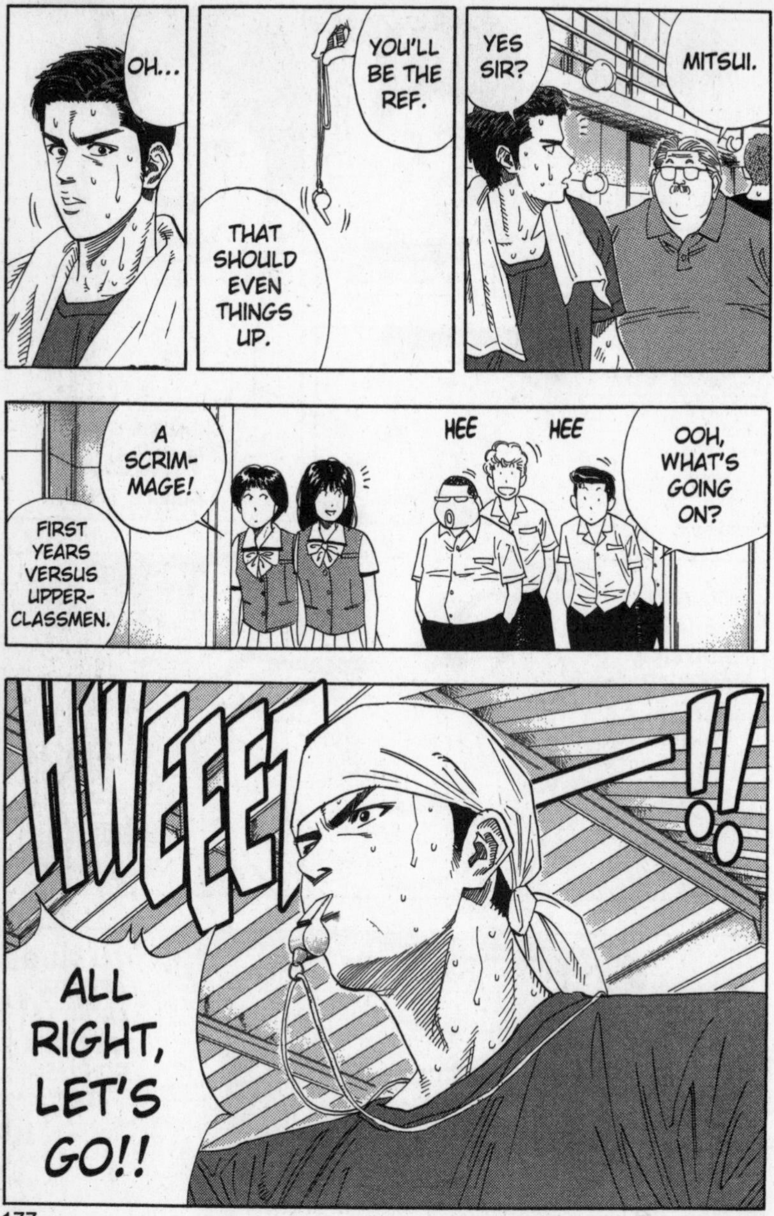
MITSUI.
YES SIR?
YOU'LL BE THE REF.
THAT SHOULD EVEN THINGS UP.
OH...
OOH, WHAT'S GOING ON?
HEE
HEE
A SCRIM-MAGE!
FIRST YEARS VERSUS UPPER-CLASSMEN.
HWEEET—!!
ALL RIGHT, LET'S GO!!

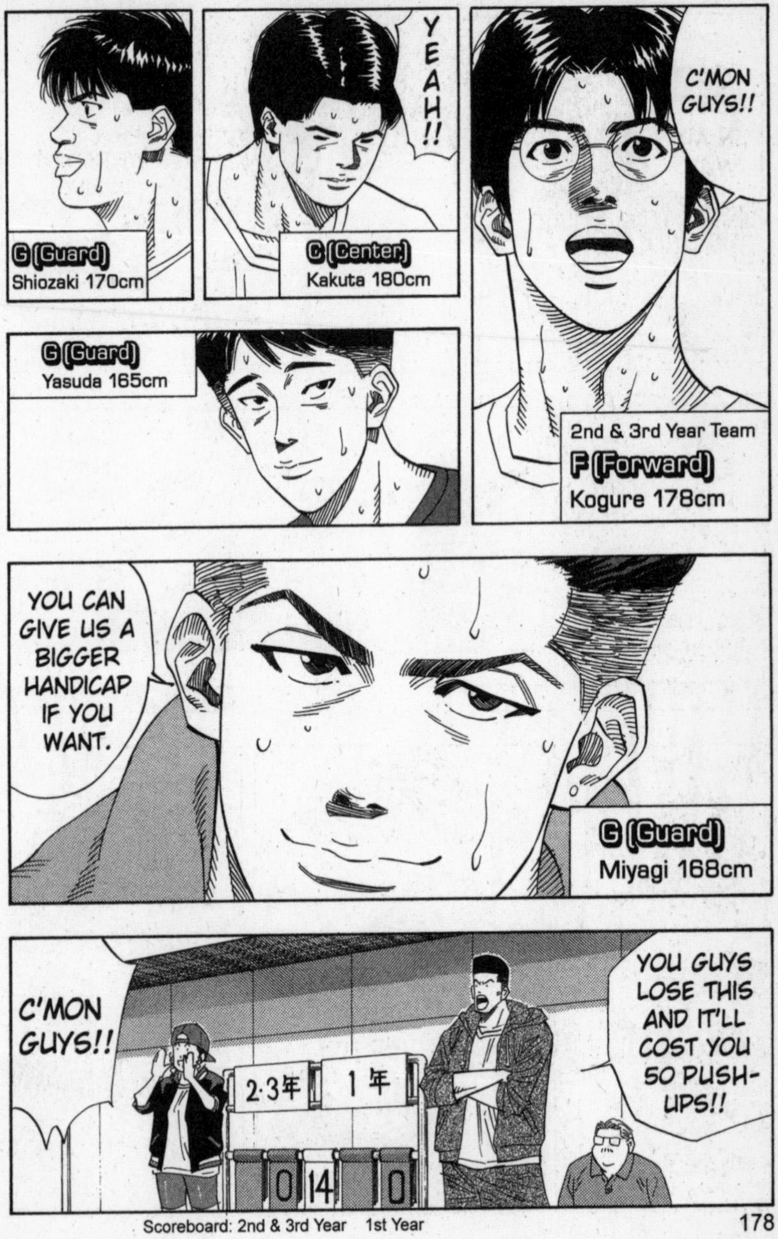
C'MON GUYS!!
2nd & 3rd Year Team
F (Forward)
Kogure 178cm
YEAH!!
C (Center)
Kakuta 180cm
G (Guard)
Shiozaki 170cm
G (Guard)
Yasuda 165cm
YOU CAN GIVE US A BIGGER HANDICAP IF YOU WANT.
G (Guard)
Miyagi 168cm
YOU GUYS LOSE THIS AND IT'LL COST YOU 50 PUSH-UPS!!
C'MON GUYS!!
2·3年
1年
0 14
0

Scoreboard: 2nd & 3rd Year 1st Year

READ THIS WAY

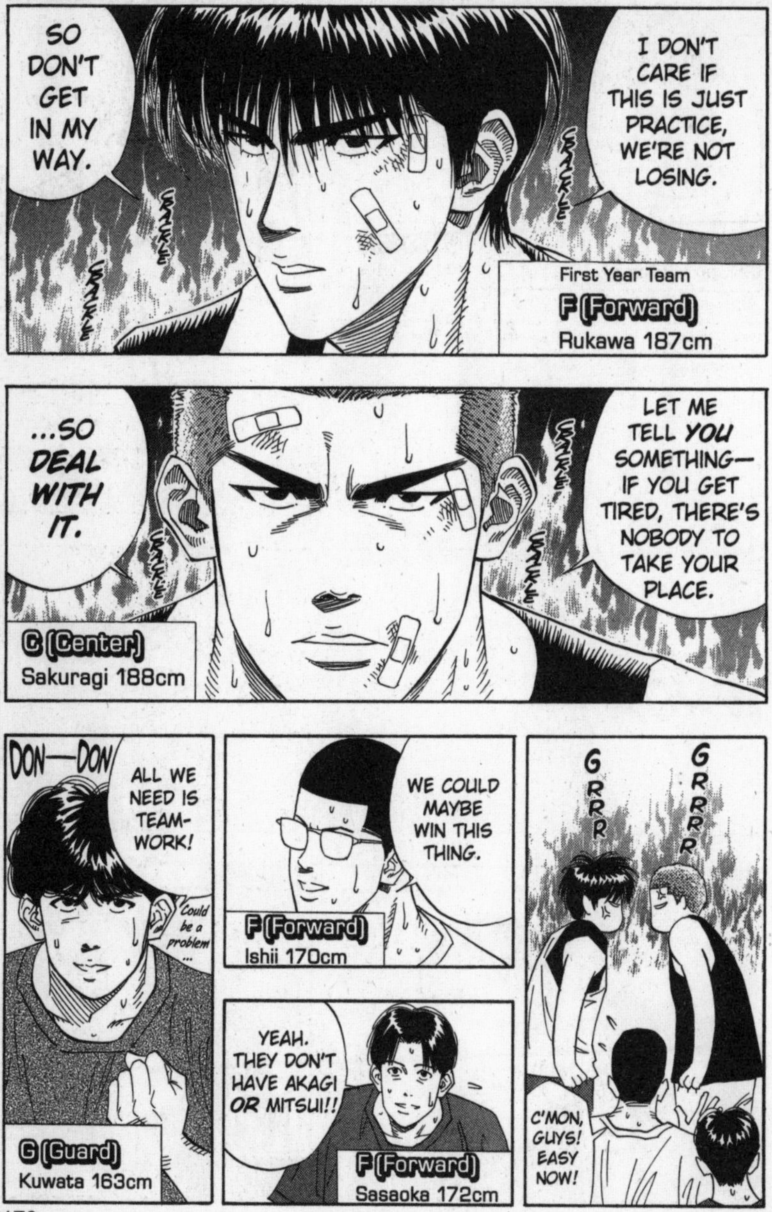
I DON'T CARE IF THIS IS JUST PRACTICE, WE'RE NOT LOSING.
SO DON'T GET IN MY WAY.
First Year Team
F (Forward)
Rukawa 187cm
LET ME TELL YOU SOMETHING— IF YOU GET TIRED, THERE'S NOBODY TO TAKE YOUR PLACE.
...SO DEAL WITH IT.
C (Center)
Sakuragi 188cm
GRRR
GRRRR
C'MON, GUYS! EASY NOW!
WE COULD MAYBE WIN THIS THING.
F (Forward)
Ishii 170cm
YEAH. THEY DON'T HAVE AKAGI OR MITSUI!!
F (Forward)
Sasaoka 172cm
DON—DON
ALL WE NEED IS TEAM-WORK!
Could be a problem...
G (Guard)
Kuwata 163cm

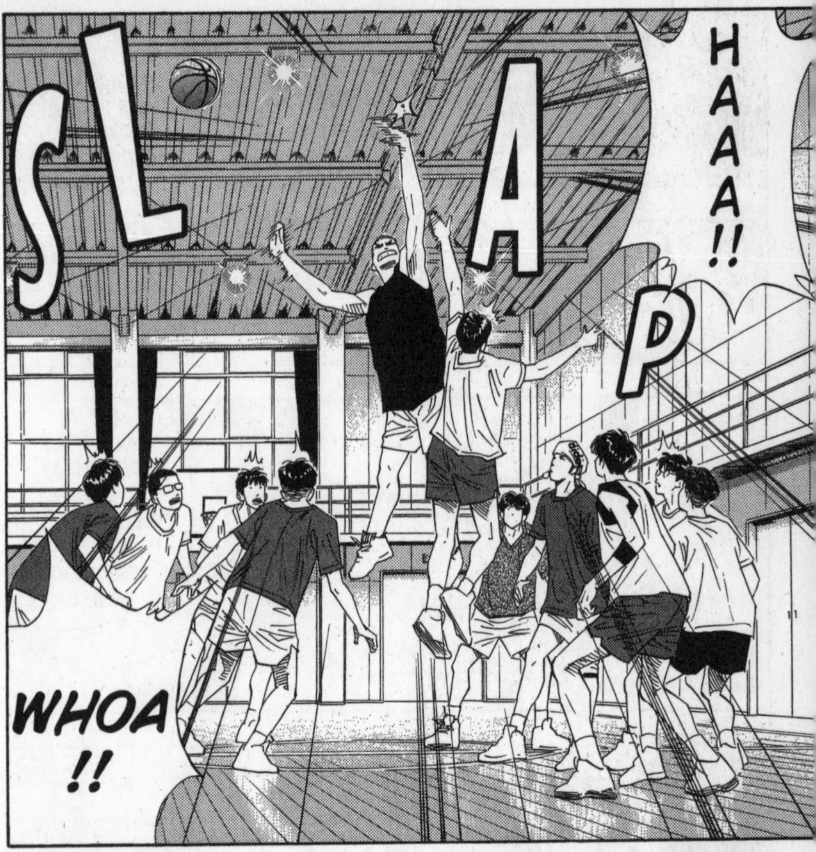
HAAA!!
SLAP
WHOA!!

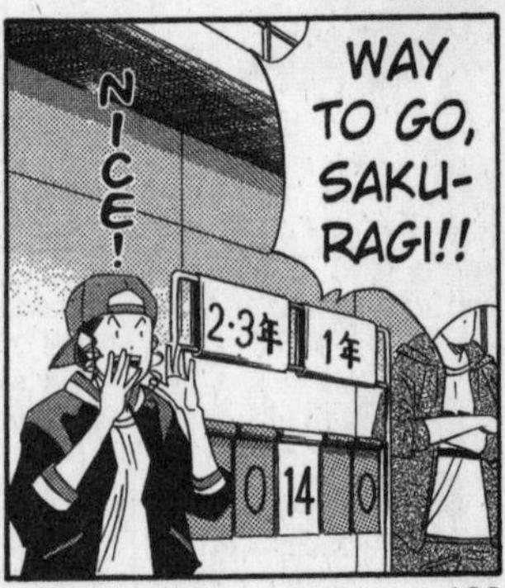
WAY TO GO, SAKURAGI!!
NICE!
2·3年
1年
0
14
0

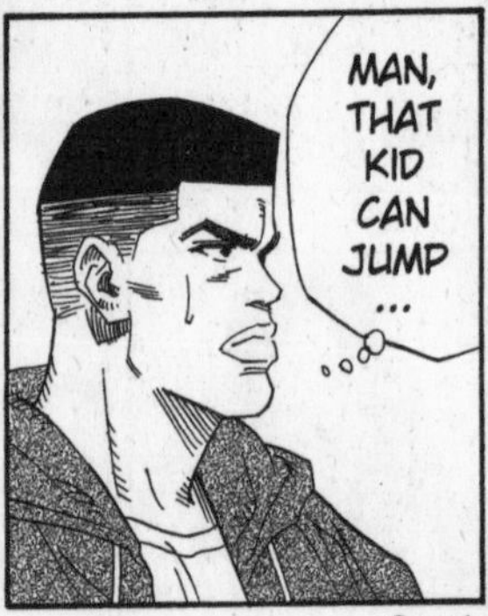
MAN, THAT KID CAN JUMP...

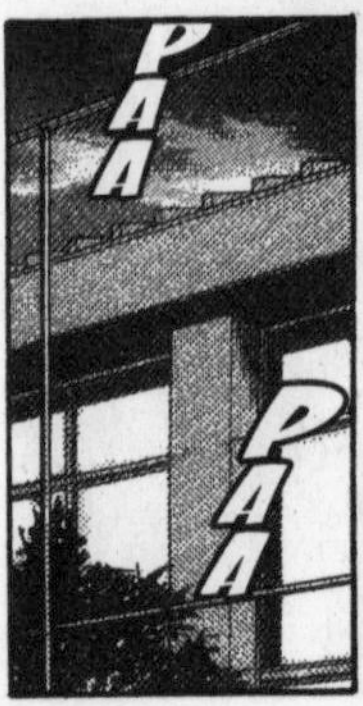
PAA
PAA

Scoreboard: 2nd & 3rd Year 1st Year

READ THIS WAY

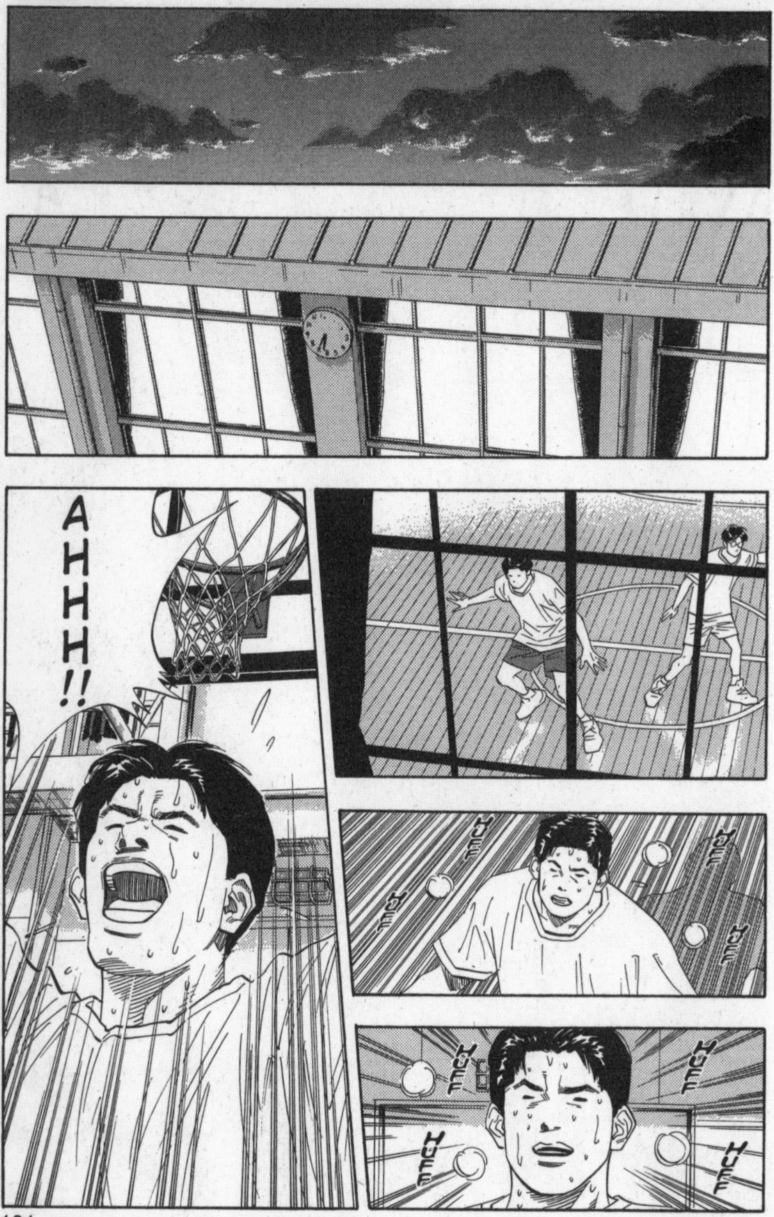
HUFF
HUFF
HUFF
HUFF
HUFF
HUFF
HUFF
AHHH!!

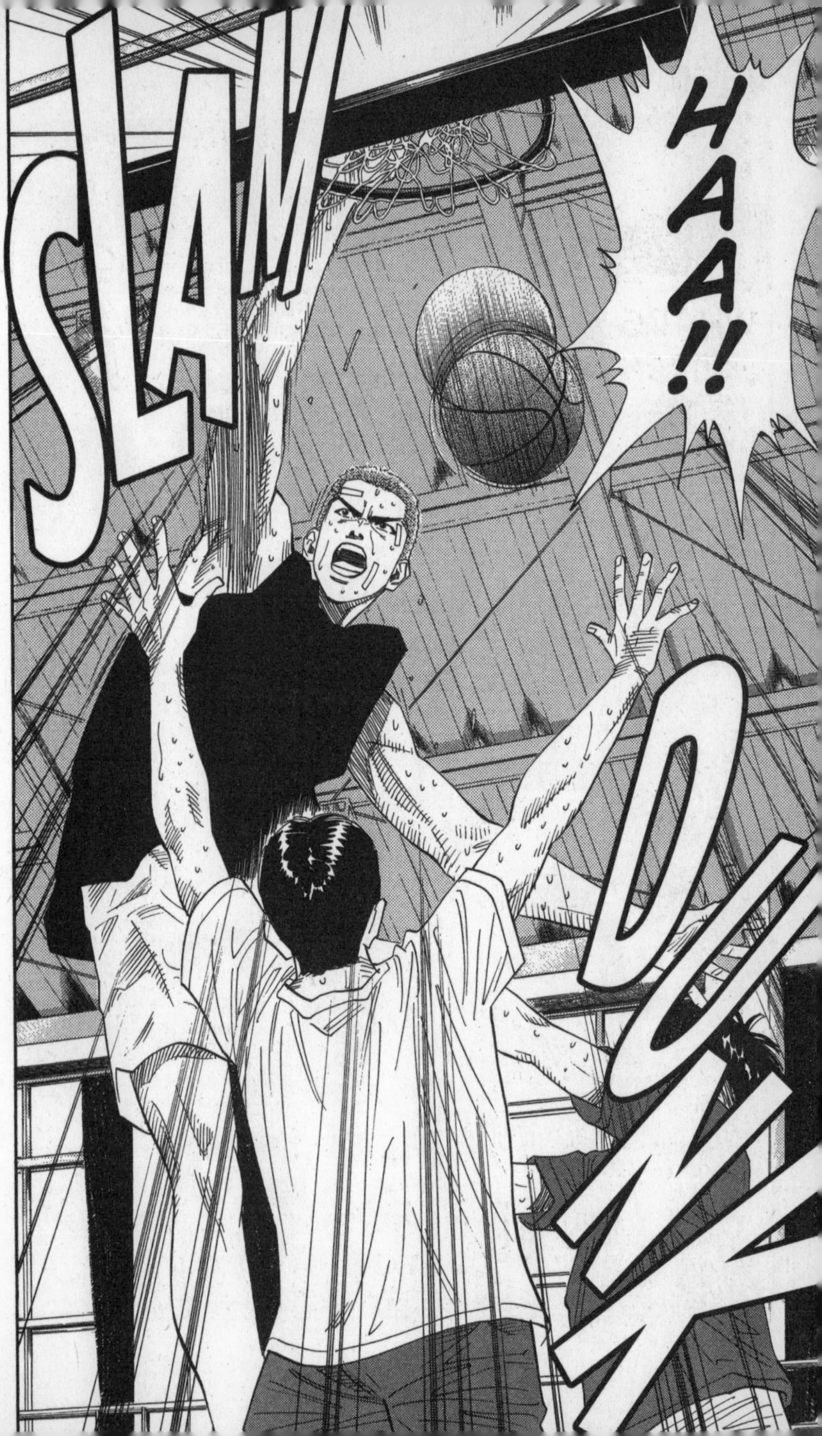
HAA!!
SLAM
DUNK

READ THIS WAY

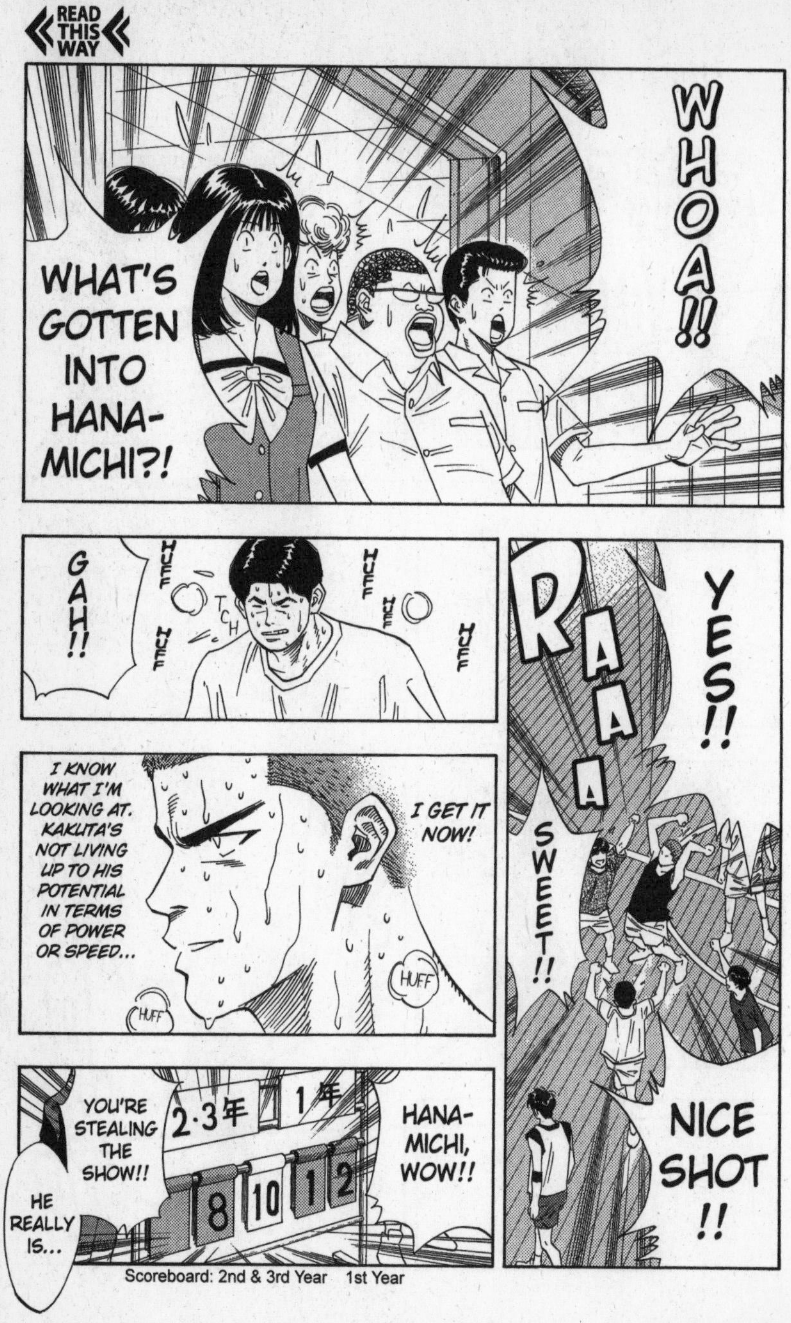
WHOA!!
WHAT'S GOTTEN INTO HANA-MICHI?!
RAAAA
YES!!
SWEET!!
NICE SHOT!!
HUFF
HUFF
HUFF
TCH
HUFF
HUFF
GAH!!
I GET IT NOW!
I KNOW WHAT I'M LOOKING AT. KAKUTA'S NOT LIVING UP TO HIS POTENTIAL IN TERMS OF POWER OR SPEED...
HUFF
HUFF
HANA-MICHI, WOW!!
1年
2·3年
YOU'RE STEALING THE SHOW!!
HE REALLY IS...
8
10
12
Scoreboard: 2nd & 3rd Year 1st Year

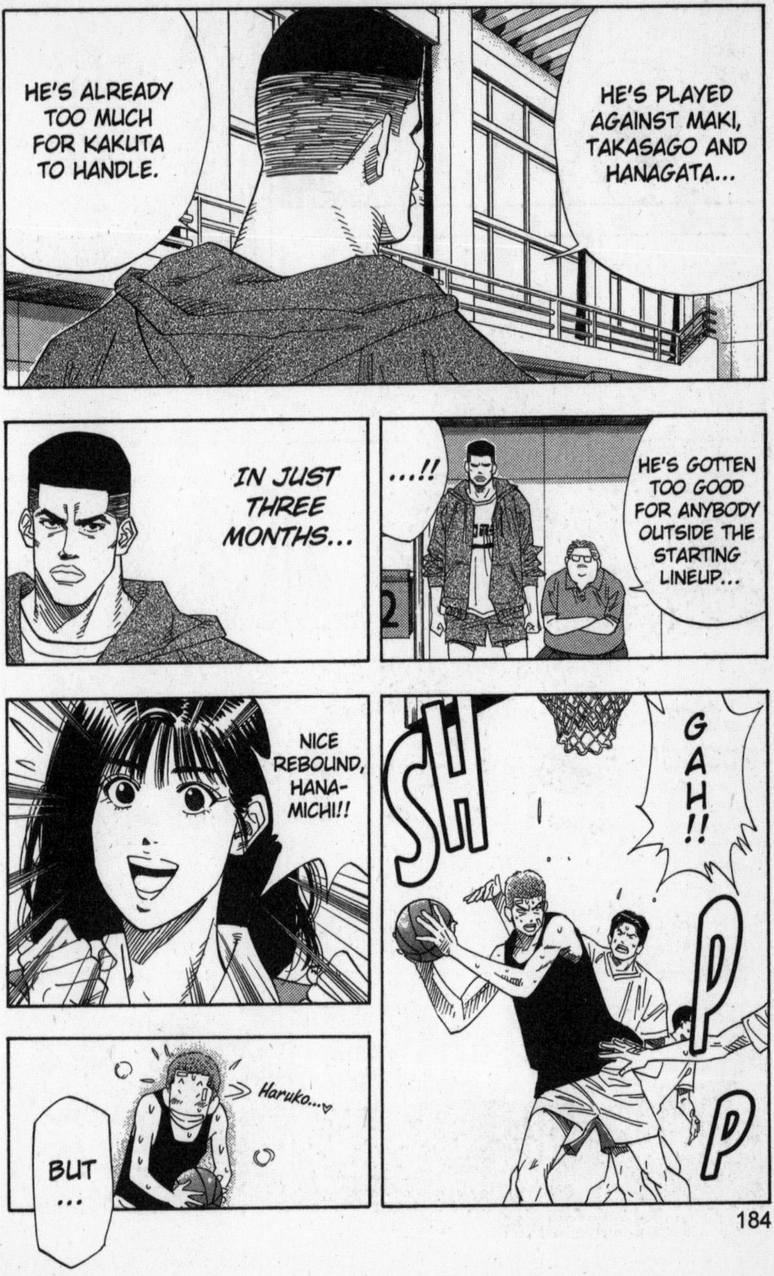
HE'S PLAYED AGAINST MAKI, TAKASAGO AND HANAGATA...
HE'S ALREADY TOO MUCH FOR KAKUTA TO HANDLE.
HE'S GOTTEN TOO GOOD FOR ANYBODY OUTSIDE THE STARTING LINEUP...
...!!
IN JUST THREE MONTHS...
GAH!!
SHPP
NICE REBOUND, HANA-MICHI!!
Haruko...♡
BUT ...

READ THIS WAY

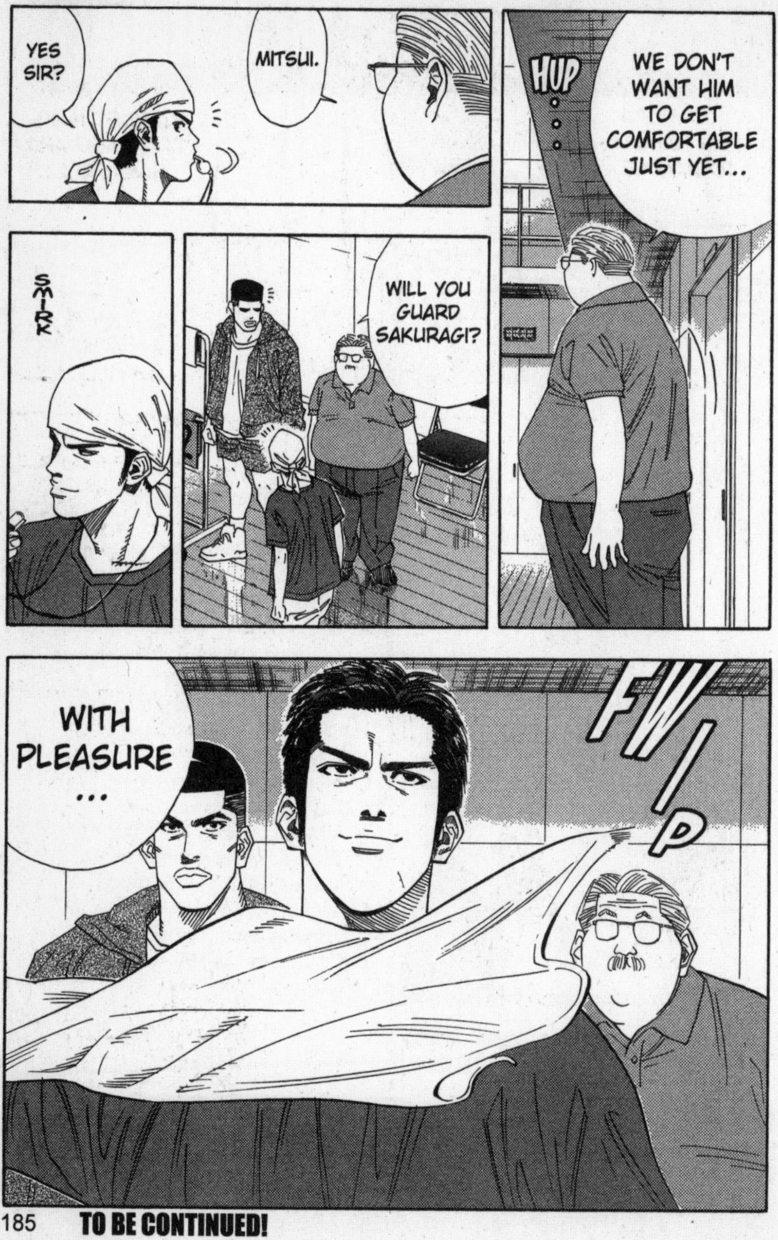
HUP
WE DON'T WANT HIM TO GET COMFORTABLE JUST YET...
MITSUI.
YES SIR?
WILL YOU GUARD SAKURAGI?
SMIRK
FWIP
WITH PLEASURE ...

TO BE CONTINUED!

Coming Next Volume

Thanks to an impressive showing during a scrimmage between Shohoku's rookie and veteran players, Coach Anzai decides to give Sakuragi a crack at playing center. And though the game reveals several of Sakuragi's weaknesses, it also highlights just how far his technique has come in a very short amount of time. With but three days until the game against Takezato, Sakuragi is placed on a new and grueling training regimen: he must make 500 shots each and every day!

ON SALE JUNE 2011

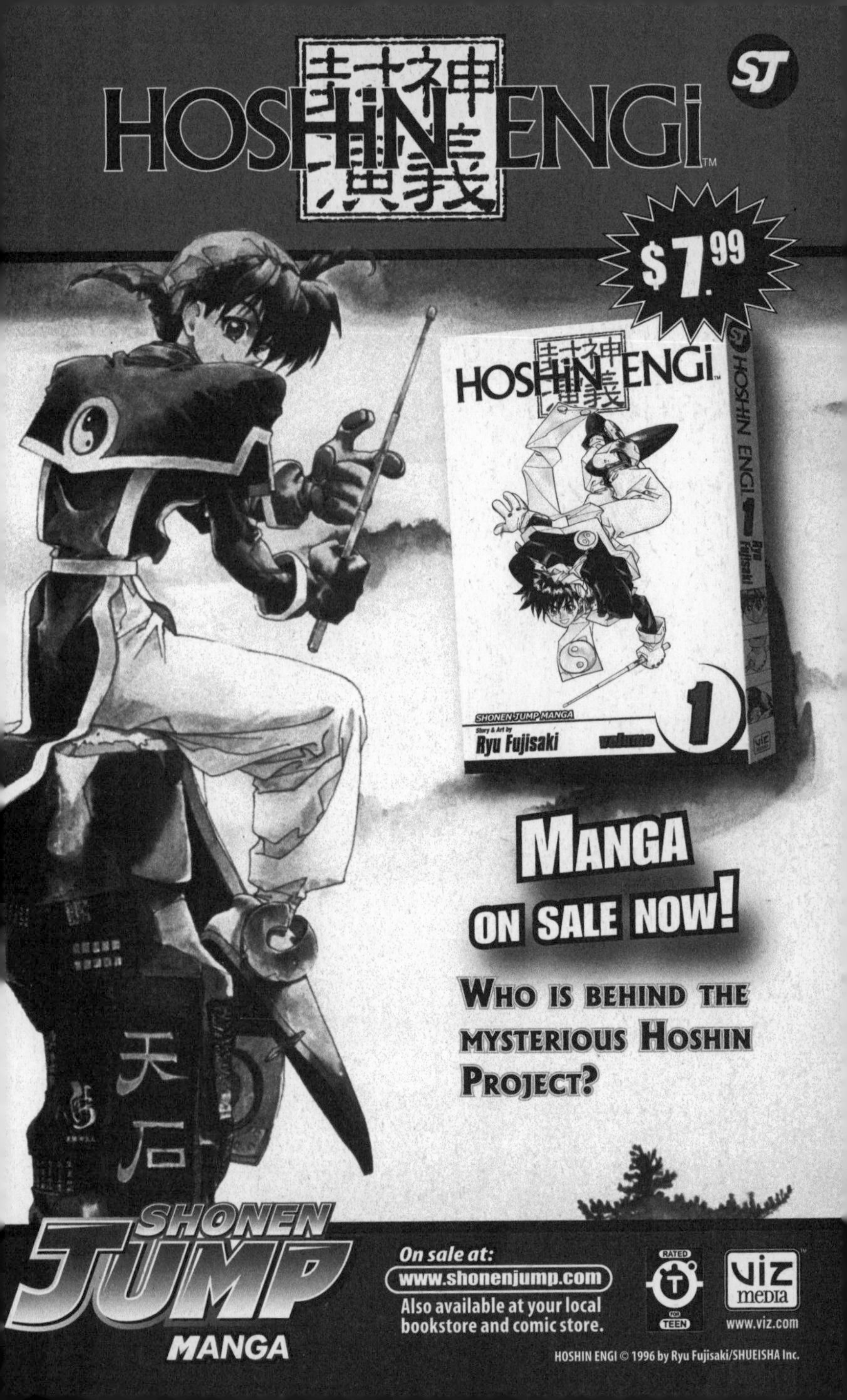
封神演義
HOSHIN ENGI™
SJ
$7.99
HOSHIN ENGI
SHONEN JUMP MANGA
Story & Art by
Ryu Fujisaki
volume 1
MANGA
ON SALE NOW!
WHO IS BEHIND THE MYSTERIOUS HOSHIN PROJECT?
SHONEN JUMP MANGA
On sale at:
www.shonenjump.com
Also available at your local bookstore and comic store.
RATED T FOR TEEN
VIZ media
www.viz.com
HOSHIN ENGI © 1996 by Ryu Fujisaki/SHUEISHA Inc.

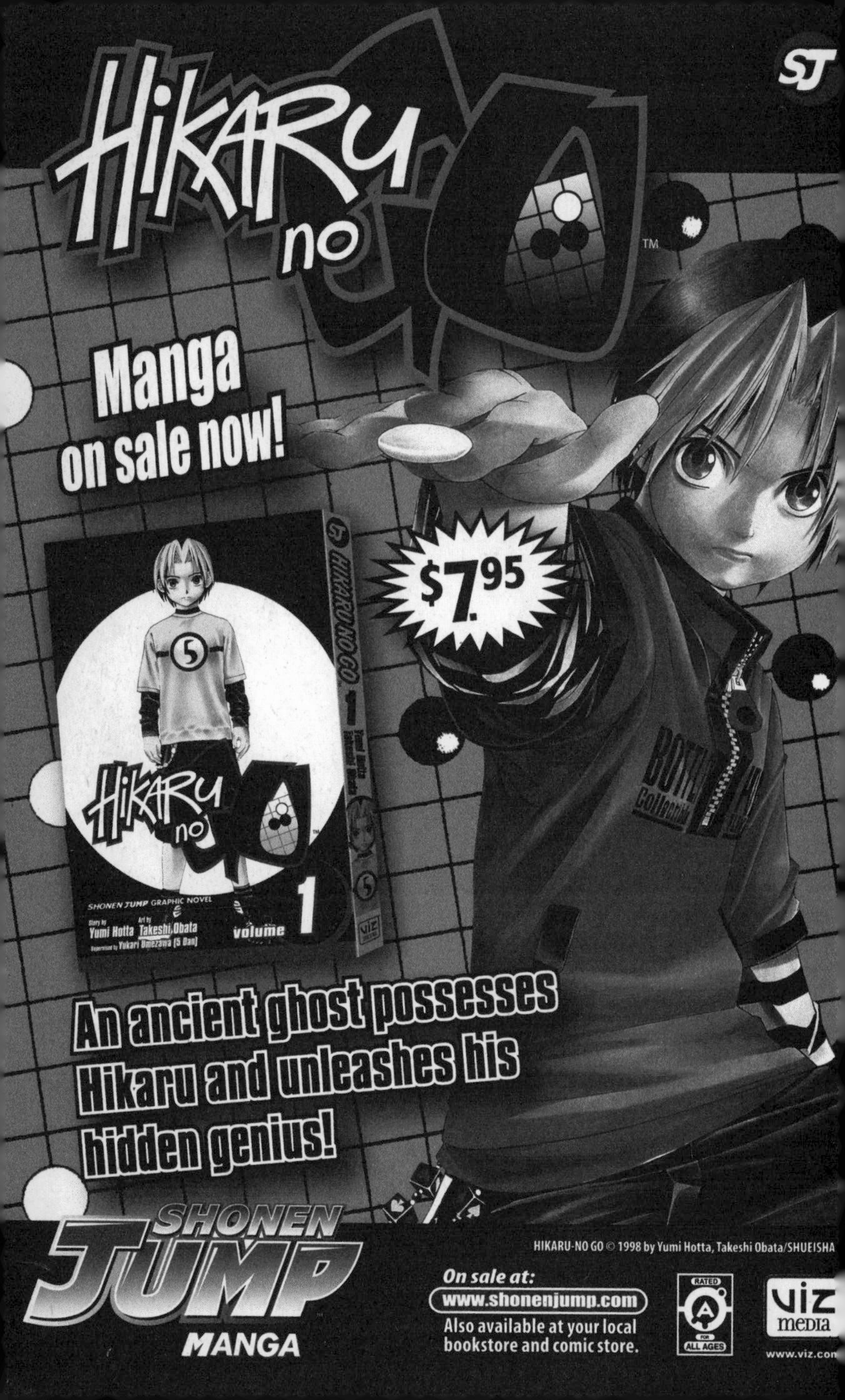
SJ
Hikaru no Go™
Manga on sale now!
$7.95
SHONEN JUMP GRAPHIC NOVEL
Story by Yumi Hotta Art by Takeshi Obata
Supervised by Yukari Umezawa (5 Dan)
volume 1
An ancient ghost possesses Hikaru and unleashes his hidden genius!
SHONEN JUMP MANGA
HIKARU-NO GO © 1998 by Yumi Hotta, Takeshi Obata/SHUEISHA
On sale at:
www.shonenjump.com
Also available at your local bookstore and comic store.
RATED A FOR ALL AGES
viz media
www.viz.com

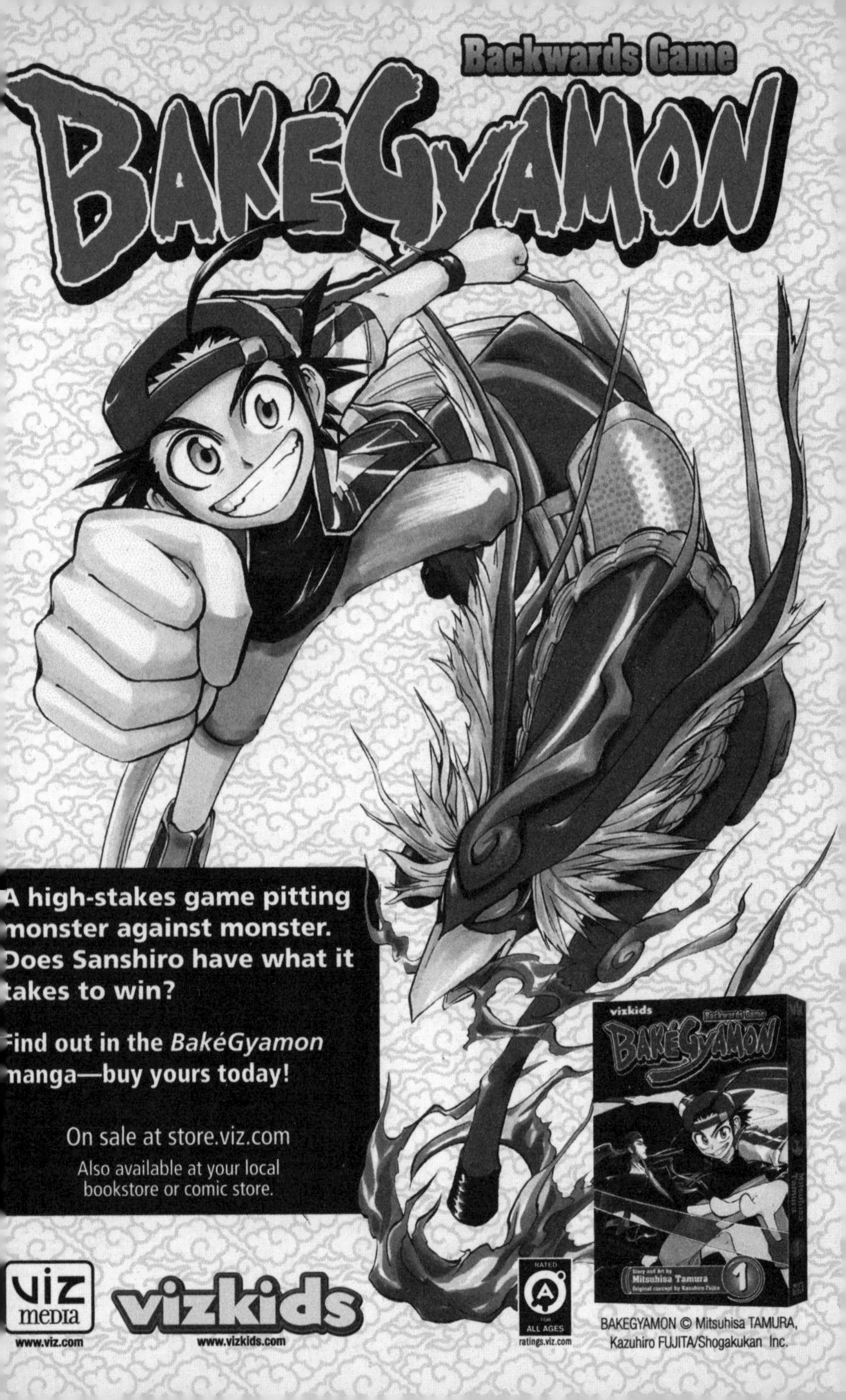
Backwards Game
BAKÉGYAMON
A high-stakes game pitting monster against monster. Does Sanshiro have what it takes to win?
Find out in the *BakéGyamon* manga—buy yours today!
On sale at store.viz.com
Also available at your local bookstore or comic store.
vizkids
Backwards Game
BAKÉGYAMON
Story and Art by Mitsuhisa Tamura
Original concept by Kazuhiro Fujita
1
VIZ MEDIA
www.viz.com
vizkids
www.vizkids.com
RATED
A
FOR ALL AGES
ratings.viz.com
BAKEGYAMON © Mitsuhisa TAMURA, Kazuhiro FUJITA/Shogakukan Inc.